T5-CQF-414

3 3073 00263430 9

DATE DUE

89668422	JUN 3 1 1995
DEC 28 1996	
NOV 2 6 1996 JUN 1 1 1999	

GAYLORD

PRINTED IN U.S.A.

VIOLENT BEHAVIOR:
Social Learning Approaches to Prediction, Management and Treatment

Other books from Banff International Conferences on Behavior
Modification available from Brunner/Mazel

Behavior Modification and Families (Banff VI)
Behavior Modification Approaches to Parenting (Banff VI)
The Behavioral Management of Anxiety, Depression and Pain (Banff VII)
Behavioral Self-management: Strategies, Techniques and Outcome (Banff VIII)
Behavioral Systems for the Developmentally Disabled: I. School and Family Environments (Banff IX)
Behavioral Systems for the Developmentally Disabled: II. Institutional, Clinic and Community Environments (Banff IX)
Behavioral Medicine: Changing Health Lifestyles (Banff X)

VIOLENT BEHAVIOR:
Social Learning Approaches to Prediction, Management and Treatment

Edited by

Richard B. Stuart, D.S.W.

Department of Family and Community Medicine
School of Medicine
University of Utah
Salt Lake City, Utah

SETON HALL UNIVERSITY
McLAUGHLIN LIBRARY
SO. ORANGE, N. J.

BRUNNER/MAZEL, *Publishers* • New York

RC
569.5
V55
V57

Library of Congress Cataloging in Publication Data
  Main entry under title:

  Violent behavior.

    "One in a continuing series of publications sponsored by the Banff International
Conferences on Behavior Modification."—Pref.
    Includes bibliographies and indexes.
    1. Violence—Congresses. 2. Wife abuse—Congresses. 3. Child abuse—Congresses. 4.
Behavior modification—Congresses. I. Stuart, Richard B. II. Banff International Confer-
ence on Behavior Modification. [DNLM: 1. Social adjustment—Congresses. 2.
Violence—Congresses. 3. Violence—Therapy—Congresses.
W3 BA203 11th 1979v / BF 575.A3 V795 1979]
RC569.5.V55V57   616.85'82   81-2851
ISBN 0-87630-262-2   AACR2

Copyright © 1981 by Brunner/Mazel, Inc.

Published by
BRUNNER/MAZEL, INC.
19 Union Square
New York, New York 10003

All rights reserved. No part of this book may be reproduced by any process whatsoever,
without the written permission of the publisher.

MANUFACTURED IN THE UNITED STATES OF AMERICA

In Memorial

The partners and all those who have attended past Banff Conferences on Behavior Modification mourn the tragic deaths of Dr. Park O. Davidson and Mrs. Sheena Davidson. Park and Sheena were among the founders of the Banff Conferences and were a consistent source of intellectual stimulation and warm feelings at each meeting during the past 12 years. Their deaths in an auto accident on December 21, 1980, brought to a sudden end two careers that had not only contributed much in innovative content, but also had served as a model of effective professional life both to their colleagues at Banff and to psychological and health-service providers across Canada and around the world.

Among Dr. Davidson's accomplishments were a tenure as Associate Dean of Graduate Studies at the University of Calgary, Director of Clinical Psychology Training at the University of British Columbia, and President of the Canadian Psychological Association. Through recent work in varied NATO conferences, Dr. Davidson extended his influence well beyond the North American continent. Among Mrs. Davidson's accomplishments were her services as a member of the Faculty of Nursing at the University of British Columbia and her many and varied activities in an ongoing effort to humanize health-care delivery.

But for those who have participated in one or more Banff Conferences and who had an opportunity to know Park and Sheena, their loss is far greater than the silencing of two profound professional voices. For all who knew them the Davidsons were a model of compassionate concern, wit, personal warmth, and responsible friendship, qualities that will be replaced with great difficulty, if at all. Therefore, it is with a mixture of great sorrow and awesome respect that we wish to dedicate the present volume to the memory of two fine professionals who managed also to be splendid human beings.

RICHARD B. STUART and L. A. (GUS) HAMERLYNCK

v

Preface

This is one in a continuing series of publications sponsored by the Banff International Conferences on Behavior Modification. The conferences are held each spring in Banff, Alberta, Canada, and serve the purpose of bringing together outstanding behavioral scientists to present and discuss data related to emergent issues and topics in the field of behavior modification. Thus, the International Conferences, as a continuing event, have served as an expressive "early indicator" of the developing nature and composition of behavioristic science and scientific application.

Distance, schedules, and restricted audiences preclude wide attendance at the conferences. Consequently the publications have equal status with the conferences proper. They are not, however, simply publications of the papers presented at the conferences. Major presenters at the Banff Conferences are required to specifically write a chapter for the forthcoming book, separate from their informal presentation and discussion at the conference itself.

The original conference, held in 1969, had as its theme "Ideal Mental Health Services." The policy consciously adopted at that conference, and followed ever since, was to identify for each year's theme those behavioral researchers who could best identify the state of the art. In 1969 the conference faculty were Nathan Azrin, Ogden Lindsley, Gerald Patterson, Todd Risley and Richard Stuart.

The conference topics for the first five years were as follows:

1969: I. IDEAL MENTAL HEALTH SERVICES
1970: II. SERVICES AND PROGRAMS FOR EXCEPTIONAL CHILDREN AND YOUTH
1971: III. IMPLEMENTING BEHAVIORAL PROGRAMS FOR SCHOOLS AND CLINICS
1972: IV. BEHAVIOR CHANGE: METHODOLOGY, CONCEPTS, AND PRACTICE
1973: V. EVALUATION OF BEHAVIORAL PROGRAMS IN COMMUNITY, RESIDENTIAL AND SCHOOL SETTINGS

Beginning in 1974, the Banff Conference books have been published by Brunner/Mazel and the interested reader may obtain copies of these earlier publications from the publisher. The conference topics and faculty were:

1974: VI. BEHAVIOR MODIFICATION AND FAMILIES

Frances Degen Horowitz	Bradley D. Bucher
Todd R. Risley,	Stephen M. Johnson,
Hewitt B. Clark and	Orin D. Bolstad and
Michael F. Cataldo	Gretchen K. Lobitz
Elaine A. Blechman and	Sander Martin,
Martha Manning	Stephen Johnson,
L. Keith Miller,	Sandra Johansson and
Alice Lies,	Gail Wahl
Dan L. Pettersen and	Martha E. Bernal,
Richard Feallock	Leo F. Delfini,
John B. Conway and	Juell Ann North and
Susan L. Kreutzer	Gerald R. Patterson
Paul M. Rosen	John A. Corson
Lief Terdal,	Victor A. Benassi and
Russell H. Jackson and	Kathryn M. Larson
Ann M. Garner	Robert F. Peterson

and
BEHAVIOR MODIFICATION APPROACHES TO PARENTING

Donald R. Green,	Virginia Tams and
Karen Budd,	Sheila Eyberg
Moses Johnson,	Karen E. Kovitz
Sarah Lang,	Barclay Martin and
Elsie Pinkston and	Craig Twentyman
Sara Rudd	Wallace L. Mealiea, Jr.
Barbara Stephens Brockway and	Martin E. Shoemaker and
W. Weston Williams	Terry L. Paulson
Edward R. Christophersen,	Joe H. Brown
James D. Barnard,	A. M. Gamboa, Jr.,
Dennis Ford and	John Birkimer and
Montrose M. Wolf	Robert Brown
Buell E. Goocher and	Margaret Steward and
David N. Grove	David Steward
Merihelen Blackmore,	Peter D. McLean
Nancy Rich,	W. Doyle Gentry
Zetta Means and	Allison Rossett and
Mike Nally	Todd Eachus

1975: VII. THE BEHAVIORAL MANAGEMENT OF ANXIETY, DEPRESSION AND PAIN

Donald Meichenbaum and	Peter Lewinsohn
Dennis Turk	Anthony Biglan and
Ernest G. Poser	Antonette M. Zeiss
Peter McLean	Wilbert E. Fordyce

1976: VIII. BEHAVIORAL SELF-MANAGEMENT: STRATEGIES, TECHNIQUES AND OUTCOMES

Frederick H. Kanfer
Gary E. Schwartz
Todd R. Risley
Marvin R. Goldfried
G. Alan Marlatt and
Janice K. Marques
William R. Miller
Richard R. Bootzin
Richard M. McFall
Carol Landau Heckerman and
James O. Prochaska
Peter Suedfeld

Lynn Buhler and
Reta McKay
Richard B. Stuart
Frances Phillips,
Jackie Hooper,
Cathy Batten,
Molly Dexall,
Dave Beamish,
Tom Pollok and
Gordon McCann
Albert J. Stunkard

1977: IX. BEHAVIORAL SYSTEMS FOR THE DEVELOPMENTALLY DISABLED: I. SCHOOL AND FAMILY ENVIRONMENTS

R. L. Schiefelbusch
Kern A. Olson and
Max W. Rardin
Stephen I. Sulzbacher and
Kathleen A. Liberty
Hyman Hops,
Hill M. Walker and
Charles R. Greenwood
Edward R. Christophersen and
Bobby W. Sykes
Robert G. Wahler,

George Leske and
Edwin S. Rogers
Gerald M. Kysela,
Kathleen Daly,
Martha Doxsey-Whitfield,
Alex Hillyard,
Linda McDonald,
Susan McDonald and
Julie Taylor
Sander Martin and
Bruce Graunke

and
BEHAVIORAL SYSTEMS FOR THE DEVELOPMENTALLY DISABLED: II. INSTITUTIONAL, CLINIC, AND COMMUNITY ENVIRONMENTS

Todd R. Risley and
James Favell
Richard P. Swenson,
Tom Seekins and
Chrys Anderson
Timothy Plaska and
Gregory Ragee
H. Robert Quilitch
Michael F. Cataldo and
Dennis C. Russo
Eric Trupin,

Lewayne Gilchrist,
Roland D. Maiuro and
Gayle Fay
Dean P. Inman
Gary Martin and
Angela Pallotta-Cornick
Steven P. Schinke
G. Thomas Bellamy,
Dean P. Inman and
Robert H. Horner

1978: X. BEHAVIORAL MEDICINE: CHANGING HEALTH LIFESTYLES

G. Terence Wilson
Ethel Roskies and
Richard S. Lazarus
Stanley Schachter
Ovide F. Pomerleau
John H. Milsum
Richard B. Stuart

Lizette Peterson,
Donald P. Hartman and
Donna M. Gelfand
Aurea Cormier,
Marielle Prefontaine,
Helen MacDonald and
Richard B. Stuart

Lynn Alden   Janet Alexander
Peter E. Nathan   J. Allan Best
Sandy Keir and   Park Davidson
Richard Lauzon   G. Alan Marlatt and
Nathan Maccoby and   Judith R. Gordon

The Banff conferences have been more than places at which theories and research data are presented and discussed. They have stimulated planning and research in selected areas, and have helped to bring together policymakers, program administrators, researchers, and clinicians in an effort to stimulate the adoption in practical settings of many of the programs that have been discussed during the conference proceedings.

Many people have devoted their energies and talents to the continued success of the Banff Conferences. Primarily, of course, we wish to acknowledge the guest faculties who develop, present and discuss topics found in this volume and its predecessors. The staff and resources of the Banff Centre, which has been the site of the Conferences, have also contributed greatly to their success. Other members of the Conference Planning Committee should be singled out for their substantial help and guidance: They are Drs. Park O. Davidson and L. A. Hamerlynck. Special thanks are due as well to Ms. Suzanne Vaughan for her aid in conference administration, and to Mrs. Elaine Bennett who very ably assisted in every aspect of the editing of this volume.

R.B.S.

Contents

Contributors

GENE G. ABEL
Department of Psychiatry,
College of Physicians and Surgeons
Columbia University
and
Sexual Behavior Clinic,
New York Psychiatric Institute

THOMAS W. AIKEN
Department of Special Education,
University of Southern California

JUDITH V. BECKER
Department of Psychiatry,
College of Physicians and Surgeons
Columbia University
and
Sexual Behavior Clinic,
New York Psychiatric Institute

KAREN L. BURKE
Mental Health Clinical Research
Center
for the Study of Schizophrenia,
UCLA Department of Psychiatry,
Camarillo State Hospital

ALLEN M. COLE
Department of Psychology,
University of Utah

THOMAS P. DOWD
Father Flanagan's Boys' Home
Boys Town, Nebraska

DONALD G. DUTTON
Department of Psychology
University of British Columbia

MICHAEL R. FENN
Department of Psychology
University of Utah

DEAN L. FIXSEN
Father Flanagan's Boys' Home
Boys Town, Nebraska

BARRY FLANAGAN
Department of Psychiatry,
College of Physicians and Surgeons
Columbia University
and
Sexual Behavior Clinic,
New York Psychiatric Institute

xiii

LEE W. FREDERIKSEN
*Virginia Polytechnic Institute and
    State University*

ROBERT PAUL LIBERMAN
*Mental Health Clinical Research
    Center for the Study of
    Schizophrenia,
UCLA Department of Psychiatry,
Camarillo State Hospital*

RUDY LORBER
Oregon Social Learning Center

JANICE K. MARQUES
*California State Department of
    Mental Health, Sacramento*

BARRINGER D. MARSHALL, JR.
*Mental Health Clinical Research
    Center for the Study of
    Schizophrenia,
UCLA Department of Psychiatry,
Camarillo State Hospital*

WILLIAM D. MURPHY
*Department of Psychiatry,
University of Tennessee Center for
    the Health Sciences, Memphis*

LOUIS J. PALMA
*Father Flanagan's Boys' Home
Boys Town, Nebraska*

ELERY L. PHILLIPS
*Father Flanagan's Boys' Home
Boys Town, Nebraska*

NANCY RAINWATER
*Veterans Administration Medical
    Center and University of
    Mississippi Medical Center*

JOHN B. REID
Oregon Social Learning Center

RICHARD B. STUART
*Department of Family and
    Community Medicine
School of Medicine
University of Utah*

JEROME S. STUMPHAUZER
*Department of Psychology and
    Psychiatry,
University of Southern California
School of Medicine*

PAUL S. TAPLIN
National Asthma Center

CHARLES W. TURNER
*Department of Psychology
University of Utah*

ESTEBAN V. VELOZ
*Coordinator,
EL CENTRO Anticrime Program,
Los Angeles*

LENORE E. WALKER
*Department of Psychology
Colorado Women's College
and
Director and Principal Investigator
Battered Women Research Center,
    Denver*

VIOLENT BEHAVIOR:
Social Learning Approaches to Prediction, Management and Treatment

1
Violence in Perspective

RICHARD B. STUART

Violence has been defined as acts that involve great force and are capable of and intended to injure, damage, or destroy (Miller, 1971). While some have doubted the validity of crime reports per se, victimization data have now been added to reports of police criminal action (National Criminal Justice Information Service, 1975), and have, in turn, been interpreted in the FBI's *Uniform Crime Reports*, thereby helping to present a reasonable picture of crime rates. The picture is alarming, at the very least. Murder, rape, robbery, aggravated assault, and burglary have all more than tripled during the past two decades. It is now estimated that 10% of all American households will be burglarized during the next 12 months and that at least 3% of the American population will be the victims of violent crimes this year. In fact, it has recently been concluded that an American boy born in 1974 is more likely to die by murder than an American soldier was likely to die of wounds suffered in World War II combat (Morris & Hawkins, 1977).

Not only do these crimes injure their victims materially and/or physically, but they also have significant impact upon the emotional state of both victims and nonvictims. Silberman (1978) observed that while accidents claim 10 times as many injuries as crimes, accidents are taken as a "natural" risk, while fear of crime brings terror to the lives of old and young, male and female alike. As a result of this fear, elderly people quiver hungry behind multilocked doors rather than brave the risks encountered on sidewalks leading to and from food stores. Even vigorous young men give up some of their favored haunts because of the threat of victimization during recreation, and many women and children are forced to limit their out-of-doors activities to crowded places during daylight hours so that they can go about the quiet enjoyment of their lives in safety. So pernicious are the effects of crime that it leads many to question the stability of the basic fabric of the society of which we are all members.

In order to stem the tide of the spread of crime, it is necessary for all sectors of society to contribute expertise and resources for understanding and controlling forces that generate and maintain the varied forms of violence. In this volume is found what can be regarded as the leading edge of work by a group of researchers best classified as subscribing to the tenets of the social learning theory tradition (see below). They offer recommendations for the management of violence from perspectives as widely divergent as those of the social ecologist and the psychopharmacologist. To present a context that will aid in the understanding and evaluation of each approach, this chapter offers a broad overview of the theories of violence that have been set forth during the past five centuries and concludes with a brief synopsis of each contribution.

SOURCES OF VIOLENT BEHAVIOR

Ethologists (e.g., Lorenz, 1966) and sociobiologists (e.g., Mark, 1978) offer the view that aggressive behavior is phylogenetically determined and that it is inevitable in all living organisms because it is adaptive for the survival both of individuals and their species. Extrapolations of animal studies to ethnographic reports of the violent behavior of primitives create a teasing ontogenetic link between human and infrahuman organisms. For example, Pfeiffer's (1980) observation that the South American Yanomamo people seem driven to continual warfare would seem to support the view that humans have inherited some of the worst behavioral characteristics of their forebears. However, critics of the ethological approach (e.g., Schuster, 1978) have pointed out that animal species may be aggressive in one set of conditions yet behave quite peaceably in others—a fact that would seem to belie an inexorable proclivity toward violence. In the same vein, the sociobiological thesis has been challenged by scholars like Chorover (1973) and Valenstein (1976) on grounds that violence is much more closely related to membership in certain demographic groups as opposed to others (e.g., Wolfgang, 1958). If violence were more prevalent in certain socioeconomically or racially defined groups, sociologists would be forced to explain why only a limited number of us evince supposedly ubiquitous violent predispositions. Two related traditions of writers have risen to the challenge of explaining why some but not all of us are "atavistic" in nature: These writers seek to identify the morphological correlations of or the genetic predisposition to violent behavior.

As early as 1586, J. Baptiste de la Porte concluded from a study of the cadavers of convicts that they were characterized by small ears and noses, thickened open lips, bushy eyebrows, shifty eyes, and long, thin fingers (cited by Catalano, 1979). Beard and the shape of the chin, eyes, and nose were found to differentiate criminals from law-abiding citizens by Lavater in 1775, while Franz Gall advocated using phrenology to predict crime in 1825. These impassioned arguments may have helped Morel to postulate in 1857 that some individuals were physically degenerate and therefore driven to be behaviorally degenerate as well. Shortly thereafter Lombroso offered his observations that Italian criminals differed from Italian firemen and bathers on sun-drenched beaches by their large jaws, high cheekbones, prominent superciliary arches, variant palm prints, handle-shaped or sensile ears, insensitivity to pain, acute sight, and tattooing. Lombroso went on to relate these characteristics to behavioral proclivities such as idleness, love of orgies, a desire to mutilate corpses and drink their blood, in addition to killing and a seemingly irresistible craving for evil for its own sake.

Dr. Charles Goring (1913) offered what should have been a definitive test of Lombroso's findings when he compared 3,000 British criminals with a like number of nonprisoners, including Oxford and Cambridge undergraduates. He found a disarmingly even distribution of cranial and facial irregularities in both groups and concluded that the prisoners were slightly shorter and finer in build—characteristics he attributed to their relatively poorer infant nutrition.

Rather than laying to rest the belief that crime has its physiological correlates, Goring's findings were to be challenged a quarter of a century later when Hooton (1939) published his epic two-volume research on *The American Criminal*. He studied some 10,000 criminals and a somewhat smaller group of controls and reached the conclusion that the former could be differentiated from the latter by their narrow jaws, compressed faces, and low sloping foreheads, not to mention their tattoos, which had also been noticed by Lombroso. The fact that even in his sample many criminals lacked and many law-abiders exhibited these characteristics did not deter Hooton from his insistence upon an etiological link between physiology and criminality.

More contemporary researchers have continued this same tradition by looking beneath the skin for morphological differentiators of criminality. Perhaps starting with the famed British psychologist Hans Eysenck (1964), who suggested that offenders were less conditionable than nonoffenders because of neurological differences, others (e.g., Fields & Sweet, 1975) assign the responsibility for criminality to abnormal EEG patterns (e.g., Ohlesen, Gibbs, & Adams, 1970) or frontal lobe abnormalities (e.g., Detre, Kupfer, & Taub, 1975). This kind of speculation has a stiff challenge to overcome. For example, one team of researchers (Virkkunen, Nuutila & Huusko, 1977) studied the postwar criminal behavior of all World War II Finnish veterans who had suffered frontal, temporal or occipital lobe combat injuries. They, along with others who conducted similar studies (e.g., Gunn & Bonn, 1971; Guze, 1976; MacDonald, 1958; Rodin, 1973), found that there were *no* statistically significant differences in violent crime rates by any subgroup of their brain-injured subjects and a randomly chosen group of uninjured veterans comprising a control group. Clearly, then, whether variations are at the surface or beneath the skin, there is little support for the view that criminals differ morphologically from noncriminals.

Some argue, however, that the differences must be sought at the genetic level, suggesting that our diagnostic techniques are not yet sufficient to detect the relevant manifest characteristics. Dugdale's (1888) study of the so-called "Jukes" family may have crystalized the beginning of genetic theorizing about criminality. Working as a prison inspector in New York State, Dugdale found, among the descendents of two brothers, 378 people who died in infancy, 301 illegitimates, 366 paupers, 80 habitual thieves, 171 convicts—including 10 murderers, 175 prostitutes, and 50 who were known to have spread venereal disease to some 600 other persons. While Dugdale attributed the results of his observations to environment as well as breeding, Goddard's (1912) study of the so-called "Kallikak" family ignored environment and stressed genetics, tracing an evil branch of the issue of a Revolutionary war soldier to his dalliance with a tavern maid and an honorable branch to his marriage to a "Quakeress."

These studies have been followed up by attempts to show that identical twins are more likely to share criminal or law-abiding tendencies than are fraternal twins. A German psychiatrist, Johannes Lange (1931), started the ball rolling by publishing his finding that 10 of 13 pairs of identical twins had criminal records as opposed to only two of 17 pairs of fraternal twins, the latter ratio being no greater than that expected for any pair of like-sexed siblings. Lange's research was riddled by so many flaws, such as the absence of objective criteria for differentiating identical from fraternal twins, the omission of analysis of any contributory life-history material, and single observer evaluations at every stage of the study, that it would in all probability not be publishable by contemporary standards; yet it spawned a number of prejudicial attacks upon minorities, perhaps best illustrated by Haldane's (1931) introduction to Lange's book in which it is claimed that Catholics display a genetically determined predisposition to a life of crime.

The so-called "criminal twin" studies have hopefully been laid to rest by the publication of landmark research by Christensen (1973). Working in Denmark, he showed that identical twins were more likely than fraternal twins to have common criminal patterns—but only if they lived in rural areas in which they were constantly linked and not if they lived in urban areas in which they could achieve some measure of individuality. Given these findings, it will be difficult for writers like Eysenck (1964) to continue to claim that genetics play a role superordinate to that of environment in the promotion of violence.

But the myth that criminals are Frankenstein or Quasimodo types lives on, most recently dressed up in the cloak of an extra X or Y chromosome. This theory was germinated by the observation that seven of 942 inmates in one hospital for the criminally insane had an extra Y chromosome (Casey, Blank, Street, Segall, McDougall, McGrath, & Skinner, 1966), as did nine of 315 inmates in another such institution (Jacobs, Price, & Brown, 1968). These values are beyond those that would be normally expected. Yet, despite a number of studies purporting to show a bias toward behavioral abnormality associated with genetic abnormality (e.g., Boughman & Mann, 1972; De Bault, Johnston & Loeffelnolz, 1972; Nielsen, 1971), researchers have again shown that this genetic predisposition—if indeed it exists—is secondary to the influence of environmental forces (e.g., Casey, Street, Segall & Blank, 1968), leading the British Medical Research Council to conclude that there is "no evidence which indicated that an XYY male is inexorably bound to develop antisocial traits" (Brown, Price, & Jacobs, 1968).

What the earlier physiological researchers could not find in their efforts to predict crime, the psychiatrists and psychologists ventured to provide. Beginning with Freud's (1901) *The Psychopathology of Everyday Life* and continuing through his *The Ego and the Id* (1923), it was suggested that efforts to cope with anxiety would drive the ego to resort to varied defense mechanisms (Hartmann, Kris, & Lowenstein, 1964) which would yield deviant and sometimes criminal behavior (Feldman, 1964). For example, it was believed that when ego boundaries were blurred (Federn, 1952) and instinctual energy was at its crest (Fenichel, 1945), some individuals would act in a manner that would evoke external punishment to shore up faltering superegos. Unfortunately, because of the intrinsic incompatibility between these hypothetical constructs and the currently available measurement techniques, it is not possible to put these notions to direct test and their use in *ex post facto* prediction has not been overly fruitful.

Related to the theory that violence is a manifestation of a warped personality are the catathymic and compulsive properties ascribed to certain instances of aggression. Wertham (1978) described catathymia as a multistage phenomenon in which an initial thinking disorder is precipitated by a traumatic circumstance; this crystalizes into a plan in which violence seems to be the only available option; the plan evokes intense emotional tension during which the violent act is carried out; the outburst leads to a period of superficial normality as calmness returns, eventually leading to inner equilibrium when insight is achieved. Insight is not, however, a solution to violence in the so-called compulsively aggressive person (Freeman, 1955; Guttmacher, 1963). This person is found guilty of repeated assaults on strangers with whom he has had no prior contact, resulting in no apparent personal gain, and receiving no overt social support. Unfortunately, both catathymia and compulsion are predictable after the fact but are not useful for the reliable classification of individuals prior to the commission of a crime.

A variety of psychometric efforts have been stimulated by heuristic psychodynamic theories. For example, some researchers have attempted to explain violence as the result of an explosive breakdown of efforts to overly restrict its expression in what may be termed a "pressure engine theory of aggression." They selected 37 MMPI items believed to address this tendency toward overrepression (Megargee, Cook, & Mendelsohn, 1967) and attempted to use it to predict violence in intimates (e.g., Megargee & Cook, 1975). Unfortunately, efforts by others to use the scale predictively have not been successful (e.g., Johnson, 1974), and one is forced to conclude with Megargee (1970) and Quinsey, Ambtman, and Pruesse (Note 1) that no single test is capable of accurately predicting violence, and that all may be inferior to the neurological measurements (Spellacy, 1977), the weaknesses of which have been identified earlier.

The same dim conclusions have been reached concerning the value of psychiatric diagnosis in predicting violence. Researchers have turned to concepts like "psychopathy" in attempts to prejudge patients who will or will not be guilty of violent acts, with weak and inconsistent results (e.g., Gibbens, Pond, Stafford-Clark, 1959; Hedlund, Sletten, Altman, & Evenson, 1973). Representative of studies in this area is the effort by Cocozza and Steadman (1976) to trace the validity of judgments of two psychiatrists concerning the potential dangerousness of 257 prisoners indicted for felonies and found incompetent to stand trial. During their institutionalization, the predicted group was slightly but not statistically more violent than those assessed as being nonviolent, a finding that was reversed following release from the institutions to which group members were committed. Studies like this illustrate the extent to which danger-ousness is overpredicted by psychiatric judgment, with false positive findings ranging from 55% to 99% of all such predictions (Monahan, 1978). Accordingly, it is reasonable to conclude that psychiatric diagnosis is, at best, marginally linked to the potential for violence (Mesnikoff & Lauterbach, 1975), a supposition even accepted by the Task Force on Clinical Aspects of Violent Individuals empaneled by the American Psy-chiatric Association (1974).

The soundness of predictions of violence is increased when environ-mental factors are coupled with individual judgments. In an early effort in this connection, Conrad (1966) generated seven "types" believed to be relevant to violent potential, including those raised in subcultures in which violence is encouraged, those confronting situations in which viol-ence is prompted, and those engaging in violence for financial gain. Similarly, Straus, Gelles, and Steinmetz (1980) recently generated scales that reliably postdicted intrafamilial violence in their national survey. For example, they found that violence is much more common in families in which the husband is unemployed, money is limited, spouses are under 30, more than two children reside, and either or both adults have a history of having been abused as children or of witnessing spousal abuse between their parents.

A number of different kinds of efforts have been put forth by students of the interactional sources of violence, ranging from analysis of the family as the cradle of violence through assessment of group factors to measurement and prediction of broad forces within the community and culture.

One team of researchers (Straus et al., 1980) concluded that violence is no stranger to families at all strata of society. They believe that:

> the American family and the American home are perhaps as or more violent than any other single American institution or set-ting . . . Americans run the greatest risk of assault, physical injury, and even murder in their own homes by members of their own families (p. 4).

In fact, not only is violence in the home not proscribed, it is actually *fostered* by social and philosophical traditions dating to the earliest days of our civilization.

It has been estimated that between 84% and 97% of all parents in this country use corporal punishment at some time in their children's lives (Bronfenbrenner, 1958; Erlanger, 1974). For upwards of half of the families in America, the use or threat of force continues virtually to the point at which the child leaves home (Mulligan, 1977; Steinmetz, 1974). The forms of abuse are somewhat amazing: Straus, et al. (1980) estimates that of the 46 million children between the ages of three and seven in the United States in 1975, in that year alone approximately 1.9 million were kicked, bitten, or punched by their parents; some 500,000 were "beaten up" by their parents; and some 50,000 were victimized by parents using a gun or a knife. This violence has been explained by reference to a number of social structural and interactional hypotheses (Burgess, 1978). For example, parents may abuse children because of conflicts of interest in which the child may want attention and the parent privacy; because of the simple amount of contact time that breeds opportunities for violence in settings far from the public's eye; because of high levels of intimacy and emotional contact that create many opportunities for disappointment; because children are smaller and weaker and therefore safe targets for displaced aggression flowing from the stress of other conflicts; or, most importantly, because parents simply lack the skills to do otherwise.

Statistics on spousal abuse are equally alarming: Straus et al. (1980) found in their national survey that at some time in their marriages slightly less than 1% of all spouses actually used a knife or a gun during a domestic argument, some 5% had been involved in a "beating up" incident, 16% had thrown something at the other during an argument, 18% slapped the other, and one-fourth of all couples were involved in pushing, shoving, or grabbing one another during arguments. Translating these percentages into gross numbers, they estimate that among American couples in 1975:

> over 1.7 million . . . had at some time faced a husband or wife wielding a knife or a gun, and well over 2 million had been beaten up by his or her spouse (p. 34).

The researchers cite a history of having been reared in a violent family as the single most influential determinant of spousal abuse, increasing the likelihood of violence by the male tenfold and by the female sixfold. They believe that this exposure teaches the child that the ones you love

are the ones you hit, that hitting family members is morally right, and
that violence is an acceptable last-ditch tactic. They also found varied
demographic factors to increase the probability of violence, as mentioned
earlier, and noted that couples who had the most frequent verbal arguments were also those most likely to become violent. The latter finding
stands in sharp contrast to the beliefs of those who subscribe to the
"catharsis" theory of aggression, and in strong support of the views of
others who contend that minor conflicts are little more than rehearsals
for major conflicts and should therefore be contained rather than encouraged (Berkowitz, 1973; Hokanson, 1970; Stuart, 1980a).

Beyond the family, a number of small-group interactional factors are
seen as contributing to violence (Megargee, 1970; Osman & Lee, 1978),
with aggressive behavior passing through a series of natural evolutionary
stages (Scherer, Abeles, & Fischer, 1975). For example, Kriesberg (1973)
predicated five stages in which two or more individuals move from a
precompetitive stage in which they might have either no contact or even
interact cooperatively, shift to competition, move through conflict to a
stage of restructuring, to a final stage of resolution. Many factors can
contribute to the level of violence they will express, ranging from the
extent of the individuals' use of drugs—particularly alcohol, which has
been associated with a majority of murders and other violent crimes
(Gillies, 1965; Guttmacher, 1967; Tinklenberg, 1980; Voss & Hepburn,
1968; Wolfgang, 1958)—to the availability of weapons (Berkowitz &
LePage, 1967), exposure to violent models (Bandura, 1976; Walters,
1966), and the extent of overcrowding at the time of the interaction
(Carstairs, 1969).

The availability of a social group with a set of operational values can
also precipitate violence among individuals whose own value system is
weakened (Merton, 1957, 1968), particularly when the group supports
aggression (Graham & Gurr, 1969). In their classic study of the adjustment of Polish immigrants, Thomas and Znaniecki (1927) found, for
example, that when the moral codes of the "old country" did not suit
life in the "new world," some newcomers turned for support to groups
that promoted crime as a ready means of achieving personal goals. While
perhaps not a deliberate choice, but rather the result of drifting toward
these supportive groups (Matza, 1964; Sutherland, 1947), and when
criminal opportunities existed (Ohlin & Cloward, 1960), membership
in these groups clearly provided fitting opportunities to learn criminal
patterns (Sutherland, 1939). Entry into these groups with deviant cultures was eased by shared ethnic (Blumenthal, Kahn, Andrews, & Head,
1972; Miller, 1958), occupational (Faulkner, 1973), or behavioral (Cohen

& Short, 1958) similarities between potential joiners and current group members.

At least two general phenomena have been believed to contribute to a willingness to join such antisocial groups. The first is economic deprivation (McKenzie, 1926; Burgess, 1926). This belief originated some 150 years ago when A. M. Guerry identified differential crime rates for five economically distinct areas of Paris. His work, which was made public during the 1820s, was followed up later by Mayhew (1862), who demonstrated that crime rate could be predicted from a knowledge of area-wide prevalence of population density, illiteracy, and poverty, for he viewed crime as adaptive for survival among a population lacking other more sanctioned means of competitin. Later, similar trials were undertaken in predicting the rate of crime in designated areas of Chicago (Shaw & McKay, 1942; Shaw, Zorbaugh, McKay, & Cottrell, 1929) by a team which found that crime rate diminished as a function of distance from the central business district, was relatively stable in each area over time despite shifts in population composition, was less likely to result in repeated offenses if the individual resided far from rather than near to the central business district, and tended to be associated with higher rates of truancy and other signs of social disorganization. The role of social disorganization as an area characteristic was noted by others (e.g., Lander, 1954; Reckless, 1926), although the methods used in these various studies have been questioned (e.g., Borgatta, 1968; Chilton, 1964; Gordon, 1967) and the correlations report but do not explain the relevant associations. In addition, "new society" efforts to provide economic opportunities to the disadvantaged (e.g., Moynihan, 1969) have generally not demonstrated a positive impact upon crime rates (Hackler, 1966; Weissman, 1969), so economics alone cannot be considered to be the breeding ground of crime.

The second dimension of community life that has been assigned importance as a stimulant of crime is an interaction between economics and values. As one expression of this approach, Davies (1969) has described the "J curve" for predicting mass violence. He believes that:

> revolution is most likely to take place when a prolonged period of rising expectations and rising gratifications is followed by a sharp reversal, during which the gap between expectations and gratifications quickly widens and becomes intolerable (p. 671).

He then analyzes historical events as divergent as the French Revolution, the American Civil War, and the Nazi rise to power in terms of his hypothesis. Other events appear to be necessary, however, to allow the conflict between resources and desires to elicit aggression. For example, social controls must at least temporarily relax (Silberman, 1978), as occurred when the lights went out in New York or the Germans provoked looting in Denmark when they disbanded the Danish police during their withdrawal from that country. If the controls are not relaxed, violence can also result if the controls are believed to be generally ineffective.

Armed with proviolence cultural values and organization in groups, the fires of aggression are sparked; they are fanned into flame when other social conditions are met. In a marvelously insightful treatise, Fogelson (1971) analyzed violence during the urban riots of the mid 1960s. He pointed out that one restraint against violence is concern for one's own safety. But with ghetto areas already highly unsafe places to live and with strong ideological support for protest overwhelming the motive of self-preservation, this restraint faltered. Fear of arrest is another restraint which was ineffective because such large proportions of blacks had arrest records not necessarily because they committed criminal acts but because police practice in high crime areas calls for frequent arrest on suspicion for questioning. Commitment to an orderly process of social change is another source of rioting restraint. For this to be operative, however, potential rioters must have "faith in the system," a creed that is very difficult to sustain in the face of the harsh realities of ghetto life. In point of fact, many urban poor people feel they have nothing to offer in exchange for access to resources, that they are "socially bankrupt" (Stuart, 1980a) and may resort to violence to steal what they cannot buy, to get attention that they cannot otherwise earn, to obtain revenge, or just to have the satisfaction of having done something, anything, even if that something makes matters worse (Dillon, 1972). When deprivation is real and groups of people sense their own powerlessness, any real or imagined act by a member of the dominant group in society can have the same power to trigger rebellion that closing the detonator terminal can have in setting off a blast of TNT (Liberson & Silverman, 1965).

Convincing though these arguments may be, it is important to point out that many groups who are heavily involved in aggression do not aspire to, and therefore are not frustrated by not having, the economic and social advantages of members of the dominant society (e.g., Burt, 1925; Douvan, 1956; Nettler, 1974; Stacey, 1965). In addition, violence is by no means uniform among members of activist groups or among members of rebellious communities, so the reliance upon economic and value terms of reference is as inadequate a basis for explaining violence as is the same reliance upon intraindividual factors.

It should be clear from this brief review that no one approach can claim great success in predicting violence or in serving as a foundation for programs that control aggressive behavior. Writers concerned with intraindividual factors tend to downplay the role of situational factors (e.g., Eysenck, 1964), much as writers who believe that violence is group-elicited (e.g., Shoham, Ben-David, & Rahar, 1974) tend to ignore the contribution of individual predisposition. Rather than adopting an either-or approach, a "both" approach would seem to be much more consistent with the current state of our knowledge (Revitch, 1975, 1977), and it should be one that recognizes that any conclusions must be regarded as tentative.

As a general rule, it seems wise to begin any assessment or treatment program with the assumption that the best predictor of criminal activity is the rate of such activity in the past. Wolfgang (1976), for example, reported that some 46% of all juvenile offenders had a single arrest, an additional 35% had no more than two apprehensions, and 25% had no more than three. For reasons that are not necessarily clear, his data would support the assumption that multiple offenders would continue to chalk up arrests—*other things being equal.* But many things can change. For example, if offered stress inoculation therapy (Novaco, 1979), the individual can learn to use self-management techniques to control anger, or changes in family interaction patterns can build adaptive skills while lessening aggression elicitors at home (Stuart, Tripodi, Jayaratne, & Camburn, 1976). Also, social conditions can change as a result of shifting economic factors or the creation of other constructive opportunities. Therefore, it is not possible to confidently predict future violence simply from a knowledge of violence in the past; to this must be coupled an assessment of the current situation which would have to be essentially similar to conditions in the past for the prediction to gain strength. Therefore, the second basic rule requires situational dimensions to be factored into every judgment about the potential for the recurrence or control of violence.

Because situational factors are so important in assessment, they are also important in the design of interventions. Elsewhere (Stuart, Note 2), a theory of indirect treatment has been put forth. In this approach a two-stage intervention plan is offered. First, an effort is made to modify the environment in ways that eliminate or suppress many of the prompts for the problem behavior. For example, providing adequate food and shelter can help to eliminate at least some of the prompts to steal. There are, in turn, two general strategies for accomplishing this change in stressors: The intervenor can take charge of the environment, as is the case in many instances of social reform, or the target individual can be trained to make the moves that will result in environmental changes. (Generally both tactics are combined.) Once the environment has been modified, the client is taught specific skills in responding differently to those cues for problem behavior that escape the interventionist's control. For example, money will not always be plentiful, and it is necessary to help the client learn other ways of coping with deprivation when money-motivated crime might be the likely response.

The combination of behaviors and situational observation in assessment and efforts to modify the environment and to improve the individual's skills is the basis for social learning theory (Stuart, 1980a). It is this theoretical approach that offers the background for the remaining chapters of this book. Some concentrate heavily on techniques for environmental change, while others stress skill building. The next section offers an overview of the content of these chapters so that readers will have a comparative perspective as each is studied.

ABOUT THE CHAPTERS IN THIS BOOK

Each of the 11 chapters that follow addresses issues of prediction and/or control from a perspective that recognizes the interaction between the range of forces believed to have etiological significance for violent behavior.

Turner, Fenn, and Cole begin Chapter 2 by taking aim at some insupportable prejudices that have long hindered clear thinking about crime, adopting a social learning theory and opportunity theory point of view. They begin by putting the frustration-aggression hypothesis in a proper light by recognizing that frustration may elicit aggression if the individual believes that it is beyond control, while it may elicit problem-solving or assertion when frustrating forces are perceived to fall within the span of the individual's control. The choice of responses will be mediated by a complex of sociocultural forces as viewed by this team of social psychologists. The microsocial forces include exposure to models, the nature of the immediate prompts for action, the availability of the instruments of violence, and the likelihood of apprehension. It is in the delineating of macrosocial forces, however, that the researchers demonstrate their remarkable creativity.

They speculate that when life stresses occur, individuals who have a strong sense of self-efficacy will opt for aggression, while those who doubt their ability to alter the course of events will elect to respond passively to frustration. They then point out that the rate of violent crime is a function of age and racial distribution (those in their early twenties and in racial minorities are more likely to commit violent crimes), but they then show that within age and racial cohorts it is those who are faced with the greatest relative economic deprivation who are the most violent. That is, young men whose economic opportunities are significantly more limited than those of their parents are most likely to commit violent crimes. The authors trace the recent rise in violence to the maturation of men born during the post-World-War-II baby boom, coming at a time when economic retrenchment makes it much more difficult for young men to secure economic gains than had been true for their parents. They then speculate and present data that begin to support the view that the rate of violent crime will decline as the population of men in their early twenties declines and as these dwindling numbers of men have less need to compete for scarce jobs.

The unique feature of this analysis is its combination of micro- and macrosocial explanations. All too often one finds either references to the family as the "crucible of violence" or to broad secular trends as the "birthplace of aggression." This paper, however, deftly interweaves the two traditions and lays a suitable foundation for the application papers that follow.

In Chapter 3 subcultural and social interactional causes of violence are brought into sharper focus, with an analysis of gang violence as the threat which causes the most fear in urban dwellers. Stumphauzer, Veloz and Aiken put this type of aggression into a useful perspective with their review of statistics showing that gang violence is on the rise, and present a functional analysis of the occasions of its occurrence and nonoccurrence. They extend the familiar clinical assessment models to an expanded data set in naturalistic surroundings using social anthropology's technique of participant observation, and indicate that gang violence is precipitated by adverse economic and physical environmental conditions, that it is maintained by peer reactions and inadvertently by the actions of crime reporters, victims, and law enforcement officers, and that it is a cumulative phenomenon. Through analysis of the lives of two boys who did not engage in delinquent behavior despite the fact that they lived in a high-crime area, they show that avoidance of overt cues of gang membership, use of prosocial behavior, and access to meaningful employment can all contribute to "going straight." They conclude their presentation with a brief and tantalizing description of a crime-fighting program in the barrio area of Los Angeles, one in which youths receive strong reinforcement for the emission of behaviors that restrict rather than perpetuate delinquent acts. This is a humane and rational approach

which promises greater rewards than the more often tried and rarely
successful repressive measures.

Chapter 4 focuses on inter- and intragenerational violence within families. Reid, Taplin and Lorber have done some very important things in
their analysis of the interaction patterns in abusive families. They move
from a theoretical model through an empirical test of the core assumptions in that model, and then to a partial test of the value of their findings
in the planning of an intervention program. It is all too rare for clinical
researchers to formulate a philosophy of the disorder with which they
are concerned, to test the validity of their theory, and then to expose
the theory to a parsimonious test through direct clinical application.
Working at the Oregon Social Learning Center, this forward-reaching
group hypothesized that all members of abusive families would show
higher rates of aversive behavior than would be found in nonabusive
families; that the parents in these families would have above-average
difficulties in dealing with day-to-day discipline situations; and that these
deficits could be corrected through a highly specific program aimed at
building constructive behavior-control skills. Careful observation of interaction patterns in the homes of 27 nondistressed families, 61 distressed but nonabusive families, and 27 distressed-abusive families
supported the first hypothesis. Of particular interest are their findings
that the parents in distressed-abusive families behave toward each other
in highly aversive ways, and that the children in these families are as
prone to aversive behavior as are their parents. Aggressive behaviors are
therefore the norms of these families, and the behaviors are distributed
across all of the interacting family members.

The authors also reported some rather surprising findings with regard
to their second hypothesis. For example, they observed that mothers
were more likely than fathers in abusive families to use coercive threats.
They found too that all of the parents studied tended to provide reinforcing consequences for some of their children's negative behaviors,
and that while the nondistressed parents succeeded in controlling their
children's negative behavior with one threat 86% of the time, the success
rate of the abusive parents was only 47%. Therefore, parental ineffectiveness was clearly shown to be at least one element in the etiology of
abuse of the children. Finally, the authors present initial data that demonstrate their success in reducing the rate of aversive behavior by mothers and the referred youth through use of a social learning theory based
treatment program. If the findings of these researchers are validated in
other settings, the 11 years of their effort clearly lay the groundwork
for energetic programs to promote more constructive family interaction

leading to the control of violence in the home, based upon the notion that violence is truly a whole-family affair and not just an expression of the pathology of a single family member.

The next three chapters deal with sex crimes as a special case of violence. Whether social attitudes have changed so that more women feel comfortable about reporting being victims of rape or the actual number of rapes has increased, the number of reported rapes has more than doubled during the past decade. Beyond the rise in the sheer number of violent sexual crimes, the nature of these crimes has been changing dramatically. For example, many more children are falling victims to forced sexual acts, and rapists are more likely than ever to attack strangers rather than other family members or associates. The consequences of rape for the victims, members of their families, and residents in their communities are terribly severe. Victims struggle with efforts to suppress the rage and hurt that are part and parcel of being invaded by the rapist. Family members often respond with a combination of guilt and repugnance that distorts or even destroys relationships that were premorbidly close and caring, and entire communities warp the shape of their lives in response to the fear evoked by rape victimization. For these reasons it was decided to incorporate not one but three papers on rape in this volume.

Chapter 5 deals with wife rape as one of a number of acts of domestic violence, while the remaining papers offer state-of-the-art designs for analyzing provocative and control dimensions of rape situations. Walker begins her presentation by noting that from one-fourth to one-half of all American wives are believed to be the victims of domestic violence at some time in their lives. She notes that only a multidimensional approach that takes into account both personal and situational variables can possibly account for this mass phenomenon, with sociocultural traditions actually placing a positive value on male violence as one of the most important of these causes—values shared by aggressors and victims alike. She concludes her paper with a plea for sociopolitical change as well as for research on the prevention of violence and on adequate services for its victims. The following two papers address her second request very well.

Reporting on pioneering work conducted at the University of Tennessee, Drs. Abel, Becker, Murphy and Flanagan (Chapter 6) begin their presentation with a sobering review of statistics showing that rape tends to be a repeated pattern of violence and that it is commonly associated with a level of brutality that goes far beyond that needed to coerce sexual entry. In an effort to discover the inner response patterns of sexual offenders, the authors developed psychophysical test protocols in which penile volume was measured as a response to descriptions of varied sexual scenes. Volunteer subjects were undergoing treatment for either heterosexual incest, rape or pedophilia, homosexual pedophilia, exhibitionism or frottage. They were exposed to verbal narratives of scenes in which either a child or an adult consented to or was coerced into a sexual encounter. Careful monitoring permitted the development of indicies of sexual preference such as the Pedophile Index, which quantified the value of children as stimulants to erectile responses. It is important to note that data obtained through psychophysical assessment differ from self-reported behavior (e.g., an incestuous male was found to have sexual desires for girls other than his daughter despite his verbal report that he found only his daughter stimulating). Therefore, while it is possible that inmates might learn to control their erectile responses in order to be able to mislead therapists, the direct measurement of arousal patterns can prove to be a significant aid in the assessment, treatment, and evaluation of change in sexual offenders. Given the fact that pedophiles in this sample are reported to have molested an average of over 60 children, it is clear that repeat offenses are the norm for the group, and any technique that can measure and change this potential should occupy an important role in our therapeutic armamentarium.

The final paper in this series (Chapter 7) is an exemplar for all sex offender researchers. While the foregoing paper by Abel et al. attended to the interaction between victim characteristics and offender arousal, Marques measured the impact of varied victim responses on the sexual and violent proclivities of 12 hospitalized rapists. She noted that much controversy surrounds recommendations that women beg for sympathy, assertively refuse to submit or try to establish a relationship with the rapist as means of attempting to avoid victimization, very ably summarizing the welter of recommendations and research on this subject that has appeared in the past decade. She then offered subjects tapes of scenes in which intended victims made each of these responses; penile circumference was measured and self-reports made of probable reactions. She found a significant interaction between victim responses and rapist retort on each of these dimensions, noting that no universal recommendation other than avoidance of dangerous situations, when possible, is likely ever to be defensible. Specifically, among other results were the findings that pleas for mercy tended to intensify rapists' sexual arousal, aggressive reactions tended to trigger inclinations toward violence by the rapist, sexually aroused rapists were more likely to complete the act, and rapists whose reactions were neither highly aroused nor very angry were most likely to allow their intended victims to escape without completion of the act. Marques' data address but do not resolve the issue of whether rape is a sexual or an aggressive act, offering support for the hypothesis that both emotions combine to produce a completed rape. The data also indicate that while an aggressive response by the victim may forestall the completion of the act, this response may also intensify the likelihood that considerable harm will be done to her in the event that the rapist does persist.

It is only through the extension and replication of research such as that conducted by the Abel team and by Marques that we will learn enough about the motivation and responses of potential rapists to reduce the probability of their initiating and/or culminating their vicious attacks.

In Chapter 8 Dutton addresses the problem of police response to domestic violence. While training of marital partners and parents in conflict containment strategies can pay rich dividends, as noted in the work of Reid, Taplin and Lorber, published here, these efforts will not be completely effective and the police will be summoned to separate battling members of the same family. Regrettably, Dutton notes that the police are all too seldom adequately trained to intervene in these disputes, which do, he reports, annually contribute one of the major sources of violent injury and death.

Data reported by Dutton suggest that some 85% of police effort is devoted to "order maintenance," with the remainder spent on activities that are classically regarded as "law enforcement." Domestic violence falls somewhere between these two categories, depending upon its severity. Perhaps because of its hybrid status, because it demands that officers invade the citizen's personal space in every sense of the word, and because response to these calls requires officers to deal with emotionally upset people, officers are hesitant to respond to domestic calls. Police middle management tends to downplay the value of intervention in domestic violence for varied reasons, including the fact that these activities are not generally considered to be benchmarks of police productivity and officers are generally powerless as regards the provision of effective domestic services. Dutton notes that even the general public has an ambivalent attitude toward these police activities: While the public clamors for relief when spouses become violent, there are also widely held beliefs that interactions between spouses should remain private albeit violent.

Because of these conflicting pressures, police are frequently injured while attempting to pull battling spouses to their respective corners, and their interventions are often iatrogenic with respect to repeated spousal outbursts. To combat these problems, Dutton and his associates designed a "generalist" approach to recruit training in which skills are built in all areas of response to violence wherever it occurs—in a home, on the street, or in a public building. The training includes attention to skills in many interpersonal areas such as communication, the physical management of agitated behavior, values clarification, referral for services elsewhere, and many other features of crisis control. The training is offered with a minimum of input from "outside experts" who are generally viewed with suspicion by uniformed officers, and it includes varied materials, from preprinted class notes to carefully developed "stop action" videotapes. The effect of this comprehensive program was cleverly evaluated by Dutton and his associates, who interviewed randomly chosen training-course participants some months after they completed their program, under the guise of United Way data collectors who contacted the officers in their homes. This evaluation showed that many different attitudes were changed sufficiently by program participation to demonstrate effects several months after program completion. But sadly, Dutton notes that the program has yet to achieve its full measure of success because middle managers in the subject police departments still do not support the program adequately either philosophically or materially. Until the bureaucracy can be changed, the public will have to countenance less than optimal police service for controlling violence in the sanctuary of the home.

The final three chapters of this volume address intervention issues directly. Chapter 9 is concerned with a skill-building program for institutionalized adolescents, while Chapter 10 discusses the use of drugs and environmental engineering to manage violence in mental hospitals, and the final chapter outlines a clinical program aimed at helping patients develop alternatives to violent behavior.

The paper by Fixsen, Phillips, Dowd and Palma presents a well-thought-out program for managing aggressive behavior in an institutional setting that serves delinquent and predelinquent youth. These writers, who represent a unique blend of skilled researchers who are charged with line responsibilities in the management of the Boys Town environment in which they work, employ what has elsewhere (Stuart, Note 2) been described as an "indirect" approach. They recognize that violent actions are often the product of social interaction. They make their point dramatically by beginning their paper with an extended reference to some of the inmate abuses chronicled in the landmark *Morales v. Turman* decision: When the environment is impoverished and the staff abusive, inmate violence is the most predictable response. They point out the necessity of building environments in which positive behaviors are modeled, prompted, and reinforced. Even in such settings, however, some aggressive behavior is to be expected. To mount a program of "direct" (Stuart, 1980b) interventions in these instances, they describe methods of choosing appropriate staff and building skills in minimizing rather than maximizing violent episodes. On the first point, they have developed an attractive incentive package for "teaching parent" couples whom they recruit nationally rather than relying on local residents who may not be well suited to the job. They then offer training in techniques of early intervention in which youths are taught to avoid problem-evoking situations when possible and to make alternative responses in place of violent actions.

The program described in this paper has an elegance and specificity that holds it apart from most other efforts to develop "programatic" solutions to the problem of institutional violence. These efforts to develop new treatment methods stand in sharp contrast to the more traditional efforts to legislate shifts in services for which no suitable technology is available or to professionalize services as though holders of college and graduate degrees can, by dint of their classroom training, intervene more skillfully than laymen in situations in which needed programming is lacking. Readers of this paper should be forewarned, however, that the setting in which the present techniques have been developed serves youths on voluntary placement, a fact that surely colors their attitude toward and behavior in the institutional environment. This fact may also divert from this setting youths whose aggressive behavior may be extreme. Rather than closing interest in this program to those working in institutions serving involuntarily placed, more aggressive youth, the philosophy and techniques described here would serve as an excellent model for program development in those more challenging environments. Readers should also be alert to the fact that data measuring the effectiveness of this program are not presented in the body of the paper.

While many people in the general public still subscribe to the "lunatic theory" of mental illness, supposing that the mental patient is capable of untold feats of violent madness, many in the professional community have come to regard the mentally ill as essentially benign. In Chapter 10, Liberman, Marshall and Burke begin their discussion of the use of drugs in the management of violence in mental institutions by documenting the assertion that violent behavior is very common among locked-ward patients, and that this behavior often persists in the community following discharge of the patient. By implication it can be concluded that while many mental patients are nonviolent, those who do display aggressive behavior do so with great frequency and destructiveness, greatly affecting the lives of all those around them.

This outstanding team of Camarillo State Hospital (UCLA) researchers point out that there is scant evidence that violence is the result of neuropathology. They cite some evidence that temporal or frontal lobe lesions have been associated with violent outbursts and that aggressive behavior has also been seen in patients suffering from temporal lobe epilepsy—particularly when the patient is exposed to environmental stresses and has consumed even a small amount of alcohol. Therefore, they look to the interaction between personal characteristics, learning history, and current situations to explain violence both on and off psychiatric wards. They show, for example, that many patients who presumably have a physiological predisposition to violence become aggressive primarily when they lack the social skills to fulfill their desires and when they receive strong reinforcement for coercive behavior.

Despite the fact that the functional analysis of much patient violent behavior reveals that it can be controlled through careful skill building and environmental management, the authors find a strong bias toward the effort to use—indeed seriously overuse—drugs to manage patient aggression. While they do recognize that some drugs can serve a useful function in treatment regimens, they also point out that the seemingly careless prescription of drugs that is the norm in most psychiatric settings has the effect of intensifying rather than of curbing acts of violence. On the positive side, they find that use of major tranquilizers or neuroleptics can reduce paranoid delusions that sometimes precipitate violence, that manic-depressive illness which may underlie violence can be effectively controlled by the prudent prescription of lithium, and that seizure-controlling drugs can minimize the likelihood of violence by epileptics. But they also point out that sedative-hypnotic drugs have effects resembling those of alcohol, which disinhibits aggression and is linked to a great many violent crimes, and that stimulants may directly prompt coercive behavior. Perhaps their most serious and unnerving observation is the fact that mental health professionals apply large quantities of drugs indiscriminately in the hope of achieving their positive effects, without any attempt to monitor their paradoxical impact. They then document their case through detailed descriptions of iatrogenic violence induced by medication in their own setting.

The authors conclude with recognition of the fact that drugs do have a place in the institutional management of violence, but that place is secondary to efforts to provide social learning opportunities for patients that obviate the need to resort to violence, and to offer institutional responses to deviant acts that quell rather than stimulate these destructive acts.

The paper by Frederiksen and Rainwater provides a fine example of the ways in which clinical programs are created. Working in the Veterans Administration Hospital in Jackson, Mississippi, the authors were called upon to help staff cope with the persistently violent behavior of a small coterie of patients. They began by developing a model of the etiology of violence which included recognition of the facts that their patients appeared to be deficient in social skills, held generally more negative social expectations when contrasted with other patients, had a lower arousal threshold than other patients, and generally achieved their objectives through violent acts. Elements of this model were then tested using a combination of pencil-and-paper, role-playing, and psychophysiological measures, each such measure making a significant contribution to the data base used for planning and evaluating treatment. Treatment followed a preparatory stage in which rapport was established with each patient, a skill-development phase including social skills training, relaxation training, cognitive restructuring, and training in moderating alcohol consumption, which was found to play an important role in generating certain violent acts. The generalization phase of the treatment was one of its more original and most frequently overlooked dimensions. It offered participants an opportunity to apply recently learned principles to novel situations in the context of their treatment, to view therapists modeling the target behaviors in diverse circumstances, and a gradual fading of therapeutic contacts.

Results presented in the Frederiksen and Rainwater paper are necessarily suggestive rather than conclusive because this paper reports a clinical trial involving the six patients who completed treatment—one-half of the original sample. Results were generally positive but inconsistent with regard to both the experimental measures and general clinical outcome; however, findings were strong enough to justify use of these materials and procedures in other therapeutic contexts under experimental conditions, and this paper may contain the seeds for institution-based programs that have far-reaching implications.

CONCLUSION

Even the most optimistic review of our current knowledge about the origins and control of violence would have to reveal that we are far from having sufficient data to offer conclusive recommendations. It would be pleasing to be able to say that the papers published in this volume offer this much-needed conclusive statement, but they do not. They are at best a state-of-the-art review of those areas of the management of violence with which social learning theorists have been concerned, and the absence of definitive data on many of the programs described reflects their status as evolving projects. It is hoped that readers of this book will carefully consider each programatic suggestion, contrast it with current practice in their setting, and include in a pilot test those elements of the programs that are considered to be potentially fruitful. Clearly, it will take years of openness to new ideas and the willingness to sacrifice traditional beliefs on the altar of careful research before we shall be able to make serious inroads toward meeting the challenge of accurately predicting and preventing violent behavior.

REFERENCE NOTES

1. Quinsey, V. L., Ambtman, R., & Pruesse, M. Institutional release policy and the identification of dangerous men. Paper presented at the symposium on violence in Canadian Society, Qualicum Beach, Vancouver Island, March, 1977.
2. Stuart, R. B. Indirect therapy: A means of promoting maintainable change. Paper presented at the annual meeting of the Canadian Psychological Association, Calgary, Alberta, June, 1980.

REFERENCES

ALEXANDER, F., & STAUB, H. *The criminal, the judge and the public.* New York: Macmillan, 1931.
AMERICAN PSYCHIATRIC ASSOCIATION. *Clinical aspects of the violent individual.* Task Force Report No. 8. Washington, D.C., 1974.
ANDENAES, J. *Punishment and deterrence.* Ann Arbor, MI: University of Michigan Press, 1974.
BANDURA, A. Social learning analysis of aggression. In A. Bandura (Ed.), *Analysis of delinquency and aggression.* Hillsdale, N.J.: Erlbaum, 1976.
BERKOWITZ, L. The case for bottling up rage. *Psychology Today,* 1973, 7, 24-31.
BERKOWITZ, L., & LePAGE, A. Weapons as aggression-eliciting stimuli. *Journal of Personality and Social Psychology,* 1967, 7, 202-207.
BLUMENTHAL, M. D., KAHN, R. L., ANDREWS, F. M., & HEAD, K. B. *Justifying violence.* Ann Arbor, MI: University of Michigan Press, 1972.
BORGATTA, E. On the existence of Thurstone's oblique reference solution. *American Sociological Review,* 1968, 33, 589-600.
BOUGHMAN, F. A., & MANN, J. D. Ascertainment of seven XYY males in private neurology practice. *Journal of the American Medical Association,* 1972, 222, 446-448.
BRONFENBRENNER, U. Socialization and social class throughout time and space. In E. E. Maccoby, T. M. Newcomb, & E. L. Hartley (Eds.), *Readings in social psychology,* New York: Holt, 1958.
BROWN, W. M. C., PRICE, W. H., & JACOBS, P. A. The XYY male. *British Medical Journal,* 1968, 4, 513.

BURGESS, E. The growth of the city: An introduction to a research project. In R. Park & E. Burgess (Eds.), *The city*. Chicago, IL: University of Chicago Press, 1926.

BURGESS, R. L. Child abuse: A behavioral analysis. In B. B. Lahey & A. E. Kazdin (Eds.), *Advances in child clinical psychology*. New York: Plenum, 1978.

BURT, C. *The young delinquent*. New York: Appleton, 1925.

CARSTAIRS, G. M. Overcrowding and human aggression. In H. D. Graham & T. R. Gurr (Eds.), *Violence in America: Historical and comparative prospects*. New York: Signet Books, 1969.

CASEY, M. D., BLANK, C. E., STREET, D. R. K., SEGALL, L. J., McDOUGALL, J. H., McGRATH, P. J., & SKINNER, J. L. YY chromosomes and anti-social behavior. *The Lancet*, 1966, *2*, 859.

CASEY, M. D., STREET, D. R. K., SEGALL, L. J., & BLANK, C. E. Patients with sex chromosome abnormalities in two state hospitals. *Annals of Human Genetics*, 1968, *32*, 53.

CATALANO, R. *Health behavior and the community*. New York: Pergamon, 1979.

CHILTON, R. Continuity in delinquency area research. *American Sociological Review*, 1964, *29*, 71-83.

CHOROVER, S. L. Big brother and psychotechnology. *Psychology Today*, 1973, *7*, 43-54.

CHRISTENSEN, K. O. Mobility and crime among twins. *International Journal of Criminology and Penology*, 1973, *1*, 31-45.

CLOWARD, R. A., & OHLIN, L. E. *Delinquency and opportunity*. New York: Free Press, 1960.

COCOZZA, J., & STEADMAN, H. Some refinements in the measurement and prediction of dangerousness: Clear and convincing evidence. *Rutgers Law Review*, 1976, *29*, 1084-1101.

COHEN, A. K., & SHORT, J. F. Research in delinquent subcultures. *Journal of Social Issues*, 1958, *14*, 20-37.

CONRAD, J. P. The nature and treatment of the violent offender: A typology of violence. In C. Spencer (Ed.), *A typology of violent offenders*. Sacramento, CA: California Department of Corrections, 1966.

DAVIES, J. C. The J-curve of rising and declining satisfactions as a cause of some great revolutions and a contained rebellion. In H. D. Graham & T. R. Gurr (Eds.), *Violence in America: Historical and comparative perspectives* New York: Signet Books, 1969.

DE BAULT, L., JOHNSTON, E., & LOEFFELNOLZ, P. Incidence of XYY and XXY individuals in a security hospital population. *Diseases of the Nervous System*, 1972, *33*, 590-593.

DETRE, T., KUPFER, D. J., & TAUB, S. The nosology of violence. In W. S. Fields & W. H. Sweet (Eds.), *Neural bases of violence and aggression*. St. Louis, MO: Warren Green, 1975.

DILLON, W. S. Anthropological perspectives on violence. In G. Usdin (Ed.), *Perspectives on violence*. New York: Brunner/Mazel, 1972.

DOUVAN, E. Social status and success strivings. *Journal of Abnormal and Social Psychology*, 1956, *52*, 219-223.

DUGDALE, R. L. *The Jukes*. New York: G. P. Putnam, 1888.

ERLANGER, H. B. Social class and corporal punishment in childrearing. A reassessment. *American Sociological Review*, 1974, *39*, 68-85.

EYSENCK, H. J. *Crime and personality*. London: Routledge and Kegan Paul, 1964.

FAULKNER, R. K. On respect and retribution: Toward an ethnography of violence. *Sociological Symposium*, 1973, *9*, 17-36.

FEDERN, P. *Ego psychology and the psychoses*. New York: Basic Books, 1952.

FELDMAN, D. Psychoanalysis and crime. In R. Rosenberg (Ed.), *Mass society in crisis*. New York: Macmillan, 1964.

FENICHEL, O. *The psychoanalytic theory of neurosis*. New York: Norton, 1945.

FIELDS, W., & SWEET, W. (Eds.) *Neural bases of violence and aggression*. St. Louis, MO: Warren Green, 1975.

FOGELSON, R. M. *Violence as protest: A study of riots and ghettos*. New York: Anchor Books, 1971.

FREEMAN, L. *Before I kill more.* New York: Crown, 1955.
FREUD, S. *The ego and the id* (1923) London: Hogarth, 1960.
FREUD, S. *The psychopathology of everyday life* (1901) London: Hogarth, 1960.
GIBBENS, T., POND, D. A., & STAFFORD-CLARK, D. A follow-up study of criminal psycho-paths. *British Journal of Delinquency,* 1959, *6,* 125-136.
GILLIES, H. Murder in West Scotland. *British Journal of Psychiatry,* 1965, *111,* 1087.
GODDARD, H. H. *The Kallikak family.* New York: Macmillan, 1912.
GORDON, R. On the interpretation of oblique factors. *American Sociological Review,* 1967, *33,* 601-620.
GORING, C. *The English convict.* London: Her Majesty's Stationery Office, 1913.
GRAHAM, H. D., & GURR, T. R. *Violence in America: Historical and comparative perspectives.* New York: New American Library, 1969.
GUNN, J. Y., & BONN, J. Criminality and violence in epileptic prisoners. *British Journal of Psychiatry,* 1971, *118,* 337-343.
GUTTMACHER, M. Dangerous offenders. *Crime and Delinquency,* 1963, *9,* 381-390.
GUTTMACHER, M. The normal and the sociopathic murder. In M. Wolfgang (Ed.), *Studies in homicide.* New York: Harper & Row, 1967.
GUZE, S. B. *Criminality and psychiatric disorders.* New York: Oxford University Press, 1976.
HACKLER, J. Boys, blisters and behavior. The impact of a work program in an urban area. *Journal of Research in Crime and Delinquency,* 1966, *3,* 155-164.
HALDANE, J., B. S. Foreword. In Lange, J., *Crime as destiny: A study of criminal twins.* London: George Allen & Unwin, 1931.
HARTMANN, H., KRIS, E., & LOWENSTEIN, R. *Papers on psychoanalytic psychology. Volume 4.* New York: International Universities Press, 1964.
HEDLUND, J. L., SLETTEN, I. W., ALTMAN, H., & EVENSON, R. C. Prediction of patients who are dangerous to others. *Journal of Clinical Psychology,* 1973, *29,* 443-447.
HOKANSON, J. E. Psychophysiological evaluation of the catharsis hypothesis. In E. I. Megargee & J. E. Hokanson (Eds.), *The dynamics of aggression.* New York: Harper & Row, 1970.
HOOTON, E. *The American criminal: An anthropological study.* Cambridge, MA: Harvard University Press, 1939.
JACOBS, P. A., PRICE, W. H., & BROWN, W. M. C. Chromosome studies on men in a maximum security hospital. *Annals of Human Genetics,* 1968, *31,* 344.
JOHNSON, J. H. A cross validation of seventeen experimental MMPI scales related to antisocial behavior. *Journal of Clinical Psychology,* 1974, *30,* 564-565.
KAHN, J., CARTER, W. I., DERNLEY, N., & SLATER, E. T. O. Chromosome studies in remand home and prison populations. In D. J. West (Ed.), *Criminological implications of chromosome abnormalities.* Cambridge, England: Institute of Criminology, 1969.
KRIESBERG, L. *The sociology of social conflicts.* Englewood Cliffs, N.J.: Prentice-Hall, 1973.
LANDER, B. *Towards an understanding of juvenile delinquency.* New York: Columbia University Press, 1954.
LANGE, J. *Crime as destiny: A study of criminal twins.* London: George Allen & Unwin, 1931.
LIBERSON, S., & SILVERMAN, A. R. The precipitants and underlying conditions of race riots. *American Sociological Review,* 1965, *30,* 887-898.
LORENZ, K. *On Aggression.* New York: Harcourt Brace Jovanovich, 1966.
MACDONALD, J. M. *Psychiatry and the criminal.* Springfield, IL: Charles C. Thomas, 1958.
MACDONALD, J. M. *The murderer and his victim.* Springfield, IL: Charles C. Thomas, 1961.
MARK V. H. Sociobiological theories of abnormal aggression. In I. L. Kutash, S. B. Kutash, L. B. Schlesinger & Associates (Eds.), *Violence: Perspectives on murder and aggression.* San Francisco, CA: Jossey Bass, 1978.
MATZA, D. *Delinquency and drift.* New York: Wiley, 1964.
MAYHEW, H. *The criminal prisons of London and scenes of prison life.* London: C. Griffin Bohn, 1862.
MCKENZIE, R. The ecological approach to the study of the human community. In R. Park & E. Burgess (Eds.), *The city.* Chicago: University of Chicago Press, 1926.

MEGARGEE, E. I. The prediction of violence with psychological tests. In C. D. Spielberger (Ed.), *Current topics in clinical and community psychology*. New York: Academic Press, 1970.

MEGARGEE, E. I., & COOK, P. E. Negative response bias and the MMPI Overcontrolled Hostility Scale: A response to Deiker, *Journal of Consulting and Clinical Psychology*, 1975, *43*, 725–729.

MEGARGEE, E. I., COOK, P. E., & MENDELSOHN, G. A. Development and evaluation of an MMPI scale of assaultiveness in overcontrolled individuals. *Journal of Abnormal Psychology*, 1967, *72*, 519-528.

MERTON, R. *Social theory and social structure*. Glencoe, IL: The Free Press, 1957.

MERTON, R. *Social theory and social structure*. New York: Free Press, 1968.

MESNIKOFF, A., & LAUTERBACH, C. G. The association of violent dangerous behavior with psychiatric disorders: A review of the research literature. *Journal of Psychiatry and the Law*, 1975, *31*, 415-445.

MILLER, R. B. Violence, force and coercion. In J. A. Shaffer (Ed.), *Violence*. New York: David McKay, 1971.

MILLER W. B. Lower class culture as a generating milieu of gang delinquency. *Journal of Social Issues*, 1958, *14*, 5-19.

MITFORD, J. *Kind and usual punishment*. New York: Vantage Books, 1974.

MONAHAN, J. Prediction research and the emergency commitment of dangerous mentally ill persons. *American Journal of Psychiatry*, 1978, *135*, 214-226.

MORRIS, N., & HAWKINS, G. *Letter to the President on crime control*. Chicago, IL: University of Chicago Press, 1977.

MOYNIHAN, D. *Maximum feasible misunderstanding: Community action in the war on poverty*. New York: Free Press, 1969.

MULLIGAN, M. A. *An investigation of factors associated with violent modes of conflict resolution in the family*. Unpublished MA thesis, University of Rhode Island, 1977. (Cited by M. A. Straus, R. J. Gelles, & S. K. Steinmetz, *Behind closed doors: Violence in the American Family*, New York: Anchor Books, 1980).

NATIONAL CRIMINAL JUSTICE INFORMATION AND STATISTICS SERVICE. *Criminal victimization surveys in the nation's five largest cities*. Washington, D.C.: U.S. Government Printing Office, 1975.

NETTLER, G. *Explaining crime*. New York: McGraw Hill, 1974.

NIELSEN, J. Prevalence and a two and a half years' incidence of chromosome abnormalities among all males in a forensic psychiatric clinic. *British Journal of Psychiatry*, 1971, *119*, 503-512.

NOVACO, R. W. The cognitive regulation of anger and stress. In P. Kendall & A. Hollon (Eds.), *Cognitive-behavioral interventions: Theory, research and procedures*. New York: Academic Press, 1979.

OHLESEN, W., GIBBS, F., & ADAMS, C. EEG studies of criminals. *Clinical EEG*, 1970, *1*, 101-105.

OHLIN, L., & CLOWARD, R. *Delinquency and opportunity*. Glencoe, IL: Free Press, 1960.

OSMAN, E., & LEE, C. Sociological theories of aggression. In I. L. Kutash, S. B. Kutash, L. B. Schlesinger & Associates (Eds.), *Violence: Perspectives on murder and aggression*. San Francisco, CA: Jossey Bass, 1978.

PFEIFFER, J. Seeking peace, making war. *Science 80*, 1980, *1*, 22-24.

RANSFORD, H. E. Isolation, powerlessness, and violence: A study of attitudes and participation in the Watts riot. *American Journal of Sociology*, 1968, *73*, 581-591.

RECKLESS, W. The distribution of commercialized vice in the city: Sociological analysis. *Publications of the American Sociological Society*, 1926, *20*, 174-176.

REVITCH, E. Psychiatric evaluation and classification of antisocial activities. *Diseases of the Nervous System*, 1975, *36*, 419-421.

REVITCH, E. Classification of offenders for prognostic and dispositional evaluation. *Bulletin of the Academy of Law and Psychiatry*, 1977, *5*, 1-11.

RODIN, E. Psychomotor epilepsy and aggressive behaviour. *Archives of General Psychiatry*, 1973, *28*, 210-213.

SCHEFF, T. J. The societal reaction to deviance: Ascriptive elements in the psychiatric screening of mental patients in a midwestern state. *Social Problems*, 1964, *11*, 401-413.

SCHERER, K. R., ABELES, R. P., & FISCHER, C. S. *Human aggression and conflict: Interdisciplinary perspectives.* Englewood Cliffs, N.J.: Prentice-Hall, 1975.

SCHUSTER, R. H. Ethological theories of aggression. In I. L. Kutash, S. B. Kutash, L. B. Schlesinger & Associates (Eds.), *Violence: Perspectives on murder and aggression.* San Francisco, CA: Jossey Bass, 1978.

SHAW, C., & McKAY, H. *Juvenile delinquency and urban areas.* Chicago, IL: University of Chicago Press, 1942.

SHAW, C., ZORBAUGH, F., McKAY, H., & COTTRELL, L. *Delinquency areas.* Chicago, IL: University of Chicago Press, 1929.

SHOHAM, S. B., BEN-DAVID, S., & RAHAR, G. Interaction in violence. *Human Relations*, 1974, *27*, 417-430.

SILBERMAN, C. E. *Criminal violence, criminal justice.* New York: Vantage Books, 1978.

SPELLACY, F. Neuropsychological differences between violent and nonviolent adolescents. *Journal of Clinical Psychology*, 1977, *33*, 966-969.

STACEY, B. Some psychological aspects of inter-generational occupational mobility. *British Journal of Social and Clinical Psychology*, 1965, *4*, 275-286.

STEINMETZ, S. K. Occupational environment in relation to physical punishment and dogmatism. In S. Steinmetz & M. Straus (Eds.), *Violence in the family.* New York: Harper & Row, 1974.

STRAUS, M. A., GELLES, R. J., & STEINMETZ, S. K. *Behind closed doors: Violence in the American family.* New York: Anchor Books, 1980.

STUART, R. B. *Helping couples change. A social learning theory approach to marriage therapy.* New York: Guilford Press, 1980a.

STUART, R. B. Weight loss and beyond: Are they taking it off and keeping it off? In P. O. Davidson (Ed.), *Behavioral medicine: Changing health lifestyles.* New York: Brunner/Mazel, 1980b.

STUART, R. B., TRIPODI, T., JAYARATNE, S., & CAMBURN, D. An experiment in social engineering in serving the families of delinquents. *Journal of Abnormal Child Psychology*, 1976, *4*, 243-261.

SUTHERLAND, E. H. *Principles of criminology.* Philadelphia, PA: Lippincott, 1939.

SUTHERLAND, E. H. *Principles of criminology.* Philadelphia, PA: Lippincott, 1947.

TANNENBAUM, F. *Crime and the community.* New York: Columbia University Press, 1938.

THOMAS, W., & ZNANIECKI, F. *The Polish peasant in Europe and America.* New York: Alfred Knopf, 1927.

THRASHER, F. *The gang: A study of 1,313 gangs in Chicago.* Chicago, IL: University of Chicago Press, 1927.

TINKLENBERG, J. R. Alcohol and violence. In R. Fox & P. Bourne (Eds.), *Alcoholism: Progress in research and treatment.* New York: Academic Press, 1980.

TOCH, H. The social psychology of violence. In E. I. Megargee & J. E. Hokanson (Eds.), *The dynamics of aggression.* New York: Harper & Row, 1970.

VALENSTEIN, E. S. Brain stimulation and the origin of violent behavior. In W. L. Smith and A. Kling (Eds.), *Issues in Brain/Behavior Control.* Englewood Cliffs, N.J.: Prentice Hall, 1976.

VIRKKUNEN, M., NUUTILA, A., & HUUSKO, S. Brain injury and criminality: A retrospective study. *Diseases of the Nervous System*, 1977, *38*, 907-908.

VOSS, H. I., & HEPBURN, J. R. Patterns in criminal homicide in Chicago. *Journal of Criminal Law, Criminology and Police Science*, 1968, *59*, 449-456.

WALTERS, R. H. Implications of laboratory studies of aggression for the control and regulation of violence. *The Annals*, 1966, *364*, 60-74.

WEISSMAN, H. (Ed.) *Justice and the law in the Mobilization for Youth experience.* New York: Association Press, 1969.

WERTHAM, F. The catathymic crisis. In I. L. Kutash, S. B. Kutash, L. B. Schlesinger & Associates (Eds.), *Violence: Perspectives on murder and aggression.* San Francisco, CA: Jossey Bass, 1978.

WOLFGANG, M. E. *Patterns in criminal homicide in Philadelphia.* Philadelphia, PA: University of Pennsylvania, 1958.

WOLFGANG, M. E. Seriousness of crime and a policy of juvenile justice. In J. F. Short (Ed.), *Delinquency, Crime and Society.* Chicago: University of Chicago Press, 1976.

2

A Social Psychological
Analysis of Violent Behavior

CHARLES W. TURNER, MICHAEL R. FENN,
and ALLEN M. COLE

INTRODUCTION

The following analysis focuses primarily upon a limited but important class of aggressive behaviors, namely, the violent crimes of serious assault and homicide. Three major assumptions guide our analysis of violent behavior. First, while aggression and violence are multifaceted phenomena with many antecedent conditions, these behaviors are particularly likely to be learned responses to aversive life events. Secondly, aggression is not the only response or even the most likely response to aversive events. Social learning processes determine which members of a society develop, through direct or vicarious experiences, aggression as the habitual mode of coping with aversive life events. Hence, these learning processes determine which individuals are likely to respond violently or

The present research was supported in part by NIMH funds to the University of Utah. During the preparation of the manuscript, the first author was supported by sabbatical leave funds from the University of Utah to Stanford University, and the second author was supported by an APA minority fellowship. We are indebted to Ruth Ault, Albert Bandura, David K. Dodd and Richard Stuart for their comments on an earlier draft.

nonviolently to particular aversive events in their lives. Thirdly, fluctuating population pressures (due to birth, death, and immigration rates)
have modified the number of individuals who are maximally at risk for
experiencing aversive life events. As more members of a society experience distress, more of them are likely to act violently; however, the
people experiencing the most aversive events are not necessarily the ones
most likely to behave violently.

We first discuss some of the problems that arise in defining aggression
and then review research on frustration and relative deprivation —conceptualized as aversive events—as determinants of aggression. Since
aggression is not the only response to aversive stimulation, we also review
research on social learning processes which mediate aggressive reactions.
For example, the learned helplessness model of Seligman (1975) and the
self-efficacy model of Bandura (1977) are used to account for diverse
individual reactions to aversive events. Later, we review demographic
data for long-term changes in violent crime. In this formulation we have
extended Easterlin's (1968, 1973) analysis to account for long-term
changes in homicide rates within the United States. Our model takes
special note of the evidence that different age and ethnic groups exhibit
differential risks for violent behavior. This model predicts a major reduction in U.S. violent crime rates (approximately 40% between 1975
and 1985).

Problems in the Definition of Aggressive and Violent Behavior

As a point of perspective, we briefly present some problems associated
with defining aggressive and violent behavior with respect to social and
legal implications. Because human aggression is a multifaceted phenomenon which serves many functions, it defies simple explanations. A wide
variety of antecedent instigating conditions (e.g., physical assault, environmental events, or social thwartings) increase the likelihood of aggression. Diverse factors are involved in the mitigation of aggressive behavior
(e.g., threats of punishment, retaliation, or negative self-evaluations).
The complex nature of aggression makes it difficult to offer a simple
omnibus definition of aggression (Bandura, 1979; Berkowitz, 1974). For
our analysis, the major defining attribute of aggression is behavior which
produces noxious stimuli that result in personal injury or harm. The
term violence expands the notion of aggression to include either intense
personal injury or physically destructive behavior.

Whether a particular response is *judged* to be an act of aggression depends heavily upon social labeling processes (Bandura, 1979). In general, observers of an act are more likely to label the behavior as aggression if they attribute personal responsibility and/or harmful intent to the person committing the act. Behaviors are less likely to be labeled aggressive when the observer believes that a harmful action was accidental (not intended) or that it was designed to serve a beneficial purpose. Thus, behaviors such as "accidentally" stepping on someone's foot or occupational activities such as painful medical or dental procedures would not be labeled as acts of aggression.

Legal sanctions for injurious behavior vary according to whether the behavior is labeled an aggressive act. However, these sanctions usually are not applied to someone reacting in self-defense against harmful acts of others. Thus, the act of shooting an intruder in someone's residence is rarely prosecuted if it is believed that the resident had good reason to fear for her/his life. Under some conditions, social norms other than self-defense can be used to justify retaliation. Socially sanctioned retaliation is a central theme of many fictional accounts of violence (Goranson, 1970). The protagonist usually becomes a "hero" by personally meting out "punishment" for the harmful behavior of evil characters. However, a fictional character is labeled a bully and receives negative legal and social sanctions if s/he retaliates against someone whose harmful behavior was accidental.

As these diverse observations illustrate, judgment of *intent* is central in the social labeling of aggression; such judgments are used to legitimize both personal and legal sanctions. Not all behavior which produces noxious stimuli is necessarily labeled as aggression. Indeed, there are many circumstances in which harmful behavior is condoned, justified, and/or expected.

Population Expansion, Resource Limitations, and Worldwide Violence

The potential for massive human destruction is not just an abstract possibility. The actual level of collective and individual destructiveness has already reached staggering proportions. Elliot's (1972) detailed analysis of various international records of violent confrontations indicates that at least 100 million individuals have become fatal victims of violence in the last 100 years. A large proportion of these deaths resulted from World War I (5-7 million) and World War II (35-40 million), but the revolutions and purges of the U.S.S.R. (25-30 million) and China (15-20 million) also contributed to the devastation. Regrettably, the threat of collective violence continues to be pervasive throughout the world. For example, more than a dozen major violent confrontations erupted within the first three months of 1979, resulting in tens of thousands of deaths (*San Francisco Chronicle*, 1979).*

As compared to earlier times, the annual frequency of individual violent crime has also escalated in the past few years. Ten times as many homicides occurred in the U.S. in 1975 as in 1910, while the population expanded only 2½ times over the same period. The homicide rate per 100,000 population in the U.S. doubled between 1955 and 1975 (U.S. Bureau of the Census, 1881-1978). Our analysis shows how these high rates of individual and collective violence reflect the fact that violent behavior has become an increasingly frequent response to aversive experiences. Furthermore, the increasing threat of violence in a community can intensify the perceived aversiveness of life in that neighborhood. Even a small increase in destructive acts in a local environment can drastically reduce the residents' perceived quality of life (Bandura, Note 1).

The task for the behavioral scientist is to identify the common threads which weave these forms of violence into a coherent pattern. One pervasive factor may be related to the long-term changes in the world population, which has grown rapidly over the past 150 years. The population today is approximately 10 times what it was in the 1600s and has doubled since 1930 (Ehrlich & Ehrlich, 1972) (see Figure 1). The primary reason for the expanding world population has been the decreased mortality rate from infectious disease, especially in Europe and North America.** Somewhat paradoxically, while improved agricultural, medical, and public health procedures have reduced mortality rates, these benefits have also increased the risk of violent confrontations. That is, the expanding population has intensified competition for limited social and economic resources. Even at present, a number of vital natural resources such as mineral and petroleum products are rapidly being exhausted (Ehrlich & Ehrlich, 1972).

According to the proposed model, restricted access to social and eco-

---

*Major violent confrontations were reported in Angola, Cambodia, China, El Salvador, Iran, Ireland, Israel, Lebanon, Rhodesia, South Africa, Tanzania, Uganda, and Vietnam.

**Agricultural improvements led to a large expansion in the amount and variety of food available; the improved nutrition led to greater resistance to infection. The improved public health procedures included the sanitary handling of food, especially milk, and the disposal of human waste, which reduced exposure to infection. More recent medical advances such as vaccination, anesthetics and antiseptics, sulfa and antibiotic drugs have reduced mortality due to infection.

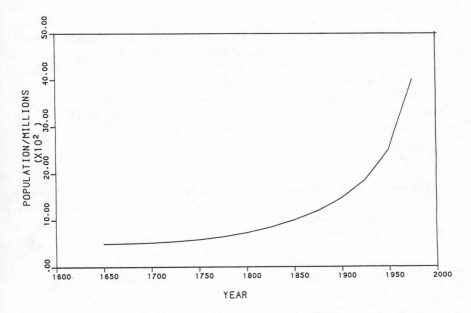

FIGURE 1. World population from 1650-1975. (Source: Erhlich & Erhlich, 1972)

nomic resources is conceptualized as an aversive event. Although high intensity aversive experiences can increase the likelihood of individual and collective violent behavior, aversive reactions do not always lead to such reactions. Those individuals objectively most deprived are not necessarily the ones most likely to engage in violence (Berkowitz, 1974; Crosby, 1976). Rather, the relative level of an individual or group's deprivation is one prime catalyst for violent encounters. Differential direct and vicarious experiences in controlling aversive events through aggression are major determinants of whether aggression is used during periods of relative deprivation.

EFFECTS OF AVERSIVE EVENTS ON SOCIAL BEHAVIOR

Frustration and relative deprivation (a difference between one's expected level and achieved level of outcomes) have been hypothesized as two contributing factors to the instigation of aggression and violence. Widely criticized as originally postulated, the frustration-aggression hypothesis has been revised to postulate that frustration only increases the probability of aggression (Berkowitz, 1974). As an extension of the frustration-aggression hypothesis, relative deprivation theory has been used to account for several important social behaviors. Easterlin (1968, 1973) employed an economic version of relative deprivation principles to account for long-term changes in family formation and dissolution, as well as changes in fertility rates. We extended Easterlin's analysis to show how the fluctuations in family size are related to short- and long-term risks of aggression during periods of relative deprivation.

The Frustration-Aggression Hypothesis

One of the early influential theories of aggression was the frustration-aggression hypothesis (Dollard, Doob, Miller, Mowrer, & Sears, 1939). This hypothesis postulated that frustration is both a necessary and a sufficient condition for aggression. That is, aggression does not occur without frustration (necessary condition), and frustration always leads to some form of aggression (sufficient condition).

Forty years of research have clearly demonstrated that the frustration-aggression hypothesis was phrased too ambiguously and too broadly (see Bandura, 1977; Baron, 1978; Berkowitz, 1974). An early problem with the proposal was the ambiguity of the term "frustration"; some uses of the term referred to environmental events (obstructions to goal-directed behavior), while other uses of the term referred to internal states of the organism (subjective experience of frustration). Although noxious stimuli and personal insults have been shown to instigate aggression, it is not clear whether these events can be defined as frustrations. Bandura (1973) has proposed that the term frustration be replaced by the construct of aversive events. Thus, insults, painful stimuli, and reductions in the level of rewarding conditions (e.g., extinction) have one property in common—they are all physically or psychologically aversive to the organism. An operational definition of the aversive property of an event can be established by determining whether an organism will work to terminate the event (Ulrich, Dulaney, Arnett, & Mueller, 1973).

Problems of operationalizing and definition aside, subsequent research demonstrated that frustration (an aversive event) is neither a necessary nor a sufficient condition for aggression. Forms of aggression do occur without apparent frustration (violating the necessary condition), and aggression is not the only or even the most frequent consequence of frustration (violating the sufficient condition). Bandura (1973, 1977, 1979) has proposed that aversive events produce many different and diverse reactions, such as increased striving, depression and apathy, as well as aggression. These diverse reactions may terminate the aversive event, thereby rendering it controllable (Seligman, 1975), or they may "blunt" the intensity of an uncontrollable aversive event (Miller & Grant, Note 2). When the aversive event can be neither controlled nor blunted, the organism may try to withdraw; if all these reactions fail, then reactions such as apathy, learned helplessness, and depression can occur (Seligman, 1975). Although most people do not use aggression as their primary response to aversive events, some people discover that aggression can be effective in terminating these experiences.

Acquisition of Aggressive Behavior Through Social Learning Processes

Researchers have identified distinct inhibiting and instigating processes which determine whether aggression is employed as a mode of terminating an aversive event (Bandura, 1979; Berkowitz, 1974). For example, social and environmental cues can produce strong *inhibitions* against aggression from such factors as: 1) threats of strong retaliation from the target of aggression; 2) threats of social sanctions for acting aggressively in some settings (e.g., in a church as opposed to a playground); 3) cues which increase the salience of negative self-evaluations for aggressive conduct (self-evaluation apprehension) (Turner & Dodd, 1979). Aversive experiences can *instigate* aggression if an individual previously has direct (Patterson et al., 1975) or vicarious (Bandura, 1979) experiences of positive and negative reinforcement for aggression. For example, within certain delinquent subcultures, aggressive behavior is positively reinforced by peers (Wolfgang, 1968). These youths quickly learn through their own direct experience or by observing their peers that aggression can be an effective method of getting what they want from other people, and for enhancing their social status in their gang.

Parental reinforcement of obnoxious, aversive behaviors. Parents may inadvertently teach their children to use coercive behaviors in response to distress (through negative reinforcement processes) even though these behaviors are contrary to the parents' child-rearing goals. A response is negatively reinforced if an aversive event is reduced or terminated following the response. Those behaviors which have effectively terminated past aversive experiences are most likely to be used on later occasions in coping with distressing events. Aggressive behavior is negatively reinforced in many families so that this form of behavior is learned as a dominant coping strategy to aversive stimulation (Patterson & Cobb, 1973; Patterson et al., 1975; Turner & Dodd, 1979). Although children of all ages may be negatively reinforced for obnoxious or aggressive behavior, the acquisition of obnoxious, coercive control can be seen as early as infancy.

Most mammalian infants display a distress cry or call which initiates caretaking responses in adults (Freedman, 1974). Similarly, the first social response of the human infant is the crying response. This response can provide the first stage in the acquisition of aversive control over others. That is, while some parents may perceive an infant's cry as an opportunity to help, most parents perceive it as an aversive or unpleasant sound (Bell, 1977). To relieve both the infant's distress and the aversiveness of the crying, a parent will typically engage in caretaking activities such as feeding, soothing, changing diapers, and comforting ministrations. If these activities end the child's crying, the parent's caretaking behavior is negatively reinforced by the cessation of the aversive crying. Since the infant's distress is terminated by the parent's ministrations, the crying behavior is also negatively reinforced for the infant. Hence, both parent and infant come under mutually interdependent negative reinforcement control (Turner & Dodd, 1979). One consequence of this arrangement is that crying and other fussing behaviors may become a coercive operant for controlling parental attention. The developing child may generalize the obnoxious behaviors to novel responses and to novel distressing situations (Gewirtz & Boyd, 1976).

The parents usually become increasingly intolerant of the child's aversive control. Consequently, they may attempt to ignore or to punish the coercive behaviors (e.g., yelling, crying, or hitting). However, the parents' responses to the child's behavior are often inconsistent. For example, parents sometimes successfully ignore a child's voluntary (operant) crying and fussing, since the child may be tired and will fall asleep after crying for a few minutes. Efforts to ignore the child's crying are not always successful, since nonvoluntary (respondent) crying may result from acute distress (a pin may be sticking the child), and the crying is likely to continue as long as the distress continues. Eventually, the parents are likely to come to the child's aid. Parents, then, are often in a dilemma trying to determine whether the child's crying reflects "real" distress or whether the child is tired and is about to fall asleep. If parents have difficulty in discriminating the two types of crying, they may yield to the voluntary (operant) crying on some occasions. The voluntary, aversive behavior of the child is negatively reinforced whenever the parents fail to correctly discriminate the two types of crying. This inconsistency is analogous to placing the child on a partial reinforcement schedule, thereby making obnoxious behavior very difficult to extinguish whenever the parents attempt to ignore the crying. The parents' inconsistency may contribute to future occurrences of tantrum or other obnoxious behaviors.

Parental reciprocation of obnoxious behavior: Crying and child abuse. On some occasions appropriate caretaking responses do not readily terminate the child's distress (e.g., teething or colicky infants can be difficult to soothe). At 3:00 a.m. the parent may be exhausted and unable to generate novel behaviors for soothing the infant. Hence, the parent's behavior does not directly lead to the termination of the child's crying. Under these circumstances the distressed parent may employ destructive techniques for terminating the unpleasant crying (e.g., neglecting or even striking the infant). Weston (1974), a criminal pathologist, interviewed 50 adults who had killed or seriously injured an infant. In most cases, the attacker initially denied responsibility for the attack. After careful interrogation, they admitted the attack, and the primary reason given for it was the uncontrollable crying of the infant. The insistent, uncontrollable, incessant crying had become so highly aversive to the caretaker that extreme measures were employed to quiet the child.

The cry of the premature infant seems to be perceived as a particularly unpleasant and aversive sound (Frodi, Lamb, Leavitt, & Donovan, 1978). A parent who is not skillful in infant caretaking is likely to be exposed to long bouts of uncontrollable crying of the infant. Also, an infant who is unwanted or who has medical problems (leading to greater caretaking obligations) may produce high-frequency, intolerable, aversive stimulation to the parent. These types of infants seem to be at greatest risk for child neglect and/or child abuse (Frodi et al., 1978). Perhaps we should not be surprised that parents may strike or abuse infants if they become highly distressed by the persistent problems of these infants.

Vicarious social learning through media portrayals of violence. In addition to the direct experience of positive and negative reinforcement for aggression, individuals also observe other people being reinforced for their aggression. Individuals are particularly likely to observe reinforced aggression when they watch media portrayals of violence. Numerous studies have demonstrated that filmed depictions of aggressive encounters can increase the level of aggression in viewers, especially when the viewers are exposed to aversive events (Bandura, 1973; Baron, 1978; Berkowitz, 1974). These studies have employed a wide range of subject samples and filmed material. Evidence from this research indicates that the effects of films can persist for at least an hour (Buvinic & Berkowitz, 1976) and possibly even for 30 days (Hicks, 1968). Filmed violence can contribute to aggression through such diverse mechanisms as: 1) lowering people's inhibitions by legitimizing aggression (as in the justified aggression scripts, Berkowitz & Geen, 1966; Goranson, 1970); 2) teaching novel aggressive acts (Bandura, 1979); 3) changing viewers' subjective probability of positive and negative consequences for aggression (Bandura, 1979); 4) desensitizing viewers to the suffering of victims (Cline, Croft, & Courrier, 1973); 5) serving as discriminative stimuli, defining the setting as one in which aggression is permitted (Ellis, Weinir, & Miller, 1971); or 6) eliciting aggressive thoughts and/or feelings which intensify preexisting predispositions to aggression (Berkowitz, 1974). However, the stimulating effects of films depend heavily on the environmental context, including the reaction of the audience with whom the film is viewed (Parke, Berkowitz, Leyens, West, & Sebastian, 1977).

Portrayals of real violence. Several studies suggest that people are likely to be stimulated to more aggression if they think they are witnessing real violence. Berkowitz and Alioto (1973) presented "war movies" to subjects and characterized them as film footage of actual wartime events or as fictional depictions of war. Subjects displayed more aggression toward someone who had previously insulted them if they believed the films depicted real rather than fictional war scenes.

Bandura (1973) has presented evidence that media accounts of airplane hijackings stimulate further hijackings. In particular, awareness of the escalation of tactics by authorities and subsequent countermeasures by hijackers seem to depend on lessons learned by hijackers through media coverage.

Berkowitz and Macauley (1971) have presented evidence that spectacularly violent crimes seem to increase the incidence of other violent crimes. Using time series methodology, Berkowitz and Macauley (1971) examined the month-to-month changes in violent crimes (rape, robbery, homicide, and aggravated assault) surrounding incidents of violence that received widespread media coverage: 1) the assassination of President Kennedy, and 2) the mass murders during the month of July, 1966. In July, 1966, Richard Speck killed seven student nurses and Charles Whitman shot numerous people walking on the streets below the University of Texas tower. Berkowitz and Macauley (1971) found significant increases in the monthly police reports of violent crimes from the period before to the period after these two sets of spectacular crimes. The researchers reasoned that the increased media coverage of these spectacular crimes could have stimulated some people to commit further crimes. However, Berkowitz and Macauley acknowledged that other interpretations are also consistent with their findings (e.g., more accurate police records). Many robberies, rapes and assaults are not usually reported to the police, but the publicity surrounding the mass killings might have increased public concern about potential or actual victimization by repeat offenders. Hence, the public might have been more likely to report real (or imagined) victimization.

Aggressive cues. Although the use of aggression as a coping response to aversive experiences may be mediated by socioenvironmental variables and reinforcement histories, the presence of aggressive cues can also increase the likelihood of impulsive aggression, especially that of homicide. An extensive body of research demonstrates that the mere presence of a firearm (aggressive cue) increases the likelihood of impulsive aggression, even if the weapon cannot be used for aggression (Turner, Simons, Berkowitz, & Frodi, 1977).

There are at least three explanations of how aggressive cues such as weapons can increase the probability of aggressive behavior. First, the frequent pairing of firearms with real or symbolic aversive events may produce a classical conditioning bonding between aggressive cues and aggressive behavior (Berkowitz, 1974). Systematic observations of crime drama television programs indicated that drawn weapons had a high rate of appearance (three to four times per hour) and a strong contingent association with physical aggression (80%) (Turner et al., 1977; Wilson & Higgins, 1977). Subsequent exposure to a cue may elicit weak classically conditioned responses which are intensified in frustrated, uninhibited subjects (Berkowitz, 1974). Secondly, weapons in media portrayals of violence are frequently paired with real or symbolic termination of aversive experiences. The weapons may serve as discriminative stimuli for positively or negatively reinforced aggressive behaviors (Ellis, Weinir, & Miller, 1971). Finally, the development of an associative bond between firearms and modeled aggression can increase the likelihood that firearms will serve as retrieval cues for previously witnessed modeled aggression (Turner & Goldsmith, 1976). All three explanations suggest mechanisms by which exposure to firearms can increase the risk of aggression (Turner et al., 1977). The instigating effects of aggressive cues is particularly likely if the cue occurs while someone is experiencing an aversive event.

Firearms, especially handguns, play a particularly important role in contributing to homicide in the United States; approximately two-thirds of all homicides result from firearms (Newton & Zimring, 1969). First, firearms are particularly lethal as compared to other weapons such as knives or blunt instruments. Secondly, firearms are readily available to most Americans; approximately two-thirds of American households contain at least one firearm. Thirdly, handguns are easily concealed so that they can be carried by an individual without being detected until the weapon is drawn. Finally, as indicated above, firearms can stimulate impulsive aggressive reactions, especially in individuals who have been highly distressed. The contribution of firearms to homicide is revealed in the statistics which show that 75% of homicides occur when a relative or acquaintance attacks the victim following an argument between the two (Newton & Zimring, 1969). Nearly two-thirds of all homicides occur when the victim is attacked with a firearm, while one-fourth of the deaths result from attacks by knives. Detailed interviews with the killers suggest that the attacks were the result of a temporary impulse, and the attackers had not expected to kill the victim (Toch, 1969).

To summarize, then, frustration in the classical sense is neither a necessary nor sufficient condition for aggression. Conceptualized as an aversive event, it can be stated that a frustrating and aversive event increases the likelihood that aggression may be used to terminate the event. But aggression is neither the only nor the most likely response to aversion. Its employment as a coping response can be mediated by increased inhibition levels against aggression (e.g., fear of retaliation) and previous direct and vicarious reinforcement for the termination of aversion by aggression. The additional presence of aggression cues in the environment, such as firearms, can also facilitate impulsive aggression as a response to an aversive event. Thus, aversive events can increase the probability of aggression, but several social learning variables influence whether the event actually produces overt aggression.

The Role of Relative Deprivation in Violent Behavior

Extensive research by economists, sociologists, and psychologists has documented that an individual's *relative* level of success or reinforcement rate is an important determinant of one's satisfaction with life's opportunities. People compare their actual achieved level of success to the performance and outcome standards to which they aspire. Their aspiration level depends upon such factors as previous success in achieving performance or outcome standards, the success of similar other people in achieving similar aspiration levels, immediate pressing biological needs, and environmental constraints to performance. Consequently, a person's *relative* rather than *absolute* level of resources becomes the more important factor in determining one's overall satisfaction; the greater the discrepancy between aspired and achieved levels of resources, the greater the dissatisfaction (Crosby, 1976).

The importance of relative rather than absolute rates of success in producing satisfaction has been demonstrated in a variety of settings. Simon (Note 3), for example, has shown that individuals who have been rapidly improving in performance are likely to set more extreme goals, while individuals making slower progress are likely to set more moderate goals. The histories of differences between achieved and aspired levels of success not only influence the goals (or behavioral objectives), but also influence these individuals' satisfaction with their performance.

Simon's findings are consistent with an analysis used by Davies (1969) to account for revolutions and riots (described as the revolution of rising expectations). Individuals whose aspirations exceed their obtained level of success seem to be vulnerable to dissatisfaction, frustration, and possibly depression or aggression. A number of riots and revolutions occurred after a period of rapidly rising economic conditions that was followed by the abrupt leveling off or decline in economic conditions (Davies, 1969). Davies reasoned that the improving economic conditions led to rising expectations for future success. When the rapidly rising economic expectations could not be achieved, the individuals became very dissatisfied with their outcomes. Presumably, the dissatisfaction increased their willingness to initiate or participate in revolutionary activities.*

There is a useful parallel between the relative deprivation hypothesis and the effects of extinction and fading processes during reinforcement. It has been shown in a number of animal species that extinction (abrupt reductions in reinforcement below "expected" levels) can instigate aggression (Ulrich et al., 1973). Analogously, an individual who has achieved relative success is likely to aspire to continuing high performance and outcome levels. An abrupt reduction in this person's achieved performance would cause the individual's achieved level to be far below her/his aspiration level. As with extinction procedures, abrupt decreases in performance and outcome gains in humans might lead to dissatisfaction and, potentially, to aggressive behavior (Ulrich et al., 1973).

It is not the initial level of reinforcement that is important; rather, it is the size and abruptness of the change. Gradual reductions in reinforcement rates (i.e., fading procedures) are not as likely to produce aggression; presumably they are not as likely to be noticed or discriminated as abrupt reductions in reinforcement. The effect of extinction procedures on aggression, then, is influenced by the relative size and abruptness of the reduction in reinforcement. If the analogy between reinforcement schedules and economic conditions holds, then we might expect a gradual reduction in economic levels (as in fading processes) to be less likely to instigate social violence than would abrupt reductions (as in extinction processes).

*Schuck (1976) has demonstrated that other variables such as perceived governmental legitimacy, coercive force (i.e., police and army) loyalty, and perceived legitimization for violent change can interact with short- and long-term deprivation to modify the risk of revolutions.

The theory of rising expectations (Davies, 1969) has not focused sufficient attention on the group most likely to participate in riots, namely young males between the ages of 16 and 34. This group is the one most likely to experience the effects of economic recessions as a major reduction in their economic opportunities, relative to their aspiration levels. Consequently, this group is more at risk for aggression and violence than other age groups. We will concentrate on this age group in accounting for changes in homicide rates due to long-term changes in economic conditions and fluctuations in population trends.

Learned Helplessness, Self-efficacy, and Aggression

The arguments previously advanced have suggested that most individuals do not characteristically respond to aversive events with aggressive behavior. Recall that Bandura (1973, 1979) proposed that many diverse responses may result from aversive events. Individual reactions may range from dependency, withdrawal, psychosomatic symptoms, and self-anesthization with drugs and alcohol, to aggression, increased achievement, and constructive problem-solving. These reactions may vary for the same person across different situations and may vary for different people within the same situation. We have adopted the concepts of learned helplessness (Seligman, 1975) and self-efficacy (Bandura, 1977) to account for the differential effects of aversive events on social behavior.

According to Seligman (1975), learned helplessness is produced when an individual learns that the outcomes s/he obtains are independent of any voluntary responses. That is, favorable or unfavorable outcomes may occur regardless of what behaviors the individual does or does not display; thus, the event is perceived as being uncontrollable by individual behavior. There is a crucial distinction between learned helplessness behavior and partially reinforced behavior. In partial reinforcement paradigms, favorable outcomes are not achieved or unpleasant events are not avoided (positive and negative reinforcement) unless the individual engages in a critical behavior. The appearance of outcomes, then, is partially dependent on the organism (i.e., outcomes can be controlled in part by individual behavior). Voluntary behaviors (such as aggression) learned under partial reinforcement procedures are very resistant to extinction (Patterson et al., 1975; Ulrich et al., 1973). However, the primary consequence of learned helplessness is that individuals believe their voluntary behavior does not make a difference in their outcomes. Their beliefs decrease the likelihood that any voluntary response, including aggression, will be employed in attempts to maintain or gain control over outcomes. Aggression, a voluntary response, would be very weak if it were acquired under learned helplessness conditions, but this response would be very resistant to extinction if it were acquired under partial reinforcement conditions.

The notion of self-efficacy in Bandura's work (1979) is closely related to the idea of learned helplessness. According to Bandura, two important determinants of behavior are 1) whether the individual believes that s/he can perform a behavior (efficacy expectation) and 2) whether the behavior will produce a given outcome (outcome expectancy). An individual may experience helplessness and/or loss of control over outcomes either because s/he cannot perform a necessary behavior (low efficacy expectation) or because s/he is not likely to receive the outcome even if s/he performs the necessary behavior (low outcome expectancy).

Individuals may display quite different reactions (e.g., aggression, depression, or apathy) to potential loss of control, depending upon their efficacy and outcome expectations (see Table 1). We might anticipate aggression to be a primary response for those individuals who believe that they can perform the required behavior but anticipate not being rewarded for their performance. This effect is similar to Ulrich's findings (Ulrich et al., 1973) that an abrupt termination of reinforcement increases the likelihood of aggression. In each instance the individual has a high efficacy expectation or sense of efficacy for successfully performing the required behavior, but experiences an abrupt loss of outcome

TABLE 1
Responses to Aversive Life Events

Controllable		Uncontrollable	
	Blunting	No Blunting	
		Withdrawal	Learned Helplessness
Assertiveness	Eating, Sex	Cults	Apathy
Achievement	Sports, TV,	Gangs	Depression
Problem Solving	Music	Runaway	Resignation
Aggression	Self Anesthization: drugs & alcohol Distracting Thoughts		Psychosomatization

Adapted from Bandura (1973), Miller & Grant (Note 3), Seligman (1975).

control (due to low outcome expectancies or loss of reinforcement). If these people have learned to successfully obtain either social or economic rewards through coercive action, they may initiate aggression in an attempt to regain the perceived or actual loss of outcomes (i.e., regain control). On the other hand, individuals with low efficacy expectations do not feel competent in dealing with their loss of control. Consequently, they are not likely to attempt to regain control over outcomes, and they are likely to experience either depression or apathy.

Changing life events, self-efficacy and aggression. As an individual matures through the life cycle, s/he will encounter a number of major life changes which can disrupt the level or rate of positive and negative consequences to which s/he has adapted. Some of the most important life events producing particularly strong positive or negative reactions are interpersonal changes (e.g., death of a spouse); a change in marital satisfaction or status; a major change in health of self or family member; and major financial or business changes (Holmes & Rahe, 1967). Frequent changes in life events can produce higher levels of stress, increase the likelihood of depression or anxiety (Johnson & Sarason, 1978), as well as increase the risk of major behavioral disruption after the event occurs.

The responses to stressful life events will vary as they do for other events of an aversive nature. Individuals with strong efficacy expectations are more likely than people with weak efficacy expectations to perceive the life event as controllable, and thus, they may attempt to control the outcomes by a voluntary response. High perceived efficacy individuals are more likely to use responses (including aggression) that previously have proven to be successful for them and/or others in terminating similar aversive experiences. Either direct experience with negatively reinforced aggression (Patterson & Cobb, 1973) or vicarious experiences with successful aggression (Bandura, 1977) can increase the likelihood of this mode of responding. However, only a small proportion of high-efficacy individuals, when exposed to aversive life events, are likely to engage in aggression to reestablish control over outcomes; that is, they may try many different non-aggressive strategies before they resort to violence.

Individuals with weak efficacy expectations, on the other hand, are likely to perceive the stressful life events as uncontrollable (Bandura, 1977; Leventhal, 1970; Seligman, 1975). These individuals may try to minimize the intensity of the aversive event by engaging in "blunting" strategies (Miller & Grant, Note 3). For example, they may engage in activities previously proven to be pleasant (e.g., eating and/or sexual behavior, listening to music, or sports) or may attempt to minimize the intensity of the aversive experience by self-anesthization with drugs or alcohol. If these blunting activities prove inadequate, the individual is likely to withdraw or perhaps display symptoms of learned helplessness, depression or apathy, including loss of appetite for eating and sexual activities (Seligman, 1975; Miller & Grant, Note 2). In short, changing life events can produce diverse reactions, depending upon whether the event is perceived to be controllable or uncontrollable, and whether "blunting" activities adequately minimize its aversive intensity.

Life changes and the age structure of crime. While individuals of all ages experience aversive life events, young people (under 30 years of age) report that they experience more frequent and more aversive life events than is reported by individuals over 30 years of age (Masuda & Holmes, 1978). The life changes of adolescence (14-18) and young adulthood (18-24) seem to be particularly important in contributing to this age group's higher risk of violent crime. The median age of arrest for different crimes (robbery, assault, etc.) was computed from values reported in the FBI's *Uniform Crime Reports.* Adolescents aged 14-16 are most involved in status-related crimes (i.e., acts which are not illegal for older persons) such as alcohol consumption and running away from home, or potentially thrill-seeking crimes such as vandalism, shoplifting, burglary, and auto theft.

Older teenagers (16-18), in the initial stages of entering the labor force, begin to commit more serious crimes such as robbery, aggravated assault, and rape. Most homicides are committed in the 15-34 age range, but the crime is especially likely to occur in the 20-25 age range. These violent acts are frequently committed under the influence of alcohol. Carefully controlled research has demonstrated that the physiological effects of alcohol do increase the likelihood that people will respond aggressively to an aversive event (Shuntich & Taylor, 1972). Nonetheless, violent crimes seem to be especially likely for those individuals who do not have easy access to legitimate occupational opportunities (Cloward & Ohlin, 1960).

The opportunity to commit a crime is also limited by a person's social experiences. For instance, as we move up in the age range, we find that individuals aged 25-30 are most likely to commit assaults against their children and spouses. These crimes usually require someone to be married for several years before s/he has children or a spouse against whom assaults may be committed.

Arrests for public intoxication, driving under the influence, and public vagrancy (which typically involve alcohol abuse) become more frequent in the 30-35 age range. Unlike the alcohol-related assaults in younger people, nonviolent problems occur in older individuals. As people become even older members of society, their risk of self-inflicted injuries such as suicide increases substantially (median age is 65). Collectively, the arrest and suicide data indicate that people are maximally at risk to either commit or engage in antisocial and inappropriate behaviors at different ages and/or stages in their lives.

During adolescence, several important demands and changes occur which can change the likelihood of being arrested. Physically, young adolescents 10-14 years of age undergo major hormonal changes associated with puberty; one result is that they experience an enormous growth in size and strength. As adolescents mature and achieve the physical appearance of adulthood, they are more likely to be responded to as adults, especially by teachers and employers who did not know them when they were younger. Important social changes also occur as adolescents receive increased pressure to achieve peer and heterosexual adjustments. Consequently, major shifts in social behavior begin to occur as adolescents assume the responsibilities of adulthood.

The important markers for this transition from adolescence to young adulthood, then, are leaving school, leaving home, getting married, and participating in the labor force by seeking employment. Most males pass through these transitions during the 18-24 age range, with proportionately fewer blacks than whites in the labor force within this age range (U.S. Census Bureau, 1881-1978; Taeuber & Taeuber, 1971).

Balanced against the increased autonomy and freedom of late adolescence is the decline in financial support. When adolescents leave home, the degree of financial support may drop substantially, especially for adolescents from low-income families. The increased autonomy and control over personal decisions may be sharply limited by this loss of financial support. These limitations may be particularly burdensome for those individuals who have access only to low-income, dead-end jobs.

The 18-24-year age range probably experiences the most relative deprivation during economic recession; they are most likely to lose their jobs or to remain unemployed. They are most likely to experience uncertain, irregular employment, often in low status jobs at low salaries. As a result, they may experience a substantial decline in their standard of living as compared to the time when they were at home with their parents (Easterlin, 1968, 1973). When the decline in the standard of living (achieved level of outcomes) is considerably lower than the standard of living they have been accustomed to and aspire to, the result is relative deprivation. Thus, during an economic recession when relative deprivation is highest for this age group, we might anticipate an increase in aggressive and/or violent criminal behavior as a means of coping with the aversiveness of the situation.

Black males experience even more difficulties than white males in making the transition into the labor force. For both groups, job-seeking tends to increase substantially after the age of 16. Labor force partici- pation rates for black males in the 16-24 age group indicate that they were more likely than white males to participate in the labor force in 1956, but the participation rate of white youth was greater than that of blacks in 1975 (U.S. Census Bureau, 1976). There are two variables that contributed to the change from 1956 to 1975. First, an increasing num- ber of black youths remained in school for the 18-24 age range in 1975, thus postponing their entry into the labor force. Secondly, a growing number of black youths "dropped out" of the labor force. The second factor resulted in part because of the disillusionment with legitimate labor force opportunities (Cloward & Ohlin, 1960; Wolfgang, 1968). The proportion of young black males aged 16-20 who sought but did not find jobs in 1975 (50%) was approximately double that of white males (25%) in the same age group (U.S. Census Bureau, 1976).

The higher risk of black versus white arrest rates for a particular age group corresponds to the ratio of black to white unemployment in that age group. The crimes for which blacks are arrested at rates much greater than whites (adjusted per 100,000 representative population) occur primarily in the 18-24 age group (Uniform Crime Reports, 1977, p. 180-184). For example, the ratio of black to white arrest *rates* of crimes committed by the 18-24 age group are: robbery = 5.1 times higher rate; aggravated assault = 3.0 times higher; larceny and theft = 3.2; homicide = 5.1; forcible rape = 4.7; and prostitution = 5.4. The ratio of black to white arrests for crimes committed by younger age groups (e.g., arson = 2.1 times higher; vandalism = 1.7; runaways = 1.1) or for older age groups (e.g., drunkenness = 1.8 times higher; driving under the influ- ence = 1.3) are more nearly proportional to the rates for the white population.

Severe unemployment of the type experienced by young urban resi- dents (especially black youths) undoubtedly reduces or eliminates legit- imate opportunities (Cloward & Ohlin, 1960). Those who cannot compete successfully for rewarding jobs may turn instead to shoplifting, burglary, and drug dealing. If these individuals begin to associate with groups who share similar predicaments, then criminal subcultures may emerge to model and reinforce antisocial behavior (Wolfgang, 1968).

DEMOGRAPHIC ANTECEDENTS OF AGGRESSIVE BEHAVIOR

Up to this point we have examined the development of violent behavior primarily at the individual level. In the following discussion, we
present some of the relatively rapid changes which are occurring in
modern societies. Major fluctuations in population characteristics, particularly the changing number of individuals in specific age and ethnic
groups, are at the root of many societal changes. The learning, economic
and social environments of children, adolescents and young adults have
been substantially modified by the effects of population fluctuation of
the past 75 years. However, the precise relationship between demographic variables and violent behavior is quite complex and poorly
understood (Turner & Dodd, 1979). In this discussion, some societal
trends will be outlined, along with recent research projects which have
attempted to relate demographic factors and societal changes to specific
crime rates.

Demographic Changes in Modern Society

Major changes are occurring in modern society which mirror changes
in family structure. For example, annual crime, divorce, and unemployment rates have climbed dramatically over the past decade, while
the birth rate has dropped to an all-time low (U.S. Bureau of the Census,
1960-1975). Accompanying these changes have been major shifts in
norms and values concerning sex roles. Moreover, changes in divorce
laws and factors such as smaller family size, availability of child-care
centers, and increased options for women to compete successfully in the
labor market have produced marked changes in the divorce rate (Kenkel,
1977; Turner & Dodd, 1979).

Although the changing family is often blamed for the high divorce
rate and other social ills, it may be that changes in the American family
are responses to, rather than causes of, major societal changes. In fact,
some have proposed that the rising divorce rate reflects healthy changes
in values and expectations among young people (Kenkel, 1977; Schulz,
1976). Regardless of perspective, there can be little doubt that our society
is changing in rather significant ways, and that the family institution is
involved in many of these changes, as evidenced by changes in both
divorce and birth rates (Turner & Dodd, 1979).

Demographers have long been aware that population changes can
have widespread effects on society (Heer, 1975; Merton & Nisbet, 1976).
Fluctuations in the birth rate have been linked to changes of the entire

economic and social structure, including industry and commerce, education and politics (Whelpton, 1932), to crime and delinquency (Ferdinand, 1969), alcoholism and drug addiction, and political alienation (Hauser, 1971). Still, the relationship of population to social change is not a simple one.

Long-term Changes in Homicide Rates and the Population

Along with our associate, David Dodd, we have collected a variety of U.S. national demographic data to investigate the impact of fluctuations in the birth rate as they relate to shifts in age-specific social phenomena such as crime, fertility, marriage, and divorce (Cole & Turner, 1977; Dodd, Cole, & Turner, 1977; Turner & Dodd, 1979). Collectively, these data suggest that the interacting effects of changing birth rates and economic opportunities can account for a major proportion of fluctuating crime rates in different age groups over the past 75 years. One particularly important implication of our model to account for fluctuating crime rates is that it leads to a clear prediction of a major decline (approximately 40% reduction) in property and violent crime between 1975 and 1985. The following discussion focuses primarily on the crime of homicide, but similar analyses can be applied to other crimes where long-term, age-specific data are available.

The annual frequency of homicide in the United States has increased substantially over the past 15 years, from 8,000 to 21,000 homicides. One reason for the increase is that the total population of the U.S. has grown. However, gains in the total population account for only 25% of the increased frequency of homicides. As we indicated earlier, some researchers have speculated that the dissolution of the family institution may be the root cause of the increase in crime rates (Kenkel, 1977; Yorburg, 1973). For example, they point to the fact that most (75%) of the homicides in the U.S. are committed among friends, neighbors, family members, and acquaintances and usually follow an altercation (Newton & Zimring, 1969). Moreover, other social phenomena have occurred simultaneously with the recent increases in violence among family members: a declining birth rate, an increased divorce rate, and a delay in the age of marriage. However, before conclusions about the family institution are seriously entertained as a possible cause of the recent increases in homicide, it is helpful to examine a longer temporal record of homicide rates in the United States.

The annual frequency of homicide increased from approximately 4,000 in 1900 to 16,000 in 1935, then decreased to 6,000 in 1945, rose slightly after the war, and then declined for the period 1950-1960. In the past 15 years, the annual frequency increased steadily until 1975, subsequent to which the rate has been declining. The high current rate of crime is somewhat similar to the rate which occurred during the Depression. Thus, there appear to be long-term swings in homicide rates.

The first step in identifying the changing rate of homicide over time is to remove shifts due to population changes. Most homicides are committed by young males between the ages of 15 and 34. There have been major fluctuations in the age-related composition of the population due to changing birth rates, immigration rates, and decreased mortality. Thus, we need an estimate of the relative change in population size for the group which is most at risk. The U.S. Census Bureau's (1960-1974) estimates of the number of individuals in the 15-34 age group for each of the last 75 years are presented in Figure 2. We have divided the annual *frequency* of homicide by the number of individuals aged 15-34 in each year. The results of the computation for the period 1910-1977 are presented in Figure 3. An inspection of this figure indicates that the intervals from 1930-35 and 1970-75 have been periods of unusually high homicide rates per 100,000 population of 15-34-year-olds.

This analysis is still too global in that it treats each member of the 15-

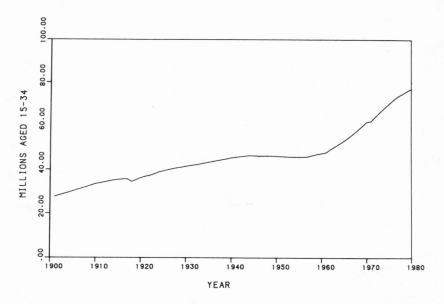

FIGURE 2. Number of 15-34 year olds in the United States from 1901-1975. (Source: U.S. Census Bureau)

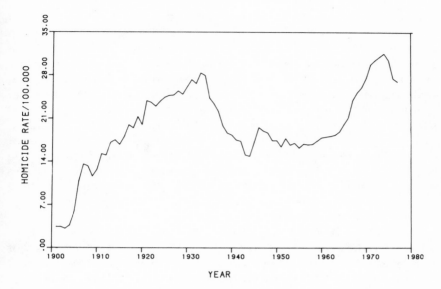

FIGURE 3. United States homicide rate (frequency ÷ number aged 15-34) from 1910-1978. (Source: U.S. Census Bureau)

34-year age group as being equally at risk for homicide. But this crime is quite age-specific; the modal age of arrest is 21 for homicide (*Uniform Crime Reports*, 1965-1976). Cole and Turner (1977) designed a statistical model to account for increased crime in each age group (e.g., 16- or 17-year-olds) from the increase or decrease of that age group in the population (e.g., the prewar baby bust and the postwar baby boom). Their model required them to obtain the rates for homicide within each specific age group. Although actual age-specific commission rates for homicide are unknown, the age-specific rates of committing homicide can be estimated from arrest data. Since these data from national samples have been carefully compiled in the *Uniform Crime Reports* of the FBI (at least since 1958), it is possible to determine the age-specific increase in homicide rates from 1958 to 1975 by the increased number of individuals in each of the age groups (14-30).

Multiple regression analyses revealed that the number of individuals in each age group (estimated from lagged birth rates) was highly correlated with changes in crime rates. That is, the changing number of individuals in a particular age group from 1960-1975 was highly correlated with the actual number of arrests of suspects from that age group ($R = .80$, $F(1,200) = 355.6$, $P < .001$).

The multiple regression equations derived from the 1960-1975 data were used to forecast the numbers of homicides to be expected from 1976-1990. This projection depends partly upon the assumption that it is possible to estimate how many people will be in each age group during the 1976-1990 time period. These estimates were based on the lagged birth records (i.e., children born in 1960 will be 20 in 1980 and 30 in 1990). When the postwar birth cohort passes beyond young adulthood into middle age during the next decade, the number of individuals in each age group will begin to decline. Due to decreasing numbers of individuals in the age group maximally at risk for crime, the regression equation predicts a 40% decline in the number of youth-oriented crimes such as homicide between 1975 and 1985-1990. Concomitantly, there will be increased rates of those crimes committed by older adults, e.g., various nonviolent, alcohol-related crimes.

Three major points emerge from a discussion of age-related crime rates. First, the arrest data clearly demonstrate that the violent behavior expressed by various age groups takes quite different forms. Violence against others is most likely from 15-34 and especially from 18-24 years of age. Perhaps the social and economic demands which living environments place on individuals may vary with age and lead to quite different forms of coping behavior. Individuals of different ages may have different efficacy expectations in coping with environmental demands, and be differentially likely to use aggression to terminate aversive events. Secondly, because of the age-specific nature of most crimes, the post World War II population wave will cause the rates of specific crimes to rise and fall as the baby boom reaches and then passes the age of risk for that crime. Although fluctuating birth rates can be linked to changing rates of violent behavior, the factors which moderate birth rates remain to be identified.

Third, the increase in birth rates was not associated with a one-to-one increase in arrest rates. For a given age group the frequency of arrests increased at a rate nearly three times greater than the expanding number of individuals within each age group. Consequently, the expanding crime rate cannot be explained solely by the increased numbers of individuals available to commit crimes. Possible explanations for such a phenomenon will now be discussed.

Comparisons of Homicide Rates in 1930-1935 and 1970-1975

The demographics of the Depression era were similar to the current period. There was a declining birth rate, a declining marriage rate, as well as an increasing homicide rate (U.S. Census Bureau, 1947-1974).

Marriage, divorce, homicide, and unemployment occur primarily within the 15-34 age group, and especially in the 18-24 age group. Individuals in this age group are also attempting to leave home and establish independent households. Since the annual rates for these social variables have co-varied over the past 60 years, it is possible that a common variable might be influencing the annual fluctuations in these social phenomena. We have attempted to identify some of the social forces which are particularly impactful on the 15-34 age group that might mediate annual fluctuations in homicide, birth rates, and marriage rates.

The Great Depression produced widespread disruptions of the world's economy; there was a massive increase in unemployment and a reduction in wages, especially for young people. According to the present analysis, this abrupt change in the economic conditions of the time created a situation of relative deprivation, one consequence of which was an upswing in violent crime. We would thus expect changes in unemployment in the Depression and in the current period to correlate with changes in the crime rates.

The annual unemployment rate obtained from the U.S. Department of Labor's records is represented in Figure 4 for the time span 1925-

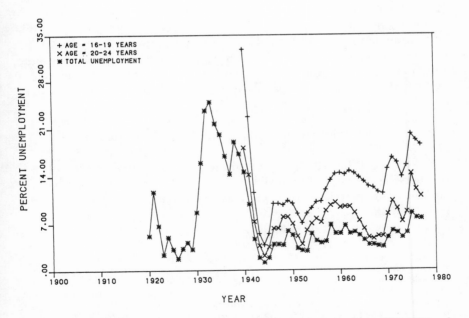

FIGURE 4. United States unemployment rates for the total population from 1920-1975 and for 15-19 and 20-24 year olds from 1940-1975. (Source: U. S. Census Bureau)

1978 (labeled total unemployment). Inspection of the figure shows that the high homicide rate of 1930-1935 does roughly correspond to the high rate of unemployment. The period from 1960 to 1975 does not appear to have such an unusually high unemployment rate that it could account for all of the increase in crime during that time interval. Recall the earlier observation that homicide is most likely to occur for individuals in the 15-34 age range. This observation would suggest that unemployment rates must be separately estimated for this age group to observe a link between unemployment and homicide. The number of individuals aged 15-19 and 20-24 unemployed each year between 1940 and 1977 are also reported in Figure 4. The age-specific rates of unemployment are not available before 1940. A comparison of Figures 3 and 4 shows that the year-by-year changes in unemployment from 1940 to 1975 in the 15-24 age group do roughly correspond to changes in homicide rates over this time interval. Historical accounts of unemployment in the Depression further indicate that the 1930-1935 period produced an unusually high level of youthful unemployment (Easterlin, 1968, 1973).

The homicide and unemployment rates are also inversely related to the fertility rate for the corresponding time interval.* That is, periods of low fertility (average number of children per woman) closely correspond to high unemployment and homicide rates. The birth rate per 1000 women aged 15-45 from 1908-1975 is presented in Figure 5. The inverse relationships among these variables over time suggests that some common factor might be at work. To explain how these variables might be related, we shift from an analysis of homicide data to unemployment data.

A Relative Deprivation Analysis of Long-term Changes in Social Behavior

Easterlin's (1968, 1973) version of the relative deprivation hypothesis has been successfully employed to explain long-term changes in unemployment, marriage, divorce, and fertility rates. In the remaining section of the paper, we extend Easterlin's model to account for long-term changes in the rates of violence.

---

*Correlations were computed between the annual fertility rate and homicide rate (per 100,000 aged 15-34) from 1925-1977 yielding an $r = -.73$. Since the observations are not independent, it is difficult to estimate the statistical significance of the correlation. The observations for the 1938-1945 period were not consistent with the other observations since there was a low birth rate and a low homicide rate. During this time, many young men were enrolled either in CCC camps or in the military (10 million by 1945). The living arrangements for young men isolated them from typical social interactions and this isolation may have contributed to the low homicide and fertility rates.

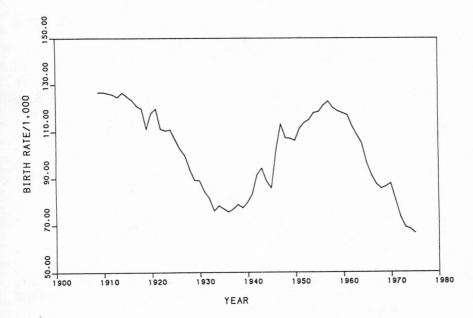

FIGURE 5. United States birth rate per 1000 women aged 15-45 from 1908-1975. (Source: U. S. Census Bureau)

Easterlin (1968) proposed that the economic condition of young people entering the labor force is a central factor in determining whether young couples will get married or, if they are married, how many children they will have. The fluctuating family size in the United States has been affected quite strongly by relative, as well as absolute, labor force opportunities (Easterlin, 1973). That is, young people are likely to become married and have children, not only as a function of their absolute income, but also as a function of their income relative to an aspired level. When individuals have more expensive tastes for consumer goods than they can afford with their income, they are likely to delay marriage, to delay having children, or to limit their family size. Easterlin's (1973) analysis reflects relative deprivation principles where the size of the gap between aspired and achieved levels of consumer consumption (i.e., relative deprivation) is assumed to be a major determinant of social behavior.

Easterlin (1968) amassed substantial evidence that the parents of the baby boom generation (which peaked in 1957) were unusually affluent, relative to their "aspiration level" for consumer goods. Consequently, they had disposable (excess) income which was available for expanding the family size. After 1957, the economic opportunities facing young married couples began to fall substantially below a level which permitted them to satisfy their "tastes" for consumer goods. Hence, the family size began to decline from 1957-1975, as the gap between aspired and achieved levels began to grow. In short, Easterlin claims that relative deprivation became greater and greater for young people from 1957 to 1975. The first symptom of relative deprivation was a declining birth rate. After 1970, the growing relative deprivation gradually influenced marriage rates so that young couples began to delay the age of marriage (Easterlin, 1968, 1973).

One of the major consequences of the later age of marriage and the smaller family size was a 35% decline in the annual birth rate from 1957 through 1975. As a consequence of fewer births, there will be approximately 35% fewer 20-year-olds from 1977 to 1995. In short, current economic conditions which influence the birth rate also produce "echo" effects a number of years later, as the current birth cohort achieves different ages (Easterlin, 1973). For example, echo effects from the low birth rate of the Depression era and high birth rate after World War II are revealed first in the low unemployment, high birth, and low homicide rates of the 1950s and then the high unemployment, the low birth, and the high homicide rates of the 1970s. The echo effect for birth, homicide, and unemployment should occur 20-25 years later than birth rate fluctuations since 15-34- (and especially, 20-24-) year-olds are maximally likely to experience these social phenomena.

As we have reasoned earlier, relative deprivation can produce many diverse reactions. If young people have, in fact, experienced more relative deprivation since 1960, then there should be increasing frequencies of those reactions which occur to aversive events such as relative deprivation (recall Table 1). Some individuals might be expected to work harder to cope with the increased perceived deprivation, if their direct and vicarious learning experiences indicate that hard work can reduce the aversive consequences of deprivation. However, increased relative deprivation can also lead to increased aggression, to "blunting strategies," to depression, or possibly to apathy (Bandura, 1977; Seligman, 1975).

Our earlier analysis of relative deprivation suggests that the objectively most deprived individuals may not be the ones who are most likely to use aggression in response to deprivation. Rather, the highly deprived group may display blunting strategies or drug abuse, apathy, or depression. They also may join social groups (e.g., religious cults) which redefine their aspiration level to a lower standard. Reduced aspiration levels can eliminate the aversive consequences of relative deprivation by making one's aspired level more consistent with achieved levels.

Extending the Analysis to Violent Behavior

Easterlin (1968), using aggregate data, constructed an estimate of relative deprivation from a measure which contrasted young adults' employment rates and/or income level to their parents' income five years earlier. A five-year lag was introduced as an estimate of the parents' financial status five years earlier when the young adults would have been adolescents and living at home with their parents. This index showed that the gap between aspired (i.e., earlier parental) and achieved income or employment levels declined from 1940 to 1957 when a minimum gap was reached. After 1957, the index indicated that the relative size of the gap increased, nearly monotonically, through 1975.

Easterlin's relative deprivation measure and the homicide rate (per 100,000 young people) demonstrate striking similarities from 1940 to 1975. While it is not possible to construct an exact measure of relative deprivation during the Depression era, we have provided a rough approximation by examining the total income and unemployment rates and relating these rates to the homicide rate. The rapid increase in unemployment from 1930 to 1935 had a greater impact on youthful employees than on middle-aged workers. Hence, this period produced increasing relative deprivation due to the expanding gap between young adult employment (1930-35) and parental employment or income five years earlier (1925-30). From 1935 to 1940, the unemployment rates for young adults began to drop, especially as compared to the high unemployment witnessed from 1930 to 1935. The relative deprivation of young people should have been decreasing during the period from 1935 to 1940.

An inspection of the homicide rates from 1925-1930, 1930-1935, and 1935-1940 indicates a rising level of homicide which reached a peak near 1935 and declined afterward through 1940. In short, the approximate analysis or relative deprivation during the Depression period does correspond roughly to changes in the homicide rate. Based on indirect evidence from 1925-1940 and direct evidence from 1940-1975, the homicide and economic data are consistent with an explanation of the long-term change in homicide rates/100,000 population from 1925-1974, as being due to a corresponding fluctuation in relative deprivation over this same time course.

Income level differences in violence. Easterlin's (1968, 1973) analysis implies that the adolescents and young adults of moderate and higher income families experience a greater level of relative deprivation than do individuals from low-income families when they leave home. That is, the offspring of high-income families would spend a higher proportion of their income to satisfy their tastes for more expensive consumer goods. By analogy, we might wonder whether higher levels of relative deprivation could lead to more aggression.

It should be recalled that aggression is only one of many possible reactions to relative deprivation. Even if offspring from high-income families did experience more relative deprivation when they left home, they still might not engage in more aggression than youths from low-income families. If they had not previously experienced direct or vicarious "negative reinforcement" for aggression when exposed to aversive events, they would not be as likely as other groups to display aggression when subsequently exposed to aversive events such as relative deprivation.

Several lines of research suggest that there are occasions in which moderate- to high-income families express more aggression than low-income families. Stark and McEvoy (1970) reanalyzed data from a national survey of self-reported, non-wartime violence from different ethnic, sex, and income groups. The data indicated that moderate- and high-income individuals were more likely to say that they had "hit," "kicked," or "punched" someone than was reported by low-income individuals. It is possible that these high-income people might have been more likely to remember, or more willing to report their attacks on others. Still, the data suggest that individuals from high-income backgrounds may display more aggression than low-income individuals, in contrast to what is normally assumed to be true.

A second line of research is more compelling in its suggestion that some types of violent reactions do occur more frequently in the offspring of high-income individuals. The analysis of participants of riots and revolutions strongly suggests that these events are precipitated by young adults from moderate- to high-income families.

Sears and McConahay (1970) observed that the cities in which riots occurred in the mid-1960s, such as Watts (Los Angeles) and Detroit, were not seriously depressed communities. The residents of the rioting cities had better incomes, more stable homes, better jobs, and higher education levels than many non-rioting communities. Similarly, interviews with riot participants indicated that the typical rioters were young black males who were better educated and longer-term residents of the city than the non-rioters. The fathers of the rioters had a higher income than fathers of non-rioters, and they lived in better than average housing of the community and maintained stable employment. In short, the riot participants were the adolescents of the more affluent, successful members of the rioting communities, and these communities were relatively well-off compared to non-rioting communities. The most deprived individuals were not the ones most likely to participate in the riots.

Sears and McConahay (1970) explain the riots as reflecting relative deprivation due to rising expectations. To clarify the role of relative deprivation, it also might be helpful to relate evidence about these riots to Easterlin's analysis. Since the young blacks came from more affluent, better educated families, they would have developed more expensive tastes which could not be satisfied with their entry level salaries as they left home. The labor force opportunities for young blacks began to deteriorate after 1957, partly due to the increased competition for jobs among the members of the first wave of the baby boom cohort (1947 + 16 = 1963). Young black youths began to experience relatively more bleak economic prospects, at the same time that their aspiration levels had been rising due to the improved economic opportunities for their parents (from 1945-1960). In short, there might have been an abrupt increase in relative deprivation for these youths as compared to the condition of their parents a few years earlier.

A number of other riots or revolutions seem to follow the pattern just described (Davies, 1969). That is, a period of improving economic conditions, followed by a brief but abrupt reversal, served as one catalyst to the riot. By concentrating on the age group entering the labor force, the actual impact of an economic reversal becomes more apparent. Before young adults leave home, they have become accustomed to the improving economic conditions which their parents have enjoyed. The young adults have developed higher aspiration levels during the period of improving economic conditions, since their parents have more money to spend. If the young adults leave home during the time of an abrupt economic reversal, they will experience two different sources of deprivation in their economic situation. First, as with all young people, they will be required to carry a heavier financial burden for their own expenses as they leave home; individuals with higher aspiration levels will experience greater relative deprivation. In addition, young labor force entrants during a recession or depression also experience greater difficulty in finding a job than their predecessors.

A sharp reduction in labor force opportunities affects new labor force entrants the most (Easterlin, 1968; Easterlin, Wachter, & Wachter, 1978). An employer's initial reaction to a minor economic slump is to stop replacing employees who leave. Partly to maintain the morale of their staff, employers are likely to fire their experienced employees only during major recessions in the economy. A brief economic recession is likely to have its greatest effect on new entrants to the labor force, since they will not be able to find jobs during recessions, yet previous employees are likely to keep their jobs. Age and ethnic differences in unemployment data for the economic recession of 1973-1974 demonstrate the differential effects of recessions on young people (Turner & Dodd, 1979). Although the total unemployment rate doubled for all age groups, the unemployment rate for males aged 25-44 doubled from 2 to 4%, while the rate for white males aged 20-24 doubled from 9 to 18% and the rate for nonwhite males aged 16-19 doubled from 24 to 48%. These data indicate that the economic recession had its greatest effects on young, nonwhite males.

Economic recessions are also likely to intensify the relative deprivation that young people experience when they are in transition away from their parents' home. These transitional youths experience both the difficult economic times of the recession and the loss in resources which they previously had obtained from their parents (e.g., food and housing). Figure 6 represents the different levels of relative deprivation experienced by youths at different points in time as they leave home. The top line in the figure represents the disposable income of parents (coded as *) for the past 75 years. For our analysis, we have assumed that parents share some of their resources with their children. Hence, during periods of higher disposable income, parents have more resources to share with their adolescent children. Thus, teenagers' access to resources at home depends on the disposable income of their parents. After completing the transition out of their parents' home, most young adults have access to fewer resources than they experienced at home with their parents. The approximate disposable income of independent young adults is represented by the bottom line in Figure 6 (coded as +). The lines coded as an × represent transitional disposable income that young people experience as they leave home to become independent young adults. The length of the transition lines at different points in time indicate that the drop in income (or relative deprivation) differed substantially over time. For example, during the 1920-1925 and 1950-1955 periods, the level of relative deprivation was much smaller than during the 1930-1935 and 1970-1975 periods.

The two periods of high relative deprivation (1930-35 and 1970-75) also have been characterized by a declining birth rate, a delayed age of marriage, an increased probability of divorce, and an increased probability of homicide. Perhaps the high level of relative deprivation intensified the aversiveness of life experiences for youths in transition out of the home. The unusually intense level of relative deprivation among new labor force participants helps to explain why they are particularly

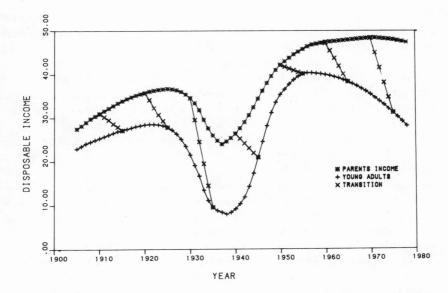

FIGURE 6. Approximate disposable income for parents (*), for young adults (+) and for youths in transition away from home (×) from 1905-1979. (Source: Easterlin, 1968; 1973; U. S. Census Bureau)

likely to participate in riots or other violent behavior as compared to younger or older members of the society.

SUMMARY

Aggression and violence are multifaceted phenomena, and many variables modify their likelihood. Aggression is particularly likely to be a learned response to aversive life events, since this behavior frequently is negatively reinforced. However, aggression is not the only or even the most common reaction to aversive life events. With both direct and vicarious learning experiences, people may learn to terminate aversive life events through intensified efforts or through "blunting" strategies (e.g., distracting activities or use of alcohol and drugs), or develop the learned helplessness reactions of depression and apathy.

It was proposed that the aversive life experiences of young adults increase the likelihood of aggression. This was evidenced by the facts that violent crime has increased dramatically over the past 20 years in the United States, and that these crimes are particularly likely to occur among young adult males. The recent increases in crime were explained by the increased number of young adults exposed to negative life events (especially economic dissatisfaction). First, there were more young adults between 1970 and 1980 because of the post World War II baby boom. Approximately 50% of the year-to-year variance in homicide can be explained by the increased number of individuals from the postwar baby boom cohort reaching the age groups of maximum risk for violence. Secondly, each member of the baby boom cohort was likely to experience more absolute deprivation since more individuals were competing for limited social and economic resources. Competition for labor force participation has been especially difficult since limited jobs had to be divided among more people. Thirdly, the baby boom cohort experienced higher levels of relative deprivation as they left home. That is, adolescents and young adults have experienced rising expectations due to the unusually favorable economic opportunities of their parents. The baby boom cohort could not readily achieve these high aspirations due to the increased competition among themselves for limited social and economic resources.

Following 1957, the growing levels of relative deprivation produced a continuing decline in the birth rate through 1975. One important consequence of the decreasing birth rate is that there will be fewer and fewer young adults entering the labor force between now and 1990.

Thus, two factors should reduce the number of individuals "at risk" for violence. First, there will be only 65-70% as many individuals in the high-risk age groups, and that factor alone leads to the prediction of a 30-35% decline in violent crime. Secondly, the smaller cohorts (individuals born in one year) will not have to divide limited resources among as many individuals as earlier birth cohorts. Hence, the later birth cohorts should experience more favorable economic conditions which would lower their perceived relative deprivation. In short, these factors lead to the prediction of a massive decrease (perhaps 40%) in violent crime by 1985-1990. However, as the postwar baby boom cohort grows older, they will experience periods of high risk for different social problems in public intoxication (aged 30-35), serious mental health problems such as depression (aged 45),* and eventually suicide (aged 65-70).

---

*The median age for first mental hospital admission (other than senility) is approximately 40 (Phelphs & Anderson, 1958). Consequently, 1985-2005 should prove to be a period of serious mental hospital problems as the aging postwar baby boom cohort reaches the age to be maximally at risk for some serious psychological and behavioral problems.

REFERENCE NOTES

1. Bandura, A. Theories of social violence. *Stanford Observer*, Stanford, California, October, 1978.
2. Miller, S. M., & Grant, R. P. The blunting hypothesis: A theory of predictability and human stress. University of Pennsylvania, January, 1979.
3. Simon, K. M. Effects of self comparison, social comparison, and depression on goal setting and self evaluative reactions. Unpublished manuscript. Stanford University, 1979.

REFERENCES

BANDURA, A. Social learning theory of aggression. In J. Knutson (Ed.), *The control of aggression*. Chicago: Aldine Publishing Co., 1973.
BANDURA, A. *Social learning theory.* Englewood Cliffs, N. J.: Prentice-Hall, Inc., 1977.
BANDURA, A. The social learning perspective: Mechanisms of aggression. In H. Toch (Ed.), *Psychology of crime and criminal justice.* New York: Holt, Rinehart & Winston, 1979.
BARON, R. A. *Human aggression.* New York: Plenum Press, 1978.
BELL, R. Q. Human infant-effects in the first year. In R. Q. Bell & L. V. Harper (Eds.), *Child effects on adults.* New York: Lawrence Erlbaum, 1977.
BERKOWITZ, L. Some determinants of impulsive aggression: Role of mediated associations with reinforcements for aggression. *Psychological Review*, 1974, *81*, 165-176.
BERKOWITZ, L. & ALIOTO, J. T. The meaning of an observed event as a determinant of its aggressive consequences. *Journal of Personality and Social Psychology*, 1973, *28*, 206-217.
BERKOWITZ, L., & GEEN, R. Film violence and the cue properties of available targets. *Journal of Personality and Social Psychology*, 1966, *3*, 525-530.
BERKOWITZ, L., & MACAULEY, J. The contagion of criminal violence. *Sociometry*, 1971, *34*, 238-260.
BUVINIC, M. L., & BERKOWITZ, L. Delayed effects of practiced versus unpracticed responses after observation of movie violence. *Journal of Experimental Social Psychology*, 1976, *12*, 283-293.
CLINE, V. B., CROFT, R. G., & COURRIER, S. Desensitization of children to television violence. *Journal of Personality and Social Psychology*, 1973, *27*, 360-365.
CLOWARD, R. A., & OHLIN, L. E. *Delinquency and opportunity.* New York: Free Press, 1960.
COLE, A. M., & TURNER, C. W. Effects on crime rates of changing birth orders during the post World War II baby boom. Paper presented at the Western Psychological Association meeting, Seattle, Wash., April, 1977.
CROSBY, F. A model of egoistical relative deprivation. *Psychological Review*, 1976, *83*, 85-113.
DAVIES, J. C. The J-curve of rising and declining satisfactions as a cause of some great revolutions and a contained rebellion. In H. D. Graham & T. R. Gurr (Eds.), *Violence in America.* New York: Signet Books, 1969.
DODD, D. K., COLE, A. M., & TURNER, C. W. Effects of post World War II baby boom on U. S. divorce rate. Paper presented at the American Psychological Association meeting, San Francisco, CA., August, 1977.
DOLLARD, J., DOOB, L., MILLER, N., MOWRER, O., & SEARS, R. *Frustration and aggression.* New Haven: Yale University Press, 1939.
EASTERLIN, R. A. *Population, labor force, and long swings in economic growth.* New York: Columbia University Press, 1968.
EASTERLIN, R. A. Relative economic status and the American fertility swing. In E. Sheldon (Ed.), *Family economic behavior.* Philadelphia: J. B. Lippincott Co., 1973.

66 *Violent Behavior: Social Learning Approaches*

EASTERLIN, R. A., WACHTER, M. L., and WACHTER, S. M. Demographic influences on economic stability: The United States experience. *Population and Development Review,* 1978, *4.*

EHRLICH, P. R., & EHRLICH, A. H. *Population, resources, environment: Issues in human ecology* (2nd ed.). San Francisco: W. H. Freeman & Co., 1972.

ELLIOT, G. *Twentieth century book of the dead.* New York: Scribner, 1972.

ELLIS, D. P., WEINIR, P., & MILLER, L. Does the trigger pull the finger? An experimental test of weapons as aggression eliciting stimuli. *Sociometry,* 1971, *34,* 453-465.

FERDINAND, T. Reported index crime increases between 1950 and 1965 due to urbanization and changes in the age structure of the population alone. In D. J. Mulvihill & M. M. Tumin (Eds.), *Crimes of violence.* Appendix 3, 1969, 145-152.

FREEDMAN, D. G. *Human infancy: An evolutionary perspective.* Hillsdale, N. J.: Lawrence Erlbaum Associates, 1974.

FRODI, A. M., LAMB, M. E., LEAVITT, L. A., & DONOVAN, W. L. Fathers' and mothers' responses to infant smiles and cries. *Infant Behavior and Development,* 1978, *1,* 187-198.

GEWIRTZ, J. L., & BOYD, E. F. Experiments in mother-infant interaction, mutual attachment, acquisition: The infant conditions his mother. In T. Alloway, L. Krames, & P. Pliner (Eds.), *Advances in the study of communication and affect,* Vol. 3. New York: Plenum Press, 1976.

GORANSON, R. E. Media violence and aggression behavior: A review of experimental research. In L. Berkowitz (Ed.), *Advances in experimental social psychology,* Vol. 5. New York: Academic Press, 1970.

HAUSER, P. M. On population and environmental policy and problems. In N. Hinricks (Ed.), *Population, environment and people.* New York: McGraw-Hill, 1971.

HEER, D. M. *Society and population* (2nd ed.). Englewood Cliffs, N. J.: Prentice-Hall, Inc., 1975.

HICKS, D. J. Short and long-term retention of affectively varied modeled behavior. *Psychonomic Science,* 1968, *11,* 369-370.

HOLMES, T. H., & RAHE, R. H. The Social Readjustment Rating Scale. *Journal of Psychosomatic Research,* 1967, *11,* 213-218.

JOHNSON, J. H., & SARASON, I. G. Life stress, depression, and anxiety: Internal-external control as a moderator. *Journal of Psychosomatic Research,* 1978, *22,* 205-208.

KENKEL, W. F. *The family in perspective* (4th ed.). Santa Monica, CA: Goodyear Publishing Co., 1977.

LEVENTHAL, H. Findings and theory in the study of fear communications. In L. Berkowitz (Ed.), *Advances in experimental social psychology,* Vol. 5. New York: Academic Press, 1970.

MASUDA, M., & HOLMES, T. H. Life events: Perceptions and frequencies. *Psychosomatic Medicine,* 1978, *40,* 236-261.

MERTON, R. K., & NISBET, R. (Eds.) *Contemporary social problems* (4th ed.). New York: Harcourt, Brace, & Jovanovich, 1976.

NEWTON, G. C., & ZIMRING, F. E. *Firearms and violence in American life.* Washington, D. C.: U. S. Government Printing Office, 1969.

PARKE, R. D., BERKOWITZ, L., LEYENS, J. P., WEST, S. P., & SEBASTIAN, R. Some effects of violent and nonviolent movies on the behavior of juvenile delinquents. In L. Berkowitz (Ed.), *Advances in experimental social psychology,* Vol. 10. New York: Academic Press, 1977.

PATTERSON, G. R., & COBB, J. A. Stimulus control for classes of noxious behaviors. In J. F. Knutson (Ed.), *The control of aggression.* Chicago: Aldine, 1973.

PATTERSON, G. R., REID, J. B., JONES, R. R., & CONGER, R. C. *Families with aggressive children.* Eugene, Ore.: Castalia Publishing Co., 1975.

PHELPHS, H. A., & ANDERSON, D. *Population in its human aspects.* New York: Appleton-Century-Crofts, 1958.

San Francisco Chronicle, various issues, 1979.
SCHUCK, J. R. Paths to violence: Toward a quantitative approach. In A. G. Neal (Ed.), *Violence in animal and human societies*. Chicago: Nelson Hall, 1976.
SCHULZ, D. A. *The changing family: Its function and future*. Englewood Cliffs, NJ: Prentice-Hall, 1976.
SEARS, D. W., & McCONAHAY, J. S. Racial socialization, comparison levels, and the Watts riot. *Journal of Social Issues*, 1970, *26*, 121-140.
SELIGMAN, M. E. P. *Helplessness: In depression, development, and death*. San Francisco: W. H. Freeman & Co., 1975.
SHUNTICH, R. J., & TAYLOR, S. P. The effects of alcohol on human physical aggression. *Journal of Experimental Research in Personality*, 1972, *6*, 34-38.
STARK, R., & McEVOY, J. III. Middle class violence. *Psychology Today*, 1970, *4*(6), 52-54, 110-112.
TAEUBER, I. B., & TAEUBER, C. *People of the United States*. Washington, D. C.: U. S. Government Printing Office, 1971.
TOCH, H. H. *Violent men: An enquiry into the psychology of violence*. Chicago: Aldine Publishing Co., 1969.
TURNER, C. W., & DODD, D. K. The development of anti-social behavior. In R. L. Ault (Ed.), *Selected readings in child development*. Santa Monica: Goodyear Publishing Co., 1979.
TURNER, C. W., & GOLDSMITH, D. Effects of toy guns and airplanes on children's anti-social free play behavior. *Journal of Experimental Child Psychology*, 1976, *21*, 303-315.
TURNER, C. W., SIMONS, L. S., BERKOWITZ, L., & FRODI, A. The stimulating and inhibiting effects of weapons on aggressive behavior. *Aggressive Behavior*, 1977, *3*, 355-378.
ULRICH, R., DULANEY, S., ARNETT, M., & MUELLER, K. An experimental analysis of non-human and human aggression. In J. K. Knutson (Ed.), *The control of aggression*. Chicago: Aldine Publishing Co., 1973.
Uniform Crime Reports, 1957-1977. Washington, D. C.: U. S. Government Printing Office.
U. S. Bureau of the Census. *Historical statistics of the United States, colonial times to 1970, bicentennial edition*. Washington, D. C.: U. S. Government Printing Office, 1975.
U. S. Bureau of the Census. *Statistical abstract of the United States*. Washington, D. C.: U. S. Government Printing Office, annual editions, 1881-1978.
WESTON, J. T. The pathology of child abuse. In R. E. Helfer & C. H. Kempe (Eds.), *The battered child*. Chicago: The University of Chicago Press, 1974.
WHELPTON, P. K. The future growth of the population of the United States. In G. H. L. J. Pitt-Rivers (Ed.), *Port Washington*, NY: Kennikat Press, 1932.
WILSON, M., & HIGGINS, P. B. Television's action arsenal: Weapon use in prime time. United States Conference of Mayors, Washington, D. C., 1977.
WOLFGANG, M. Crime: Homicide. In D. L. Sells (Ed.), *International encyclopedia of the social sciences*, Vol. 3. New York: Macmillan, 1968.
YORBURG, B. *The changing family*. New York: Columbia University Press, 1973.

3
Violence by Street Gangs: East Side Story?

JEROME S. STUMPHAUZER, ESTEBAN V. VELOZ,
and THOMAS W. AIKEN

Many people feel that we are experiencing a "new wave" of gang violence in the United States—that gangs were a severe problem in the 1950s, that they disappeared in the 1960s, and that they returned as a major social problem in the late 1970s. One certainly gets this impression from sensationalized television reporting and national news magazines. Actually, only one nationwide study of gang violence, reported by Walter B. Miller (1975, 1977), has been carried out. He investigated the extent of gangs in six major cities and did indeed find gang violence a severe problem. Various officials (court, police, probation) reported the following range in numbers of gang members in their respective cities: New York—8,000 to 40,000; Chicago—3,000 to 10,000; Los Angeles—12,000 to 15,000; Philadelphia—4,700 to 15,000; Detroit—500 to 1,250; and San Francisco—250. Contrary to popular belief, Miller found that violence by street gangs did not decrease in all of these cities in the 1960s, but, in fact, continued to grow during this period in Chicago, Los Angeles, and Philadelphia. Miller reasoned that this national misperception was due to the fact that the national news media is based in New York and Washington, areas which did experience a temporary lessening of the problem. To this we might add that Los Angeles, to a large extent, controls the entertainment industry, and the recent release of "gang movies" and related television programs may otherwise alter perception of the problem. One wonders where this leaves the rest of the populace who hear only about New York and Los Angeles yet live elsewhere. Miller found relatively high agreement in correspondents' definition of "gang" as follows:

> A gang is a group of recurrently associating individuals with iden-
> tifiable leadership and internal organization, identifying with or
> claiming control over territory in the community, and engaging
> either individually or collectively in violent or other forms of illegal
> behavior (Miller, 1975, p. 9).

Internationally, the problem is less clear. The senior author was told by participants at the March, 1979, Banff Conference that street gang and motorcycle gang violence did exist in major Canadian cities. Infor-mal information also suggests severe gang problems in Mexico, South and Central America, Hong Kong, Tokyo, and in some European cities.

Miller (1975, 1977) did find a recent increase in the severity of violence by gangs in the United States, and, therefore, some support for a "new wave" of lethal violence. Today's gang members are more violent and better armed than their predecessors; this is especially evident in their increased use of handguns, more sophisticated weaponry, and violence in schools. Nowhere is this more true than in Los Angeles, where several deaths a week are common. Los Angeles Sheriff Peter Pitchess has gone so far as to say that an urban boy in Los Angeles today is more likely to die by murder than an American soldier in World War II was to die in combat.

Police estimate that there are 200 street gangs in Los Angeles, and most of them are violent gangs in which territoriality, shootings, and extortion have become a way of life over the past 50 years, to the point where killings only reach the news if they are "unusual" (e.g., involve "outsiders"). These 200 gangs are formed chiefly by territory and, for the most part, are ethnically or racially divided into Hispanics, Blacks, Anglos, and Asians, with the majority of gangs from the first two groups. There is no question that street gang membership is also related to poverty and lower-class membership. Nearly 100 of these gangs are Chicano, reflecting the large Mexican-American population in Southern California.

Our work on the east side of Los Angeles over the past several years (in clinical psychology, community work, and education) brought us into daily contact with Chicano gangs and eventually led to our combined efforts described below. Our focus has been in East Los Angeles—a seven-square-mile, predominantly Chicano community. This area is divided, with firmly held lines, by 18 organized street gangs. East Los Angeles is patrolled by the Los Angeles County Sheriff's Department. Their statistics, reported in Table 1, reflect increasing gang violence over the years 1976, 1977, and 1978. "Gang incidents" (criminal incidents in police reports related to gangs) have steadily increased. Gang related homicides have remained fairly constant, but felonious assaults by gang members rose sharply in 1978 (Note 1).

Upon first examining the problem, it was obvious that traditional psychotherapeutic and law enforcement approaches had not been effective; indeed, there are indications that the gang problem is increasing. Ten years ago, Klein (1969, 1971) did a series of studies of juvenile gangs in Los Angeles, utilizing a detached-worker program. He concluded that such a program inadvertently increases gang cohesiveness and defeats its own purpose. Stumphauzer (1973, 1974, 1976, 1979) has reviewed the many contributions of behavior therapy to the treatment of delinquents, from token economies to group homes, outpatient treatment, and community programs. While the results are promising, the behavior therapy model did not quite fit the vast community problem we are observing around us, and it is necessary to expand the conventional behavioral theories to include other approaches with promising utility. For example, sociology and anthropology have offered *ethnography* as one such possibility. As illustrated by Wepner's (1977) volume, ethnography studies behavior in its naturally occurring settings. Simi-

TABLE 1

Police Recorded Gang Delinquency in East Los Angeles 1976-1978*

	1976	1977	1978
Number of gang incidents	737	1310	1468
Number of gang related homicides	22	20	24
Number of gang related felonious assaults	286	246	368

*Data collected by the Los Angeles County Sheriff's Department, East Los Angeles station.

larly, *ecological psychology* suggests a tie between a stream of behavior and its environmental conditions of geography, space, time, etc. (Barker, 1968; Wahler, House, & Stambaugh, 1976; Evans & Nelson, 1977).

While adapting these models and beginning to study gang delinquency directly in the community, an interesting phenomena came to our attention: the nondelinquent, nongang member in the same neighborhood. We thought it especially important to understand this instance of naturally occurring self-control directly where it was happening. Our goal was to understand how both gang delinquent and nondelinquent behaviors were being taught and learned throughout a community—the *behavioral ecology*—before global, preventative strategies could be implemented.

BEHAVIORAL ANALYSIS MODEL

In general, the behavioral approach has utilized its functional method of understanding people (behavioral analysis) and its methods of treatment (behavior therapy) to focus on one patient or client at a time, or, in some cases, on small groups of individuals inside institutions (e.g., token economies). We are suggesting the utilization and expansion of the behavioral analysis concept to understand broad community problems; then this information can be directly applied in prevention and community-change programs. We believe this is necessary if behaviorism is to make a meaningful contribution both in understanding and in preventing delinquency.

The behavioral analysis model for individual treatment is clearly outlined by Kanfer and Saslow (1965, 1969). A brief outline of the seven major points covered in their behavioral analysis for the individual patient follows:

1) *Initial analysis of the problem situation.* Problem behaviors are objectified and then classified into *behavioral excesses* (those behaviors that occur too much), *behavioral deficits* (those that do not occur enough), and *behavioral assets* (good or nonproblematic behaviors).
2) *Clarification of problem situation.* Who objects to the problem behaviors and who supports them? What are their stimuli? What are their consequences?
3) *Motivational analysis.* What are the major incentives and punishers for this person? Who currently has control over them?

4) *Developmental analysis.* What are the biological limitations of this person? When and how did they develop?
5) *Analysis of self-control.* Under exactly what circumstances does the person control problem behaviors? What situations or persons change this self-controlling behavior?
6) *Analysis of social relationships.* Who are the most significant and influential people? How do they exercise their influence on this person?
7) *Analysis of the social-cultural-physical environment.* What are the norms in the person's social milieu for the problem behaviors? Would there be support in this environment for changing or improving these problem behaviors?

Each of these concepts will be expanded through analyzing a particular high juvenile crime community, a particular youth gang, and nondelinquents in that same community. We have selected a particular gang in an East Los Angeles community, Geraghty Loma, as well as much-neglected nondelinquents, to develop a behavioral ecology approach preliminary to undertaking a more thorough project. We were told repeatedly that "this is no *West Side Story*"; we had to agree that the east side of Los Angeles has its own story.

A HIGH CRIME COMMUNITY: EAST SIDE STORY?

In formulating a behavioral understanding of how delinquent behavior is learned and maintained in a particular community, we first took a broad look at the *entire* community. We did this by examining the physical, sociocultural, and economic environment of these youths, and then began examining their behavior as viewed by various factions of their social environment, beginning with law enforcement personnel. (We are hopeful of meeting later with parents and teachers.) A more thorough analysis of this community is found elsewhere (Stumphauzer, Aiken, & Veloz, 1977).

Our first task was to define and describe the community (Kanfer, Note 2). This community has a psychological identity in that residents say that they are *from* Geraghty Loma. It also has a physical identity: The community is a series of hills three miles square bounded by fenced freeways to the north and east and by major streets on the south and west sides.

Geraghty Loma comprises two census tracts, and therefore we have a fund of demographic data on this community. The following information was gathered from the 1970 U.S. Census and from the Los

Angeles County Sheriff and Probation Departments. The community is a densely populated area with 15,310 residents, of which over 90% are of Mexican descent. The median family income of the community was $8,705 in 1970. The community, for the most part, has small, single-dwelling living units with many rear, add-on houses. It is a residential neighborhood with no major businesses. The community has three elementary schools, but there is no junior high or high school within the two census tracts for its 1,479 adolescents. There is a small clinic, one park, and several "mom and pop" grocery stores.

A behavioral analysis of the community was conducted through cooperation with the Los Angeles County Sheriff's Department patrols, with 10 veteran peace officers helping responding to a structured survey. Data were collected on behavioral excesses, including youths' use of firearms, felonious assault, robbery, burglary and car theft. Similar data were collected on such behavioral deficits among the youth as truancy, unemployment and poor community relationships, and such assets as strong family relationships, competitive skills, artistic abilities and the capacity for "smooth talking."

Problem behaviors were identified by parents who had lost control of the youths, and by community residents and law enforcement officials who were, respectively, harassed by juveniles and called upon to curb deviant acts. The law enforcement effort was hampered by youths who intimidated the local citizenry who refused to bear witness to their illegal acts. Many residents who have attempted to stand up to the gang have been threatened and beaten; some residents have been killed. As a consequence, community residents generally report incidents only when anonymity is guaranteed. Delinquent behavior is therefore reinforced, not only by the almost complete removal of any possibility of aversive consequences, but also by the enhancement of the intimidator's prestige.

Whereas community residents maintain the behavior by ignoring it, other groups maintain the behavior by attending to it. Peer groups reinforce inappropriate or "loco" behavior by praising or otherwise rewarding it. The media (television, newspapers, etc.) also reinforce gang activity by sensationalizing gang exploits and cliques in the news. It is also possible that some police officers may be encouraging gang violence and thereby increasing the excitement incurred in some aspects of policing gang activity. Many officers prefer busy nights over slow, quiet nights when there is "no action."

Most officers interviewed did not see themselves as having a "punishing" effect on gang delinquent behavior, but rather feel they simply "keep a lid on it." A review of the arrest records of several gang members in the census tracts revealed that, even though convicted many times, these individuals had not received any punishment whatsoever.

THE VIOLENT STREET GANG: LA VIDA LOCA

The Geraghty Loma street gang has been in existence for well over 50 years, dating back to the early 1920s. It began initially for both social and self-protective purposes and has grown steadily ever since. The current barrio gang member is easily identified by the gang uniform: khaki pants, camp or prison jacket, plaid Pendleton shirt, and head bandana or brim hat. Moreover, many of the gang members (*vatos*) are decorated with tattoos such as a tear drop beside the eye, an insignia representing a *barrio* gang, or a dramatic announcement of their predominate life-style such as "*Mi Vida Loca*" (My Crazy Life).

There are anywhere from 300 to 400 core gang members, according to residents, community agencies, and gang members themselves, with hundreds more "on reserve," retired, or otherwise diverted to other activities or life-styles. There is no one gang leader; rather, the gang is broken up into ranks in a pattern which seems to follow the military model. Ranks are divided roughly by age into groups—what Cartwright (1975) calls a vertical gang. In addition, approximately 150 to 200 girls identify with the gang.

A group of older (age 22 to 55) members are commonly referred to as the *veteranos* (gang veterans) who are, in a sense, retired soldiers holding administrative, decision-making positions. On interviewing various community factions, it was reported that the *veteranos* have been responsible for preventing gang warfare on many occasions. However, they have also been accused of actually providing the necessary weaponry and drugs to the gang members, thus stimulating, modeling, and maintaining gang activity.

For Geraghty gang members, problem behaviors occurring most frequently include shootings, drug or alcohol abuse, extortion, street fighting, and vandalism. The more *loco* (wild, crazy, or risky) the behavior, the greater the social reinforcement. In fact, the very presence of the police in the barrio may stimulate the gang members to take even greater risks.

School attendance is a behavioral deficit. There are no high schools located in Geraghty Loma; school attendance would involve going into a rival gang's territory. Nonemployment seems to be due to the lack of vocational training and job opportunities. Those without work will seek other means of obtaining money (robbery, burglary, and extortion).

Among many of the gang members, there is some degree of self-control, given certain stimuli. Many behaviors (gang beatings, shootings, extortion, etc.) will not occur if an older adult (particularly a woman) is present. There is some evidence that the "code" of never harming a mother, a young child, or an old man is breaking down, especially in the recent practice of opening fire on houses without knowing (or caring) who is inside.

Learning Gang Violence: A Model

The preliminary findings of the community and gang analyses are summarized in the Figure, in which the learning of gang violence is formulated in terms of antecedents (stimuli or setting events) which lead to gang violent behavior, and results or consequences which maintain the behavior. This model and our findings thus far suggest a variety of very strong reinforcers for gang violence. Many of these reinforcers give gang members the kind of attributes that make them especially effective models for teaching further gang violence to their younger peers, as

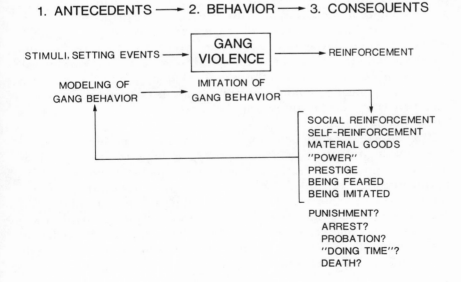

LEARNING GANG VIOLENCE

1. ANTECEDENTS ——► 2. BEHAVIOR ——► 3. CONSEQUENTS

STIMULI, SETTING EVENTS ——► GANG VIOLENCE ——► REINFORCEMENT

MODELING OF GANG BEHAVIOR   IMITATION OF GANG BEHAVIOR

SOCIAL REINFORCEMENT
SELF-REINFORCEMENT
MATERIAL GOODS
"POWER"
PRESTIGE
BEING FEARED
BEING IMITATED

PUNISHMENT?
ARREST?
PROBATION?
"DOING TIME"?
DEATH?

suggested by the considerable literature on modeling and imitation (Bandura, 1969). Thus, we suspect that a cycle (as indicated by the loop in Figure 1) is being maintained. Reinforced gang members model violence which is then imitated, reinforced, and so on.

What about the negative side? Little or no evidence was found to suggest that any effective aversive consequence or punishment is at work to suppress gang violence. Few arrests are made and very few convictions follow because of lack of evidence and intimidation of witnesses. In addition, arrest and/or imprisonment are often inadvertently reinforcing in that they give the youths higher status on their return to the community. Probation "camp jackets" are often worn with pride. Gang affiliations are maintained or even strengthened in the California camp and prison systems. Fear of death is often not a concern. In fact, gang members who die in "battle" are often revered by their "homeboys" with honor rolls painted on walls. In summary, there is strong preliminary evidence for the continued learning of gang violence and little reason to expect any decrease.

Behavioral Analysis of Youths Who Stay Out of Gangs

Our research thus far has shown that the comprehensive delinquency-learning program going on within the target census tracts offers such potent, pervasive reinforcers that there is a high probability that any given adolescent would become involved in a gang or delinquent lifestyle. However, there are some adolescents who, according to the delinquency research and literature of the last 50 years, should become delinquent, and yet, despite discouraging odds, go on to lead productive, even exemplary lives. How is this done? What are the factors involved in learning nongang, nondelinquent behavior in a neighborhood where such behaviors may be contrary to social norms and thus be aversively responded to as well?

By conducting several behavioral analyses of these nondelinquents in this same high gang-violence community, we hope to determine how they learn, utilize, and teach alternative, incompatible, noncriminal behavior. It is likewise hoped that it can be determined how these youths control their behavior with respect to avoiding potential trouble situations; that is, what kinds of trouble-avoidance strategies are used to stay out of trouble. Such analyses would have direct application: Determination of how these youths stay out of trouble might be applied directly in community-wide delinquency prevention.

While video and audiotape interviews were being conducted with members of a barrio clique within the high-crime census tracts being investigated, the authors became aware of two brothers (Caesar, aged 23, and Richard, aged 15) who live in this barrio and who, although they visit with this clique and are accepted by them, openly disavow any participation in delinquent behavior generally and in violent gang behavior specifically. Arrangements were made to conduct an in-depth behavior analysis interview with these brothers directly in their barrio. A structured, open-ended interview and observation following Kanfer and Saslow's (1965, 1969) behavior analysis model were audiotaped. To evaluate the motivational aspects of the interview, a reinforcement survey patterned after Cautela and Kastenbaum (1967) was utilized. A more in-depth analysis of these brothers is found in Aiken, Stumphauzer and Veloz (1977).

Definite asset behaviors reported and observed in Caesar include: 1) restoring old cars; 2) dressing plainly, or as he calls it, "nonviolently," with no outstanding gang insignia; 3) knowing as many *vatos* (bad dudes) from as many different cliques as possible; and 4) being a particularly articulate speaker. Asset behaviors listed by the younger brother, Richard, include: 1) fixing up bicycles for himself and for neighborhood kids; 2) dressing like his older brother (e.g., blue Levis, white T-shirt, and tennis shoes—no gang affiliation clothing); and 3) attending school regularly.

Behavior excesses are not necessarily a focal point of the study, as one would not theoretically expect them with nonproblematic adolescents. Caesar discusses what he considered his deficits, which are: not attending school (he quit after one year of college to help his family), not working regularly, and lack of marketable job skills. He also feels that he should be more deeply involved with helping his "homeboys." Richard sees his deficits in the area of schoolwork. According to Richard, "I want to be smart like my older brother, but I just don't know."

A discussion of the assets, deficits, and excesses reveals that restoring old cars was positively reinforcing for Caesar because of monetary gains received on resale, formal social praise received for his efforts (he has won trophies for his cars in custom auto shows), and informal social praise received from family, friends, and community residents who respect his abilities. In addition, he has gained self-reinforcement through pride in his accomplishments. Richard, on the other hand, shows a unique talent for being able to strip down, repair, and rebuild bicycles, with such ability being modeled after his older brother's work on cars. According to Richard, neighborhood kids value him highly because of his bicycle-repairing abilities. Major environmental aversive stimuli are discussed by Caesar: "I'm afraid that I might be in the wrong place at the wrong time and be mistaken for someone that I'm not and get shot, getting killed, or having someone hassle with my family." Richard discusses his fears of being harassed by the strong cliques at school—an occasional actuality rather than an imagined fear. Richard likewise expresses concern about police harassment and the possible victimization of his family. Caesar and Richard both attribute a good deal of their nondelinquent behavior to specific models in their environment. Caesar states that an older *veterano,* a former felon named Hood, was instrumental in helping him to formulate a code of conduct within which to live in the barrio. Richard emphasizes that when his father left, it was his older brother who provided the appropriate modeling experience.

The brothers agree that they can control their own behavior relative to avoiding trouble. Both state that they do not drink, smoke, or use any drugs, and further state that they have never been arrested (observed and corroborated by researchers and other raters). Caesar states that he could envision situations where he would lose control, however, particularly if his family were threatened. An interesting pattern of self-control emerges when it comes to defining trouble situations and how each of the brothers identifies and avoids them. Both brothers use past experience and observations of their present environment to evaluate the possibility of any danger. Problem situations that are seen as potentially dangerous and are therefore avoided are identified by the brothers as: a) strangers gathering on the street or groups of youths driving in a car; b) parties, weddings, or other social gatherings where liquor is served or marijuana or pills are used; c) clothing or speech that is associated with a specific barrio which might lead to challenges from another barrio; and d) activities that are likely to attract attention from the police (i.e., owning or driving a low-rider automobile). The mere presence of police was viewed as potentially dangerous.

Caesar and Richard use different strategies to avoid trouble; the decision on what to do or how to act after the problem situation has been defined and evaluated depends primarily on the situation. Richard generally uses more trouble-avoidance strategies—walking away from potentially dangerous situations. Caesar, however, generally relies on his ability to manipulate the environment if the source of the trouble is his peers, although he will use avoidance strategies when the potential source is the police.

Caesar and Richard make use of *inner dialogues* to define, evaluate, decide, and reinforce their own behavior in trouble-avoidance situations.

This phenomenon may well lend itself to study from a cognitive behavior modification perspective (see Mahoney, 1979; Meichenbaum, 1977). Caesar also states that he gets to know as many of the gang members from as many of the barrios as he possibly can, and is teaching his brother to do the same.

Caesar feels it is difficult to remain nondelinquent because of police harassment by deputies who "can't tell a vato from a straight dude, and that's what they're getting paid for."

Incentives for being nondelinquent seem to be rare in this barrio. Caesar and Richard express cogent complaints that there are job opportunities and programs for ex-offenders, and that gang activity is always publicized. Caesar graduated from high school and stayed out of trouble, yet there is no program for him or others like him. Richard further states that his easygoing manner and politeness are often taken as a sign of weakness by peers and as insincerity by some teachers. However, Caesar sheds some interesting light on how gang members will take it upon themselves to keep some kids from getting into trouble: "If you are a straight dude, often the gang members will try to keep you straight. They'll tell you to go home before trouble starts. They'll say, 'Hey man, don't screw up like us. You have a chance to make something of yourself, don't blow it and end up like us. Maybe you'll make it and come back and help us someday.'"

Both brothers concede that school is important because of work skills that can be learned, but stress that many "good" kids don't attend because they would have to cross into rival barrio cliques' territory and because they are often ashamed of their own learning (language) weaknesses. Good teachers are seen as being properly educated and having the appropriate credentials and mental attitudes to work in primarily Mexican-American schools. Caesar recalls that many of his teachers lacked both of the above qualifications, and many were indifferent to the particular needs of the Mexican-American student. Richard stresses that it is sometimes difficult to stay out of trouble at school because of the strong gang influence there. He states that he doesn't think school is offering him much because he is in high school now and still can't read, but he states that at least he is not getting into any trouble there.

It does appear that some individuals are learning to be nondelinquent and that many factors influence that development. However, this has simply been the study of two such young people. Aiken (Note 3) has just begun an extension of this line of research by systematically studying several nondelinquents in this same community. Specifically, nondelinquent youths who have delinquent brothers are being located through the Los Angeles County Probation Department. If their families fit the multiple causation, high-risk theory of delinquency (low socioeconomic status, severe social and family problems) and agree to participate, they are given vibra/tactile "beepers" and a pocket-sized record booklet. For one week they are beeped on a random schedule. When beeped they are to record specific information regarding location, activity, company, and reinforcement. It is hoped that this direct sampling of behavior can be expanded to gang members as well. Further planned studies of non-gang members include an investigation of naturally occurring self-control and utilization of these successful nondelinquents and their self-control strategies in a prevention program.

CONCLUSIONS AND A COMMUNITY ANTI-CRIME PROGRAM

A model for the behavioral analysis of gang delinquents, nondelinquents, and their community environment has been presented. Although preliminary in nature, results strongly suggest that the approach has utility for understanding a broad community problem, perhaps for intervention and, more importantly, prevention.

Gang violence and incompatible nondelinquency were both found to follow the principles of learning and were more easily understood within their social, ecological contexts. This community and the larger economics and politics of the area do much to support and encourage gang violence. It would seem that four kinds of interventions (or their combination) logically follow from our preliminary findings: 1) environmental stimuli (setting events including poverty, unemployment, etc.) need to be changed; 2) the multifaceted material and social reinforcements for violence need to be reduced; 3) effective punishments need to be consequated; and 4) behavior incompatible with gang violence (both in current gang members and in nondelinquents) needs to be further stimulated, modeled and reinforced. Easier said than done! To some extent, we found evidence that the fourth intervention was already naturally occurring in this community with an unknown number of "nonproblem" (even "model") youths, and this group is being studied further.

A community-based anti-crime program for the east side of Los Angeles was developed, based in part upon our findings, and was recently funded by the Law Enforcement Assistance Administration of the U.S. Department of Justice (Rodriquez, Veloz, & Stumphauzer, Note 4). Six neighborhood programs are now dealing with crime in their particular sections of the community and include such diverse activities as: escort services to senior citizens provided by gang members; a hotline and block organization program; a mothers' rumor control and violence blockade program; a gang youth and senior citizen community redevelopment program; a residential treatment program; two newsletters; and a youth communication training and theatrical group. While all of the four interventions listed above are included to some degree, two are especially utilized. First, several of the programs reduce the reinforcement for gang membership and violence by direct intervention (blockade, hotline, and removal of social reinforcement). Second, virtually all of the programs are encouraging and reinforcing behavior that is incompatible with gang violence. For example, it is quite a new behavior for a gang member to suddenly begin escorting senior citizens so that they do not get robbed, to help clean up high-crime properties, and to write and perform anti-crime plays. It is too early to tell what effects will be evident as far as longer-term individual changes in these youths or decreases in gang violence are concerned. There is considerable room for further refinement of research, but also for encouragement.

REFERENCE NOTES

1. Crime statistics for East Los Angeles, Los Angeles County Sheriff's Department, 1976, 1977, & 1978.
2. Kanfer. F. H. Personal communication, July 1, 1976.
3. Aiken, T. W. Behavior analysis of nondelinquent invulnerable adolescents from a high juvenile crime community by way of experimental sampling. Unpublished doctoral dissertation, University of Southern California, 1980.
4. Rodriguez, A., Veloz, E.V., & Stumphauzer, J.S. East Los Angeles anti-crime project. Proposal submitted to the Law Enforcement Assistance Administration (U. S. Department of Justice), 1978.

REFERENCES

AIKEN, T. W., STUMPHAUZER, J. S., & VELOZ, E. V. Behavioral analysis of nondelinquent brothers in a high juvenile crime community. *Behavioral Disorders*, 1977, *2*, 212-222.
BANDURA, A. *Principles of behavior modification.* New York: Holt, 1969.
BARKER, R. G. *Ecological psychology.* Stanford: Stanford University Press, 1968.
CARTWRIGHT, D. S. The nature of gangs. In D. S. Cartwright, B. Tomson, & H. Schwartz (Eds.), *Gang delinquency.* Monterey, CA: Brooks/Cole, 1975, 1-22.
CAUTELA, J. R., & KASTENBAUM, R. A. A reinforcement survey schedule for use in therapy, training, and research. *Psychological Reports*, 1967, *20*, 1115-1130.
EVANS, I. M., & NELSON, R. O. Assessment of child behavior problems. In A. R. Ciminero, K. S. Calhoun, & H. E. Adams (Eds.), *Handbook of behavioral assessment.* New York: Wiley, 1977, 603-681.

82 *Violent Behavior: Social Learning Approaches*

KANFER, F. H., & SASLOW, G. Behavioral diagnosis. *Archives of General Psychiatry*, 1965, *12*, 529-538.
KANFER, F. H., & SASLOW, G. Behavioral diagnosis. In C. M. Franks (Ed.), *Behavior therapy: Appraisal and status*. New York: McGraw-Hill, 1969, 417-444.
KLEIN, M. W. Gang cohesiveness, delinquency, and a street-work program. *Journal of Research in Crime and Delinquency*, 1969, *7*, 135-166.
KLEIN, M. W. *Street gangs and street workers*. New York: Prentice Hall, 1971.
MAHONEY, M. J. Cognitive issues in the treatment of delinquency. In J. S. Stumphauzer (Ed.), *Progress in behavior therapy with delinquents*. Springfield, IL: Charles C Thomas, 1979, 22-33.
MEICHENBAUM, D. H. *Cognitive behavior modification*. New York: Plenum, 1977.
MILLER, W. B. *Violence by youth gangs and youth groups as a crime in major american cities*. Washington, DC: U.S. Department of Justice, 1975.
MILLER, W. B. The rumble this time. *Psychology Today*, 1977, *10* (May), 52.
STUMPHAUZER, J. S. (Ed.), *Behavior therapy with delinquents*. Springfield, IL: Charles C. Thomas, 1973.
STUMPHAUZER, J. S. *Six techniques of modifying delinquent behavior*. Leona, NJ: Behavioral Sciences Tape Library, 1974.
STUMPHAUZER, J. S. Modifying delinquent behavior: Beginnings and current practices. *Adolescence*, 1976, *11*, 1-28.
STUMPHAUZER, J. S. (Ed.) *Progress in behavior therapy with delinquents*. Springfield, IL: Charles C. Thomas, 1979.
STUMPHAUZER, J. S., AIKEN, T. W., & VELOZ, E. V. East side story: Behavioral analysis of a high juvenile crime community. *Behavioral Disorders*, 1977, *2*, 76-84.
United States Census Bureau Report: Washington, D.C., 1970.
WAHLER, R. G., HOUSE, A. E., & STAMBAUGH, E. E. *Ecological assessment of child problem behavior*. New York: Pergamon, 1976.
WEPNER, R. S. (Ed.) *Street ethnography: Selected studies of crime and drug use in natural settings*. Beverly Hills: Sage, 1977.

4

A Social Interactional
Approach to the Treatment
of Abusive Families

JOHN B. REID, PAUL S. TAPLIN,
and RUDY LORBER

The conceptualization of child abuse presented in this paper focuses on certain aspects of the everyday interaction of parents and their children which might be significant determinants of child abusive acts. No attempt has been made to propose a comprehensive theory of child abuse. Instead, interactional variables will be described which are regarded as essential to an eventual understanding of the abusive process. The ideas to be presented apply primarily to families with children between the ages of three and 13 years.

The present social interactional conceptualization of child abuse is predicated on the assumption that many parents physically abuse their children as a futile last effort to achieve control, or at least some degree of balance, in parent-child relationships. It is further postulated that one major cause for such a breakdown in family equilibrium is a lack of skill

The present research was supported by funds from Grant # MH 25548, 31017, and 33067. The writers wish to thank G. R. Patterson for his careful critiques of earlier versions of this manuscript.

by the parents in teaching their children appropriate social behaviors and in handling discipline situations. The result is a parent who correctly perceives that he or she has lost control of the child and thus feels dominated by the child. A growing feeling of parental hostility toward the child is also likely to be present. At some point in such a relationship, the parent strikes out and the result is often an injured child.

The interactional approach to child abuse which is described here is bidirectional in that parents and children are both regarded as active participants in the abuse process. Two key aspects of parent-child interaction are hypothesized as leading to abuse: lack of parental skill in effectively handling day-to-day discipline confrontations, and high rates of aversive behaviors by both parents and children.

A number of studies have been reported which are relevant to the proposed relationship between poor parental disciplinary skill and child abuse. In one study, Young (1964) reported that 100% of severely abusive families and 91% of moderately abusive families were characterized by inconsistent and ineffective parental discipline. Discipline in these families was reported as having little corrective value and often seemed to be administered for its own sake. In another study, Elmer (1967) found that parents in abusive families used a wide variety of disciplinary measures in an inconsistent fashion.

A presumed correlate of poor parental disciplinary skill is the frequent occurrence of disruptive, out-of-control child behavior. Field studies supporting this relationship have shown erratic parental punishment in the backgrounds of delinquents (Glueck & Glueck, 1950; Jenkins, 1968; McCord, McCord, & Howard, 1961). Several laboratory studies have also explored the relationship between poor disciplinary skill and child behavior. Parke and Deur (1972) reported that inconsistent parental punishment was clearly less effective in controlling child behavior than punishment provided on a consistent schedule. Furthermore, Deur and Parke (1970) reported that inconsistently punished children showed the most persistence in responding in the face of a new schedule of continuous punishment, as well as showing the greatest resistance to extinction. An observational study by Patterson (1976) found that parents in families characterized by highly aggressive children employed less effective punishers than parents in nondistressed families. Lack of parental disciplinary skill was suggested by the finding that aggressive children were twice as likely as normal children to continue aggressive behavior following parental punishment.

Evidence that abusive families display highly aversive patterns of family interaction comes from several sources. A naturalistic observation study by Burgess and Conger (1978) revealed that parents in abusive families were relatively more aversive in daily interactions than were parents in nondistressed families. This finding characterized mothers more strongly than fathers. Although these investigators reported that children in abusive families were not different from children in nondistressed families, the data were not analyzed separately for children who were the actual victims of abuse. A survey study by Straus (1978) found that families in which violence between husband and wife occurred also had high rates of violence directed at children. The rate of severe violence directed at children was 129% greater in these families than in families in which no marital violence occurred. Gil (1971) found that 25% of a nationwide sample of child abuse cases involved children described as persistently annoying or overactive. Similarly, Gelles (1973) has pointed out that child abuse case studies frequently indicate that parents complain of numerous toileting mistakes, incessant crying, and persistent noncompliance in their children.

The importance of poor parental disciplinary skills and aversive patterns of family interaction in the etiology of child abuse is underscored in the classic survey research conducted by Gil (1969; 1970; 1971). Gil reported that 63% of child abuse incidents occurred in the context of parental disciplinary action, and that most cases of child abuse were part of a prevailing pattern of family interaction. It is quite possible to interpret these findings in the context of the studies of parental ineffectiveness and family aversiveness which have previously been discussed. If both of these factors are operative, it is likely that disciplinary situations will occur frequently in abusive families, and it is also likely that these situations will not be adequately resolved. As a result, it is hypothesized that there will be an increase in the likelihood of an escalation of normal disciplinary measures into physical child abuse.

If it is the case that many child abuse acts are the end product of poor parental disciplinary skills and/or a difficult, out-of-control child,* then three predictions follow. First, all members of abusive families would display more aversive behaviors toward one another in their daily lives than is the case for members of either nondistressed or distressed but not abusive families. Second, abusive parents would demonstrate severe problems in dealing with day-to-day discipline situations. Third, a treatment program designed to teach consistent and nonphysical child man-

---

*Note, for example, the studies reviewed by Friedrich and Boriskin (1976) which suggest that abused children tend to have more than their share of constitutional defects. Factors such as these may well predispose abused children to be difficult to raise.

agement skills should significantly reduce the daily aversive behavior of all members of abusive families. The data to be presented later in this paper provide preliminary evaluations of these hypotheses.

The formulation described here has focused on interactional variables as antecedents of abuse. However, social psychological variables are also likely contributors to the abuse process. Factors such as social isolation of the family (e.g., Elmer, 1967; Young, 1964), crises in the lives of potential abusers (Justice & Duncan, 1976), parental unemployment (Gil, 1970), and low infant birth weight (Friedrich & Boriskin, 1976) may increase the likelihood of child abuse. Any combination of these factors may also increase the probability of occurrence of the family processes outlined in this paper or increase the likelihood of the escalation of those processes into child abuse.

DESCRIPTION OF TREATMENT

For many years, our group at the Oregon Social Learning Center has been working with distressed families referred for help with child conduct problems. The treatment and data collection techniques used with these families have developed gradually over the course of 11 years of work. The primary location of the treatment and data collection is in the homes of these families rather than in the laboratory. The parents in the families are trained to use child management techniques with their children.

Treatment Tactics

The set of treatment techniques was developed in the course of several studies completed between 1966 and 1975 (e.g., Patterson, 1974a, b; Patterson & Brodsky, 1966; Patterson, McNeal, Hawkins, & Phelps, 1967; Patterson, Ray, & Shaw, 1968; Patterson & Reid, 1970; Reid, 1967). The approach which evolved from this work contains the following basic components.

a. All family members are systematically observed in the home during baseline, at several points during intervention, at termination, and periodically during 12 months of follow-up.
b. The parents are instructed in social learning theory and its applications to child management. Educational materials include social learning oriented programmed texts on child management (Patterson, 1971; Patterson & Gullion, 1968), films, and videotapes. Discussion

between parents and therapists and modeling of treatment techniques by the therapists are also part of the training program.

c. The parents are taught to pinpoint, observe, and record specific behaviors of their children. They are also instructed in the employment of appropriate consequences for child behavior, and in the use of time-out.

d. Both parents and children are involved in negotiation sessions which result in the creation of family programs designed to alter reinforcement and punishment contingencies within the family.

The description of treatment presented here is not intended to be complete—there are many subcomponents and procedures—but to give the reader a general idea of the steps. A complete description of the treatment program is available elsewhere (Patterson, Reid, Jones, & Conger, 1975).

OBSERVATION DATA COLLECTION PROCEDURES

The observation code used in this research was initially developed in 1967 (Reid, 1967), and has been revised several times. The code currently used is described by Reid (1978). The code was designed to give a sequential account of a subject's behaviors and the reactions of other family members to those behaviors in terms of 29 categories. During an observation session, each family member is the subject of two five-minute observations. During each five-minute observation, the behavior of the subject is recorded each six seconds using the 29 code categories. Each time the subject's behavior is coded, the reactions to that behavior which are given by other family members are also coded. Thus, it is possible to calculate the rate at which any of the 29 behaviors occurs for each family member, and its immediate positive or negative consequences.

In our research, we have been primarily interested in a composite of the categories which we call Total Aversive Behavior (TAB). The TAB score is made up of the sum of the following 14 categories which are seen by parents as highly aversive: Cry, Command Negative, Dependency, Destructiveness, Disapproval, High Rate, Humiliation, Ignore, Negativism, Noncompliance, Physical Negative, Tease, Whine, and Yell. TAB scores are calculated by adding together the rates per minute for all 14 aversive behaviors. Although several other research measures have been developed, only these observation data are relevant to the present report.

A good deal of research has been carried out to demonstrate that the coding system produces reliable and stable data. This research has been described extensively in other publications (e.g., Jones, Reid, & Patterson, 1975; Reid, 1978).

COMPARISON OF NONDISTRESSED, DISTRESSED, AND DISTRESSED-ABUSIVE FAMILIES

Over the last several years, the therapeutic and assessment techniques described in the previous section were employed in three treatment studies (Fleischman, 1976; Patterson, 1974a; Reid, Rivera, & Lorber, 1979). A total of 88 distressed families and 27 nondistressed control families participated in these three studies. Each of the 88 distressed families was referred to the project because of the conduct problems of one or more of their children. The 27 nondistressed families were recruited through the local newspaper and were selected for study on the basis of having no apparent child management problems (Patterson, 1974a). A *post hoc* search of the clinical records and referral information of the 88 distressed families revealed significant evidence of physical child abuse in 27 families.* Thus, the data to be reported in the present paper were collected in the homes of 27 nondistressed families (N), 61 distressed families (D), and 27 distressed-abusive families (DA) with both child conduct problems *and* evidence of child abuse. Demographic data for the three groups are presented in Table 1. All families participated in six to 10 baselines observation sessions, which utilized the observational coding system previously described. All the families in the D and DA groups received at least four weeks of the intervention described previously, and then participated in two posttreatment observation sessions.

Baseline Data

Total Aversive Behavior (TAB). The TAB score, which was described previously, is a summation of rates per minute for 14 categories of aversive behavior. Table 2 presents the baseline rates of TAB scores for parents and their referred children in each of the three groups.

As can be seen in Table 2, the mean rates of TAB scores are higher

---

*Significant evidence of child abuse consisted of the following kinds of information: a) previous court action because of child abuse; b) secondary referral problem was child abuse; c) parental self-report of abuse; d) abuse witnessed by observers.

TABLE 1
Demographic Data

	Nondistressed (N=27)	Distressed (N=61)	Distressed-Abusive (N=27)
Age of referred child:			
Mean	8.7 years	9.2 years	7.9 years
Range	5-14 years	3-14 years	3-12 years
Sex of referred child:			
Male	100%	91%	86%
Female	0%	9%	14%
Birth order of referred child:			
Mean	3	3.4	2.8
Range	2-5	1-7	1-8
Proportion of intact families	67%	75%	63%
*Socioeconomic level:**			
Mean	3.9	4.4	5.2
Range	1-7	1-7	2-7

*Based upon the system developed by Hollingshead and Redlich (1958), in which Class 1 denotes higher executive or professional employment, Class 4 denotes clerical work, and Class 7 denotes unskilled labor.

TABLE 2
Mean Rates per Minute during Baseline
of Total Aversive Behavior

	Nondistressed (N)	Distressed (D)	Distressed-Abusive (DA)	F	df	p
Mothers						
$\bar{x}$	.26	.30	.61	11.34	2, 111	.001
N	27	60	27			
SD	.18	.24	.48			
Fathers						
$\bar{x}$	.21	.24	.35	1.41	2, 77	n.s.
N	18	45	17			
SD	.22	.24	.35			
Referred children						
$\bar{x}$	.28	.52	.83	4.94	2, 112	.01
N	27	61	27			
SD	.36	.59	.67			

TABLE 3

Baseline TAB Rates (Directional) for Family Members in Distressed-Abusive,
Distressed-Nonabusive, and Nondistressed Comparison Families

| | Distressed-Abusive | | Distressed-Nonabusive | | Nondistressed | | Comparisons | | |
| | | | | | | | DA/D[1] | DA/N[2] | D/N[3] |
	Mean	SD	Mean	SD	Mean	SD	p	p	p
TC→M**	.0391	(.0302)	.0501	(.0624)	.0104	(.0112)	n.s.	.001	.001
M→TC**	.0577	(.0903)	.0385	(.0421)	.0098	(.0097)	n.s.	.03	.001
TC→F*	.0264	(.0247)	.0255	(.0407)	.0084	(.0190)	n.s.	.05	.05
F→TC*	.0272	(.0263)	.0206	(.0206)	.0087	(.0096)	n.s.	.03	.02
M→F*	.0628	(.2245)	.0034	(.0037)	.0018	(.0023)	.05	.05	.09
F→M*	.0700	(.2556)	.0039	(.0056)	.0021	(.0027)	.05	.05	n.s.

TC: Target Child   [1]DA/D: Distressed-Abusive vs. Distressed-Nonabusive
M: Mother   [2]DA/N: Distressed-Abusive vs. Nondistressed
F: Father   [3]D/N : Distressed-Nonabusive vs. Nondistressed

*Main effect for groups significant at $p < .05$
**Main effect for groups significant at $p < .01$

for all members of abusive families in comparison to their counterparts in either nondistressed or distressed but nonabusive families. Analyses of variance (ANOVAs) revealed significant differences between groups for mothers and referred children, but not for fathers. Subsequent comparison of the D and DA groups was significant for mothers ($t = 3.10$; $df = 85$; $p < .001$, one tailed), but not for referred children ($t = 1.22$; $df = 60$; $p < .15$, one tailed). It is reasonable to conclude that the abusive families in this sample are characterized by an overall high level of aversive behavior, significantly higher, in fact, than that demonstrated by distressed families in which there is no evidence of child abuse. Further, the highest mean level of aversive behavior was exhibited by the abused children themselves.

The data presented in Table 2 were computed without regard to the directionality of the aggressive acts. For example, the TAB rates for the children represent not only their aggressive acts toward the parents, but toward siblings as well; this is also true of the TAB rates of the mothers and the fathers. It is also the case that the TAB rates presented in Table 2 do not discriminate between aggressive acts initiated by the subject and aggressive acts which are in retaliation to the aggression of another family member. In order to get specific information about the rates at which aggressive acts were initiated among the mothers, fathers, and target children in the three groups, the rates at which aggressive acts were initiated within specific dyads were tabulated. Table 3 shows the results of that analysis. As can be seen from Table 3, both the children in the distressed-abusive and the distressed but nonabusive groups direct more aggression toward their parents than do children in the nondistressed group. Similarly, mothers and fathers in the distressed-abusive and distressed nonabusive groups direct more aggression toward the target children than do their counterparts in the nondistressed group.*

Perhaps the most surprising and potentially interesting data in Table 3 are those which describe the rates at which mothers and fathers direct aggressive acts toward each other. The mothers and fathers in the distressed-nonabusive sample show a statistically unreliable tendency to direct more aggression at each other than do their counterparts in the

---

*Looking specifically at the data for the target children and their mothers in the distressed-abusive and the distressed-nonabusive groups, there is some suggestion that, in abusive families, mothers initiate aggression to their children more than do children to their mothers, while the reverse is true in the distressed-nonabusive families. This apparent interaction, however, is not statistically reliable but suggests the possibility that abusive mothers are relatively more aggressive in their transactions with their children than are mothers in distressed but not abusive families.

nondistressed families. Mothers and fathers in the distressed-abusive group, however, are significantly more aggressive toward each other than are the parents in either the distressed-nonabusive or the nondistressed group. Inspection of the means shows that parents in the distressed-abusive group demonstrated between 15 and 30 times as much aggression toward each other as did their counterparts in the other two groups. Although this finding was not predicted, or even anticipated, it is interesting to speculate on its significance. Taken as a whole, the data in Table 3 suggest that high rates of conflict between parents and children are sufficient to produce a "distressing" family situation which may motivate the parents to seek treatment. However, it may also be the case that high rates of parent-child conflict alone are not sufficient to produce child abuse in most families. High rates of parent-child conflict combined with high rates of parent-parent conflict may add up to a family situation which is at high risk for child abuse. Tactically, these data suggest that social learning treatment programs designed to reduce parent-child conflict, and hence to reduce the probability of further abuse, may be of limited value unless coupled with a complementary intervention program designed to teach parents how to handle conflicts between themselves.

The composite TAB score utilized in the analyses discussed previously includes extremely mild forms of aversive behavior (e.g., ignore, tease, and negativism), as well as more severe forms of aversive behavior (e.g., physical attacks and threats). Therefore, individual analyses were performed on two behavior categories which appeared to be particularly aversive and intuitively likely to lead to child abuse. These two behaviors are Physical Negative (PN) (i.e., hitting, kicking, etc.) and Commands which contained a negative threat component (CN). The rates per minute for PN and CN were compared for the three groups of families. The low base rates for each of these individual behaviors prohibited analysis of directionality within dyads.

Physical Negative behavior (PN).* Mean rates per minute of negative physical contact observed in the homes of the three groups of families are presented in Table 4. It is evident that the parents and referred children in the abusive families show consistently higher rates of PN than do their counterparts in nondistressed and in distressed but non-

---

*PN is defined in the observational coding system as an attack or an attempted attack on another person. The attack must be of sufficient intensity to potentially inflict pain (e.g., biting, kicking, slapping, hitting, spanking, and taking an object roughly from another person).

abusive families. Again, the *F* ratios revealed that these differences were
significant for mothers and referred children, but not for fathers. However, the incidence of observed physical aggression was not high in the
sample (i.e., there were zero entries for over half the subjects). Therefore, the distributions of scores were highly skewed, making the interpretation of the ANOVAs described in Table 4 somewhat ambiguous.

For this reason, chi-square analyses were carried out to determine
whether the number of family members in each group who demonstrated at least one instance of physical aggression in the presence of our
observers differed as a function of type of family. These analyses indicated that more mothers in the child abuse group demonstrated physical
aggression then did mothers in either the nondistressed group (X^2 =
7.50; *1*; $p < .01$) or the distressed-nonabusive group (X^2 = 14.10; *1*; p
$< .001$). In the case of fathers, the pattern was similar but not statistically
reliable. More fathers in the child abuse group demonstrated physical
aggression than fathers in the distressed-nonabusive group (X^2 = 2.09;
1; $p < .10$). There was no significant difference between fathers in the
distressed-abusive and nondistressed groups. More children in the abuse
group showed physical aggression than children in the nondistressed

TABLE 4

Mean Rates per Minute during Baseline of Negative
Physical Behavior (PN)

	Nondistressed (N)	Distressed (D)	Distressed-Abusive (DA)	F	df	p
Mothers						
x̄	.007	.006	.030	12.82	2, 111	.001
N	27	60	27			
SD	.01	.01	.04			
%*	26	22	63			
Fathers						
x̄	.005	.003	.010	1.80	2, 77	n.s.
N	18	45	17			
SD	.02	.01	.02			
%*	11	11	29			
Referred children						
x̄	.009	.030	.040	3.14	2, 112	.05
N	27	61	27			
SD	.022	.06	.05			
%*	30	44	59			

*Percent of group making at least one negative physical contact in the presence of the observer.

group (X^2 = 4.86; *1*; $p < .05$). Although more children in the distressed-abusive group showed physical aggression than children in the distressed group, the difference was not statistically reliable (X^2 = 1.91; *1*; $p < .15$).

In summary, both the mean level and the proportion of the family members showing physical aggression were higher in the abuse group than in either of the other groups. The finding was most dramatic for mothers (i.e., the percentage of mothers in the abusive group who actually hit their children in the presence of the observers was over twice that of the other two groups). It is not only the parents who show high levels of actual aggression in these abusive families, but also the abused children themselves.

Command Negative (CN). Mean rates per minute of threatening commands observed in the three groups of families are presented in Table 5. As can be seen in Table 5, mothers, fathers, and referred children in abusive families had higher mean rates of threats than did their counterparts in the other two groups. The overall ANOVAs were significant for mothers and children, but not for fathers. As was the case with negative physical behavior, the majority of the subjects was not observed using threats, making the interpretation of the ANOVAs somewhat ambiguous.

As can be seen from Table 5, a higher proportion of mothers, fathers, and children in abusive families made at least one more threat than did their counterparts in the other two groups. Chi-square analyses revealed the following differences: More mothers in abusive families used threats than did mothers in nondistressed families (X^2 = 2.84; $p < .10$) or mothers in distressed-nonabusive families (X^2 = 5.08; $p < .05$); fathers in abusive families were not significantly different from fathers in the other two groups (X^2s = < 1); and more children in the abusive group used threats than children in nondistressed families (X^2 = 8.34; $p < .01$) or children in distressed-nonabusive families (X^2 = 2.89; $p < .10$).

Both of the above analyses provide further support for the hypothesis that the children as well as the parents in abusive families used more aversive behavior than did their counterparts in nondistressed and distressed-nonabusive families.

Consequences Provided by Parents. Because much of the previous work on child abuse reviewed in the introduction to this paper suggests that abusive parents have uncommonly severe problems in handling discipline, some exploratory analyses were conducted on the present data which compared the reactions of the three groups of parents to aversive child behaviors and compared these parents' ability to successfully ter-

TABLE 5
Mean Rates per Minute during Baseline of
Command Negative (CN)

	Nondistressed (N)	Distressed (D)	Distressed-Abusive (DA)	F	df	p
Mothers						
x̄	.020	.03	.100	6.27	2, 111	.01
N	27	60	27			
SD	.04	.09	.15			
%*	44	50	74			
Fathers						
x̄	.020	.020	.030	.52	2, 77	n.s.
N	18	45	17			
SD	.04	.04	.04			
%*	39	36	41			
Referred children						
x̄	.002	.010	.030	11.20	2, 112	.01
N	27	61	27			
SD	.005	.02	.03			
%*	14	34	51			

*Percent of group making at least one threat in the presence of the observer.

minate aversive child behaviors. In the first analysis, the in-home observational data were tabulated to ascertain the probability that a parental response to an aversive child behavior would be either positive or negative. Since, in this analysis, negative reactions are simply the reciprocal of positive reactions, only the conditional probabilities for positive reactions to aversive child behaviors are given in Table 6. As can be seen from Table 6, the mothers and fathers in the three groups do not differ to any significant extent. It is of some interest to note that even the parents in nondistressed families provide positive consequences for approximately two out of three aversive child behaviors. It should be noted, however, that many of the aversive child behavior categories are only mildly noxious and hence do not readily address parents' typical response to significant child problem behaviors or to discipline confrontations.

A more relevant question concerns those sequences in which the child displays an aversive behavior and the parent responds to the child in an aversive manner. That is, to what extent is the parent able to successfully stop a child's aversive behavior with an aversive reaction? To examine this issue, all parent/child interactions were tabulated in which the child displayed an aversive behavior followed by an immediate aversive re-

TABLE 6
The Probability that, Given a Parent Reacts Immediately
to an Aversive Behavior of the Child, the Parental
Reaction Will Be Positive

	Distressed-Abusive	Distressed	Nondistressed
Mothers*	.663	.646	.716
Fathers*	.700	.726	.705

*Neither main effect nor comparisons were statistically significant.

action by the parent. These sequences were then examined to ascertain the probability that the child would subsequently and immediately continue displaying the aversive behavior. Thus, the following conditional probability was calculated for each parent/child dyad: the probability of a child aversive response at T_3 given a child aversive response at T_1 and a parent aversive response at T_2, where T_1, T_2, T_3 are consecutive intervals. The higher the conditional probability, the more likely is the child to continue behaving in an aversive manner despite a disapproval or reprimand by the parent.

The mean conditional probabilities for the parent/child dyads in each of the three groups are presented in Table 7. Both mothers and fathers in the nondistressed families failed in terminating only about 14% of child aversive behavior sequences with one negative reaction. The parents in the distressed-nonabusive families were less effective (i.e., a failure rate of about 35%). The fathers in the distressed-abusive families were not reliably different from their counterparts in the other two groups in terms of their success in terminating child aversive behaviors. The mothers in distressed-abusive families, however, were least effective of all groups in stopping aversive child behavior by reacting negatively to it (i.e., a failure rate of 53%). Their rate of failure is almost four times that of mothers in the nondistressed group when it comes to successfully intervening in child aversive behavior sequences.

It is also interesting to note that within the nondistressed and distressed-nonabusive families, the mothers and fathers have nearly identical success rates. In the distressed-abusive families, however, mothers show twice the failure rate of the fathers. Although these data partially support the hypothesis that abusive parents, particularly mothers, have extreme difficulties in handling discipline confrontations, it is impossible from these data to pinpoint the exact reason. It could be that the aversive behavior displayed by the children in abusive families is harder to control than that displayed by children in the other two groups. This interpretation is partially supported by the data presented earlier, which showed that children in abusive families displayed the highest levels of the most aversive behaviors (Physical Negative and Command Negative). However, those highly aversive child behaviors happened only infrequently in the present study.

Another possibility, and one which merits further study, is that even though mothers in the abusive families punish at about the same rate as mothers in the other two samples, their punishment is less skillful. This latter interpretation fits more closely with our clinical impressions to date and with the observations of previous investigators, such as Elmer (1967) and Young (1964). If it is the case that mothers in abusive families display skill deficits in handling discipline confrontations, then social learning approaches to the treatment of abusive families which focus on parent training may prove highly effective.

Preliminary Treatment Data

In the previous section, data were presented to support the contention that many child abusive acts occur as part of an overall pattern of aversive behavior in family relationships. If a family with preadolescent children learns to handle its conflicts in a physical manner, escalations in conflicts

TABLE 7

The Probability that a Child Will Immediately Continue Aversive Behavior at Interval Three, Given that S/he Initiated an Aversive Behavior at Interval One and the Mother or Father Reacted Aversively at Interval Two (Consecutive Six-Second Intervals)

	Distressed-Abusive		Distressed-Nonabusive		Nondistressed		Comparisons DA/D[1] DA/N[2] D/N[3]		
	Mean	SD	Mean	SD	Mean	SD	p	p	p
Mothers**	.530	(.369)	.351	(.264)	.143	(.222)	.05	.001	.01
Fathers*	.264	(.312)	.338	(.345)	.132	(.300)	n.s.	n.s.	.05

[1]DA/D: Distressed-Abusive vs. Distressed-Nonabusive
[2]DA/N: Distressed-Abusive vs. Nondistressed
[3]D/N : Distressed-Nonabusive vs. Nondistressed

*Main effect for groups not significant
**Main effect for groups significant at $p < .01$

may well be accompanied by injury to the weaker family members (i.e., the children). If this formulation has some validity, then one would expect that a treatment program designed to teach parents effective and nonphysical child management skills would reduce the aggressive conduct of all family members. As was previously stated, both groups of distressed families were treated after the initial evaluation. The treatment program took the general form outlined previously. Relevant to the present paper are preliminary outcome data for the abusive families.

Posttreatment observation data were collected in 24 of the 27 distressed-abusive families. At present, we have completed only an analysis of the pre-post TAB rates for the target members of these families.

Separate analyses of changes in TAB scores from baseline to termination were performed for mothers, fathers, and referred children in 24 abusive families. These analyses are summarized in Table 8. Results indicated significant reductions in TAB rates for mothers and referred children, but not for fathers. These analyses of changes in TAB scores strongly suggest that the overall level of hostility in these families decreased as a function of parent skill training. The finding that fathers showed no reliable change on this measure should be interpreted in light of the fact that they did not differ significantly from fathers in the other two groups before treatment.

FINAL COMMENTS

The data reported in this paper must be regarded in a tentative manner for several reasons. First, the division of treated families into distressed and distressed-abusive was made after the fact. It is possible that some families in the distressed group were, in fact, abusive. Second, the distressed-abusive group is not necessarily a representative sample of

TABLE 8
Rate per Minute of Total Aversive Behavior:
Baseline to Treatment Termination

	Baseline	Termination	t	p
Mothers ($N = 24$)	.64	.42	2.01	.05 (one-tailed)
Fathers ($N = 15$)	.38	.34	<1	n.s.
Referred children ($N = 24$)	.93	.69	2.10	.05 (one-tailed)

the population of abusive families. All families who received treatment
were referred because of child conduct problems. It is possible that a
significant number of abusive families do not demonstrate such chronic
child conduct problems. Home observational data from a representative
sample of abusive families (referred primarily for child abuse) must be
carried out to put the present data in perspective. However, it should
be noted that a majority of the abusive families studied by Young (1964)
and by Elmer (1967) demonstrated such problems, and the study by Gil
(1969) indicated that almost two-thirds of child abuse episodes occurred
in the context of discipline confrontations. Finally, it should be noted
that the interaction patterns examined in this paper were observed after
the child abuse incidents had occurred. It seems likely that these problems prevailed prior to the occurrence of the abusive act, an aspect of
these families not addressed in the present research.

The results of the present study strongly suggest that the child is not
a passive participant in the abuse process. Rather, the abused children
observed in this study were, because of constitutional defect, temperament, or ineffective parenting, extremely difficult to handle. The mothers and children in the abusive families were significantly higher on most
measures of aversive behavior than were their counterparts in the distressed and control families (as were the fathers, but not significantly
so). This suggests that these families are characterized by an overall
tendency to handle problems in a coercive, physically aggressive manner.
In such families, escalation in parent/child conflicts seems likely to lead
to an increased probability that the child will be injured. To turn such
a family around, it is argued that all members must be taught nonphysical
alternatives to conflict resolution. Therapeutic endeavors aimed solely
at the intrapersonal dynamics of abusive parents are inadequate because
they do not address the children's aversive behaviors or the parent's lack
of child-management skills, both of which contribute to the escalation
process which can lead to injury. The dynamics of the abusive parents
must be considered, but the development of nonphysical child management skills is viewed by the present writers as absolutely critical. It is
obviously the case that the type of intervention strategy outlined here
must be integrated with procedures to deal with a wide range of problems, such as social isolation, economic deprivation, and alcoholism,
which are frequently associated with child abuse.

The treatment data presented in this paper *suggest* that intensive training in parenting skills can be highly effective in reducing the level of
parent/child conflict in abusive homes. Two further steps are necessary
to properly evaluate the utility of such a parent-training approach to

this problem. First, the therapeutic strategy must be expanded in such a way that aggressive behaviors by parents are pinpointed for specific intervention. Second, the assessment methodology for the evaluation of treatment outcome must be expanded to include repeated and long-term medical examinations of the children, record searches for reabuse following treatment, and attitudinal, self-concept, and intellectual measures. The data presented here suggest that such an endeavor may be worthwhile.

REFERENCES

ANDERSON, E. C., & BURGESS, R. L. *Interaction patterns between same- and opposite-gender parents and children in abusive and nonabusive families.* Paper presented at the meeting of the Association for the Advancement of Behavior Therapy, 1977.

BARNHART, J. The acquisition of cue properties by social and nonsocial events. *Child Development*, 1968, *39*, 1237-1245.

BURGESS, R. L. Child abuse: A behavioral analysis. In B. B. Lahey & A. E. Kazdin (Eds.), *Advances in child clinical psychology.* New York: Plenum Publishing Corp, 1979, in press.

BURGESS, R. L., & CONGER, R. D. Family interaction in abusive, neglectful, and normal families. *Child Development*, 1978, *49*, 1163-1173.

BURGESS, R. L., & CONGER, R. D. *Family interaction in abusive, neglectful, and normal families.* Paper presented at the meeting of the Society for Research in Child Development, 1977. (a)

BURGESS, R. L., & CONGER, R. D. Family interaction patterns related to child abuse and neglect: Some preliminary findings. *Child Abuse and Neglect: The International Journal*, 1977, *1*, 269-277. (b)

CAIRNS, R. B. Meaning and attention as determinants of social reinforcer effectiveness. *Child Development*, 1970, *41*, 1067-1082.

DEUR, J. L., & PARKE, R. D. The effects of inconsistent punishment on aggression in children. *Developmental Psychology*, 1970, *2*, 403-411.

ELMER, E. *Children in jeopardy: A study of abused minors and their families.* Pittsburgh: University of Pittsburgh Press, 1967.

FLEISCHMAN, M. J. *Controlled metamorphosis: Taking social learning from the laboratory to the field.* Paper presented at the meeting of the American Psychological Association, Washington, D.C., September 1976.

FRIEDRICH, W. M., & BORISKIN, J. A. The role of the child in abuse: A review of the literature. *American Journal of Orthopsychiatry*, 1976, *46*, 580-590.

GELLES, R. J. Child abuse as psychopathology: A sociological critique and reformulation. *American Journal of Orthopsychiatry*, 1973, *43*, 611-621.

GIL, D. G. Violence against children. *Journal of Marriage and the Family*, 1971, *33*, 637-648.

GIL, D. G. *Violence against children: Physical child abuse in the United States.* Cambridge, Massachusetts: Harvard University Press, 1970.

GIL, D. G. Physical abuse of children: Findings and implications of a nationwide survey. *Pediatrics*, 1969, *44*, 857-864.

GLUECK, S., & GLUECK, E. *Unraveling juvenile delinquency.* Cambridge, Massachusetts: Harvard University Press, 1950.

HOLLINGSHEAD, A. B., & REDLICH, F. C. *Social class and mental illness.* New York: Wiley, 1958.

JENKINS, R. L. The varieties of children's behavioral problems and family dynamics. *American Journal of Psychiatry*, 1968, *124*, 1440-1445.

JONES, R. R., REID, J. B., & PATTERSON, G. R. Naturalistic observations in clinical assessment. In P. McReynolds (Ed.), *Advances in psychological assessment.* Vol. 3. San Francisco: Jossey-Bass, 1975.

JUSTICE, B., & DUNCAN, D. F. Life crisis as a precursor to child abuse. *Public Health Reports*, 1976, *91*, 110-115.

McCORD, W., McCORD, J., & HOWARD, A. Familial correlates of aggression in nondelinquent male children. *Journal of Abnormal and Social Psychology*, 1961, *62*, 79-93.

PARIS, S. G., & CAIRNS, J. B. An experimental and ethological analysis of social reinforcement with retarded children. *Child Development*, 1972, *43*, 717-729.

PARKE, R. D., & DEUR, J. L. Schedule of punishment and inhibition of aggression in children. *Developmental Psychology*, 1972, *7*, 266-269.

PATTERSON, G. R. The aggressive child: Victim and architect of a coercive system. In L. A. Hamerlynck, E. J. Mash, & L. C. Handy (Eds.), *Behavior modification and families. I. Theory and research. II. Applications and Developments.* New York: Brunner/Mazel, 1976.

PATTERSON, G. R. Intervention for boys with conduct problems: Multiple settings, treatments, and criteria. *Journal of Consulting and Clinical Psychology*, 1974, *42*, 471-481. (a)

PATTERSON, G. R. Retraining of aggressive boys by their parents: Review of recent literature and follow-up evaluation. In F. Lowy (Ed.), Symposium on the Seriously Disturbed Pre-school Child, *Canadian Psychiatric Association Journal*, 1974, *19*, 142-161.(b)

PATTERSON, G. R. *Families: Applications of social learning to family life.* Champaign, Illinois: Research Press, 1971.

PATTERSON, G. R., & BRODSKY, G. A behaviour modification programme for a child with multiple problem behaviours. *Journal of Child Psychology and Psychiatry*, 1966, *7*, 277-295.

PATTERSON, G. R., & GULLION, M. E. *Living with children: New methods for parents and teachers.* Champaign, Illinois: Research Press, 1968.

PATTERSON, G. R., McNEAL, S. A., HAWKINS, N., & PHELPS, R. Reprogramming the social environment. *Journal of Child Psychology and Psychiatry*, 1967, *8*, 181-195.

PATTERSON, G. R., RAY, R. S., & SHAW, D. A. Direct intervention in families of deviant children. *Oregon Research Institute Research Bulletin*, 1968, *8* (9).

PATTERSON, G. R., & REID, J. B. Reciprocity and coercion: Two facets of social systems. In C. Neuringer & J. L. Michael (Eds.), *Behavior modification in clinical psychology.* New York: Appleton-Century-Crofts, 1970. pp. 133-177.

PATTERSON, G. R., REID, J. B., JONES, R. R., & CONGER, R. E. *A social learning approach to family intervention. I. Families with aggressive children.* Eugene, Oregon: Castalia Publishing Company, 1975.

REID, J. B. Reciprocity in family interaction. Unpublished doctoral dissertation, University of Oregon, 1967.

REID, J. B. (Ed.) *A social learning approach to family intervention. II. Observation in home settings.* Eugene, Oregon: Castalia Publishing Company, 1978.

REID, J. B., RIVERA, G. H., & LORBER, R. A social learning approach to the treatment of stealers: An outcome study. Unpublished manuscript, Oregon Social Learning Center, 1979.

STRAUS, M. A. *Family patterns and child abuse in a nationally representative American sample.* Paper presented at the Second International Congress on Child Abuse, London, England, 1978.

YOUNG, L. *A study of child neglect and abuse.* Princeton, New Jersey: McGraw-Hill, 1964.

5

A Feminist Perspective
on Domestic Violence

LENORE E. WALKER

The analysis of violent behavior between family members who live together and love each other has been a fertile ground for researchers and mental health professionals for the past 10 years. Child abuse was the first area to receive scrutiny, and then, more recently, battered women. Still waiting to be let out of the closet are incest, marital rape, parent abuse, and granny-bashing. Nonstranger homicide has been studied (MacDonald, 1971; Wolfgang, 1958), and now newer ways of analyzing spousal murders in the broader context of spouse abuse are beginning to be utilized (Schneider & Jordan, 1978; Walker, 1979). Clearly, the image of the family as a tranquil oasis where one can retreat in order to soothe the bruises from the outside world is simply not true.

Sociologists (Straus, Gelles, & Steinmetz, 1980) who conducted the first national epidemiological survey of domestic assault concluded that physical violence occurs at home between family members more often than it occurs between any other individuals or in any other setting except for wars and riots. The statistics available on incidence are meager and replete with the inaccuracies and underreporting expected when trying to obtain data on a shameful secret behavior. Estimates vary from 28% of all American couples (13 million) engaging in physical assaults in one year (Straus et al., 1980) to 50% of all women seriously psycho-

102

logically or physically abused at some point in their lives (Walker, 1979). In one year over two million children in the United States used a gun or knife on a sister or brother; almost two million adults used lethal weapons in attacking their spouses; and over one million young children were assaulted by the same weapons (Straus et al., 1980). This violence occurred in families across all demographic characteristics: all ages, races, ethnic groups, and socioeconomic and educational levels.

Police estimate that between 25 and 85% of all murders occur between people who are not strangers to one another. In Kansas City, analysis of the homicide patterns indicated that, in 85% of the murders, police had been called to the homes from one to five times previously. The rape research also indicates a higher percentage of violent acts committed between people who know each other than between strangers (Chappell, Geis, & Geis, 1977). Despite the television and movie version of violence as street shoot-outs between men, the data indicate these scenes are rarely repeated in real life. It is much more likely that the most unsafe place to be is in your own home. This is especially true if you are a woman.

The purpose of this paper is to review the current research and discuss the theories which have been used to gain understanding of domestic violence within the past five years. Several current major research projects will also be discussed to demonstrate new models, and all will be critiqued from a feminist point of view.

Family analysts typically look at the various forms of domestic violence as discrete events rather than as an interrelated system dysfunction. The medical model that has permeated the child abuse field has been broadened to link sociological variables such as unemployment or unusual stress with intrapsychic problems of the abuser (Helfer & Kempe, 1974), but still utilizes a pathology model to understand and treat the offenders. Gelles (1974) has placed child abuse on one extreme of a continuum that places normal child discipline on the other. This emphasis is on a sociological model of analysis with norms changing for various cultures. While it is true that the data have not yet demonstrated a direct link between wife abuse and child abuse, I propose that this is due to inadequate methodology and a failure to look beyond the discrete form of domestic violence initially found, rather than to the lack of relationship. Even where there is no overt physical trauma, watching their father beat up their mother is a most insidious form of abuse that children often experience. I shall concentrate on descriptors relating to battered women in this paper, as it is the area in which I have greatest expertise. However, I believe much of what is said applies to all forms of domestic violence.

For a feminist, the issue of domestic violence takes on a special perspective. "A feminist is a person who advocates political, social and economic equality between men and women" (Gardner, 1979). By definition, a feminist psychologist and researcher would be especially sensitive to locating such inequality, should it occur within a specific area such as family violence, and could best measure sexism's impact on the problem. While it is true that on the surface all the forms of domestic assault have a commonality in the violent acts that are committed, a feminist perspective also notes that there is commonality in the sexism expressed. Thus, while the general area of violence in the culture needs to be studied in order to shed more light on domestic violence, violence against women should be a special area of interest.

THEORIES OF CAUSATION

Numerous theories about the causes of spouse abuse have been proposed. Some have looked toward historical roots (Flick, 1978); patriarchal (Dobash & Dobash, 1978) and religious (Davidson, 1978) ideology; facilitative cultural values (Martin, 1976; Pizzey, 1974) and institutional sanctions (Fields, 1978; Kremen, 1976; Roy, 1978); sociological factors (Gelles, 1974; Steinmetz, 1978; Straus, 1978); masochism and other intrapsychic personality characteristics (Gayford, 1975; Snell, Rosenwald, & Robey, 1964; Starr, 1978); learned helplessness (Walker, 1978b); intermittent reinforcement in a cycle of violence (Walker, 1978a, 1979); and cognitive distortion through causal attribution (Frieze, 1977).

These theoretical orientations have developed out of different approaches, often reflecting the biases and training of their proponents. Data have come from epidemiological studies, individual clinical interviews, organizational analyses, reviews of historical literature, and treatment programs. Analysis has been both deductive and inductive, often using nonrandom empirical data to provide checks and balances. Despite the limitations of the studies undertaken so far, they represent a welcome creativity in a field that formerly has yielded little understanding that could be translated into applied programs to eliminate such violence from family life. The sexist biases apparent in many of our established theoretical orientations have been documented (Groth, 1978); therefore, all models for understanding violence need a feminist scrutiny—a major purpose of this analysis.

It seems reasonable that a multideterminist theoretical orientation probably makes common sense, given the overlap of so many theories. Indeed, most current writers propose an interactionist model. For the purposes of discussion, I shall group the theories into several distinct models: feminist-political, sociocultural, and psychological. It is understood that no combinations and interactions should be excluded by this arbitrary classification. Because of my own theoretical biases, I shall briefly review the first two categories and then describe the psychological theories in greater depth.

Feminist-political

The theoretical orientation most clearly associated with a feminist-political stance is that all violence is a reflection of unequal power relationships, and the most unequal of all occurs between men and women; thus sexism is at the root of all violence. Some writers hold this stance to the exclusion of others (Dobash & Dobash, 1978; Pleck, Pleck, Grossman, & Bart, 1978). It appears that such a militant position is taken because of political considerations, including the need to be taken seriously as feminists, and the fear that confused data may be used against needed social reform programs.

Most feminists stress the historical legal precedents of male supremacy. Prior to patriarchal religion, women and men are thought to have lived in equality. As men assumed the role of protector of their women and accepted responsibility for or paternity of their children, they were given the right of discipline and chastisement over their property. Until recently, laws gave a man the right to beat his wife, provided he used a stick no wider than his thumb. When those statutes were eliminated from our legal code, an informal system of benign neglect and different standards for prosecution were the substitution.

Leidig (1978) has described numerous acts of violence committed by men against women. In addition to the battering of women, these include rape, girl-child incest, pornography, prostitution, and sexual harassment. Leidig asserts that all men benefit from violence against women, even if they do not engage in it themselves. Some of these benefits have been documented by Brownmiller (1975) and include subservience, passivity, decreased mobility, and less independence. Many studying wife abuse have presented detailed evidence of how a sexist society actually facilitates the beating of women (Chapman & Gates, 1978; Dobash & Dobash, 1978; Fields, 1978; Martin, 1976): Police, courts, hospitals, and social services all refuse to provide women adequate protection. Psychologists, too, have learned how to keep the family together at all costs—even if the individual's mental health or life is at stake. As a result, within the last four years a grassroots woman-dominated movement has developed one of the most successful nationwide alternative care systems, providing safety, shelter, and treatment for battered women, literally on shoestring finances (CAABW, 1979).

My own feminist analysis of wife-battering is that sexism is an underlying cause of all violence against women. An unequal power relationship between men and women is the underbelly of all violence. Men fight with other men to prove they are not sissies; women show passive faces to the world while struggling to keep their lives together without letting men know how strong they really are for fear of hurting their men's masculine image. And men beat up women in order to keep themselves on top of this whole messy heap. Little girls and boys learn these sex-role expectations through early socialization. This sex-role stereotyping conditions little girls to believe they have no voluntary control over their lives, which can then result in the psychological condition of learned helplessness. The current research at the Battered Women Research Center is looking at whether such a conditioning process occurs and, if so, if it is part of the battered woman's early socialization, as I hypothesize, or merely part of her relationship with a specific batterer (Walker, 1977). In either case or both, it may be one explanation of why she remains in such a violent home.

It has been difficult for feminists to link all forms of domestic violence together because of the commonly held belief that child abuse deserves more attention, since women are adults and more likely to protect themselves. While it is important to understand that this is not true, that women are often at the mercy of men who are physically stronger, and that women, therefore, become victims, it is also important not to infantilize women by trying to protect them as we would children. The learned helplessness explanation could be misinterpreted and used to justify inadequate treatment alternatives, as have other psychological analyses. Nevertheless, while understanding the difficulties in trying to apply a feminist critique to psychological insights, and knowing it may only be a stop-gap measure, I take that risk in the hopes of preserving those psychological tenets which can help save some women now and also combat violence against women. From a feminist point of view, however, no matter how useful psychology might become, violence in the family will not be stopped until profound changes, eliminating sexism, are made in our social structures and in our child-rearing patterns.

Sociocultural

Sociologists have long sought to understand domestic and other criminal violence. The typical research pattern, used, for example, by Wolfgang (1958), uses police reports as a first step and then goes on to collect
demographics for both perpetrators and victims. Sometimes a matched
sample of people who have not been involved with the police is used for
comparison. MacDonald (1971) and Amir (1971) used this methodology
in rape research, resulting in serious questions about conclusions based
on such data (Hursh, 1977). Gelles (1974) used it in his pioneering study
of spouse abuse, and even the Dobashes (1978) used it to analyze British
wife-beating cases. The problem with such methodology is that the sample is a biased group, since only a fraction of such cases get police
attention. In my original sample only 10% of the battered women ever
reported it to the police (Walker, 1979). It is also highly probable that
the select group who do get police or other agency attention have special
characteristics that do not make them representative. Thus, generali-
zations based on such data can be misleading and inaccurate. Dobash
and Dobash went on to develop an interview technique to gain information from women housed in battered women refuges. Although they
broadened their sample, they missed a different group of women who
were battered but not in shelter. Gelles participated with Straus and
Steinmetz in an epidemiological survey where they asked 2,000 families
in the United States questions about child and spouse abuse. He began
to suspect his original data were insufficient when he learned that 38%
of the control group had violent episodes which were previously unreported. Thus, their study was designed to gather information about
incidence levels. Given the study's design, they probably have under-
estimated it, even with a reported violence rate at almost one-third of
the population.

The Straus, Gelles, and Steinmetz sociological analysis was the first to
break away from the traditional theories of masochism as a way to understand battered women. Early on, Straus (1978) began writing about
the kind of sociocultural conditions that facilitate domestic violence. He
saw sex-role stereotyping and sexism, as well as cultural acceptance of
all violence in the name of discipline, as underlying factors. Because of
the deeply imbedded nature of domestic violence in our society, Straus
calls for a program of primary prevention as an important step in elimination of the problem. Gelles (1974) does the same for both wife abuse
and child abuse, yet he barely links the two. He demonstrates how the

cultural standard of discipline permits different cultures to tolerate various degrees of violence against children, and, like Straus, calls for prevention strategies to insure that we do not raise a new generation committed to violence as a way to resolve problems. Steinmetz (1978) has moved from wife abuse issues to a legitimate concern with sibling violence and children's violence against their parents. She has begun to draw parallels between all forms of abuse within the family context, and cites learning theory principles to explain why so many different forms of abuse occur in the same family. The opportunity for modeling is clear, and the message passed on is that "people who love you have the right to hurt you in the name of discipline."

Steinmetz (1978) has also caused a furor in the feminist political community around her speculation that the number of men who are battered by their wives is as high as the reverse. Unfortunately, this is an unfounded argument based on small differences stemming from an unrepresentative sample. The sociocultural theories place great skepticism in the concept that battering of husbands occurs as frequently and in the same situations as battering of women and children. It is essential to accept the sociocultural premise, however, that living together in a family legitimizes the use of violent behavior that would not be tolerated in any other setting.

Elsewhere, I have critiqued Straus and his colleagues' work (Walker, 1978d). I have also disagreed with their definitions of abuse. Straus limits battering behaviors to discrete units of physical abuse. This faciliates data collection, as it is relatively easy to count broken ribs and black eyes, but this definition is too narrow to permit real understanding of the problem. It is important to include extreme psychological abuse in the definition, despite the measurement problems. In my research with battered women, they insist psychological abuse is at least as powerful as physical force in perpetuating the reign of terror under which they live. The definitions of what to study make a difference in the outcome of the research, particularly in the areas of social policy.

Sociologists have looked at several other theories besides the cultural legitimization of violence in the family. The whole body of literature which analyzes the uses and abuses of power has had interesting applications to the understanding of the power dynamics between violent spouses (Rounsaville, 1978; Stahly, 1978). Arguments have been put forth, documented by limited empirical data, which state that men who beat their wives have fewer resources than do their women, and so ruling by physical strength allows them to equalize the power balance. The limited fund of resources attributed to men include poorer verbal skills, less education, lower salaries, greater stress in the outside world, more sexual dysfunctions, and fewer friends than their wives. Needless to say, the presence of such deficits does not justify use of coercive behavior. Furthermore, such a theory is really pejorative to men, implying that they do not have adequate behavioral controls when adverse social conditions occur. The movement to examine male sex roles will hopefully lead to an understanding of how men are socialized into violent behavior patterns.

Psychological Theories

The earliest studies on domestic violence were concerned with the strength of the bonding between the men and women involved. After observing that women repeatedly returned to abusive husbands, only to receive more violence, psychologists concluded that there must be a flaw in those women's personality development. I believe it was because of the intense sexuality often seen in these couples and the continued presence of the feeling of love (in addition to other feelings such as fear, anger, hatred, and pain) that these women were labeled as masochists. When the woman victim was blamed in some way, usually by detailing incidents where she provoked the man—victim precipitation theory—the man who beat her was not held responsible for his behavior. Men also were excused by being declared mentally ill, usually psychopathic (Gayford, 1975), although recent clinical observations indicate that those batterers who did come to a mental health center for psychotherapy were more likely to be diagnosed as schizoid personality, paranoid, or depressed with suicidal features (Walker, 1979). Their responsibility is further compromised by attempts to blame excessive alcohol abuse, too much stress, or a Saturday night brawl—which implies he should be forgiven because the rest of the time he behaves appropriately.

The mental illness explanation of domestic violence is still popular today, despite greater public understanding of the complexity of the problem. If we could find the cause of this disease, then a cure, it is thought, would quickly follow. Most clinicians working in this field no longer hold out such hope, understanding instead that, when one-third of the population exhibits a behavior, the underlying causes are psychosociological and epidemiological rather than individual in nature. Although researchers are now looking to identify personality characteristics and other clinical indications of battered women (Hilberman & Munson, 1978; Rounsaville, 1978; Starr, 1978; Walker, 1979) and of the batterers (Boyd, 1978; Ganley & Harris, 1978; Klingbeil, 1978; Walker, 1978c) in efforts to provide some treatment alternatives, it is generally recognized that symptoms are usually the result of living in violence and not its cause. In my research, I found the several characteristics for the battered women and their men (Walker, 1979). (See Table I.)

Perhaps the most promising theories of causation are those psychological theories which are based on social learning theory tenets. My research (Walker, 1978b) has sought to find links between Seligman's (1975) concepts of learned helplessness and battered women, while Irene Frieze (1977) has focused on attribution theory. Recent discussion in various articles in a special issue of the *Journal of Abnormal Psychology* (1978, 87:1), devoted to "Learned Helplessness as a Model of Depression," attempts to clarify the two theories so that they no longer are viewed as mutually exclusive.

The learned helplessness model is based on learning that voluntary responses do not produce expected outcomes, resulting in deficits in three areas: motivational, cognitive and emotional. The motivational deficit is seen in the limiting of further initiation of such voluntary

TABLE 1

Characteristics of Battered Women and Their Batterers

Battered Women	*Batterers*
1. Low self-esteem	1. Low self-esteem
2. Believes all myths about battering relationships	2. Believes all myths about battering relationships.
3. Is a traditionalist in the home, strongly believing in family unity and the prescribed feminine sex-role stereotype.	3. Is a traditionalist in his home, believeing in male supremacy and the stereotypical masculine sex role in the family.
4. Accepts responsibility for the batterer's actions.	4. Blames others for his actions.
5. Suffers from guilt yet denies the terror and anger she feels.	5. Is pathologically jealous and intrusive into his woman's life.
6. Presents a passive face to the world but has strength to manipulate her environment so she does not get killed.	6. Presents a dual personality—a Dr. Jekyll and Mr. Hyde.
7. Has severe stress reactions with psychophysiological complaints.	7. Has severe stress reactions, during which he uses drinking and wife-beating to cope.
8. Uses sex as a way to establish intimacy.	8. Uses sex as an act of aggression frequently to overcome impotency or bisexuality.
9. Treated as "Daddy's Little Girl" as a child.	9. Suffered from child abuse or neglect as a child.
10. Believes no one will be able to help her resolve her predicament except herself.	10. Does not believe his violent behavior should have negative consequences.

responses. The essential cognitive deficit is the expectation of uncontrollable outcomes. This is the area where causal attribution becomes evident and both generality and chronicity of helplessness deficits can be affected (Weiner, Frieze, Kukla, Reed, Rest, & Rosenbaum, 1971). The cognitive deficit then makes it more difficult to later learn that responses do produce that outcome, and depression results (Abramson, Seligman, & Teasdale, 1978). The reformulations of these theories have taken into consideration questions of how locus of control is assigned by those who succumb to helplessness or depressed affect. Issues such as probability of aversive outcome or nondesireable outcome, rather than simple noncontingency of response outcome, seems to have taken on more importance, as have formulations about the process of falling into helplessness, low self-esteem and depression.

These new formulations have particular relevance for battered women specifically and domestic violence in general. If women learn that they cannot control aversive outcomes, such as being beaten, yet also learn that they need a man to take care of them, helplessness and paralysis can result. It has been suggested that effects of early sex-role socialization patterns produce noncontingent responses for women and subsequent helplessness and depression (Radloff, 1975). Those women who accidently meet up with a batterer—and, with my estimate that 50% of all women will meet up with such a man, it can only be thought of as a chance meeting—may have the process of helplessness set off by the nature of the aversive outcome of love and violence together. The helplessness theory explains the paralysis, the lowered rate of escape responses, the cognitive deficits and attributions, the lowered self-esteem, and the emotional changes in battered women. It also can be applied to physically and sexually abused children.

Maintenance of the relationship despite the violence needs explanation beyond the learned-helplessness and attribution theory responses. The bonding that occurs in families where domestic violence occurs is unique and powerfully strong. Learning theory would suggest variable intermittent reinforcement as a factor. I (1978a, 1979) found that a cycle of violence provided the discovery of the reinforcement—kind, loving behavior during the third phase of the cycle. The first phase is one where tension builds and minor battering incidents occur. The woman accepts his abuse directed at her in the hopes of averting another acute battering incident—the explosive second phase of the cycle. Actually, she has minimal control of the outcome, as the helplessness theory would predict, and eventually he lashes out at her in a blind rage. Following this acute battering incident, the batterer becomes sorry and frightened that his behavior might cause him to lose her. He becomes kind and loving, often contrite, and tries to make it up to her by showering her with gifts and love. Sometimes he may threaten to commit suicide or his mental health status may be viewed as precarious, both likely outcomes if the woman does not quickly forgive and forget. This phase may last for a while, but soon minor incidents begin to occur, tension builds, and the cycle starts over.

BATTERED WOMEN RESEARCH CENTER*

The theories discussed in this paper have had little systematic testing against empirical data. Such scrutiny began in July 1978 at the Battered Women Research Center with a grant from NIMH** to interview 400 battered women over a two-year period. While an important part of the grant calls for data collection just to provide information about battered women, other hypotheses more carefully measure learned helplessness and the cycle theory of domestic violence. The women who volunteer comprise a self-referred group of physically and psychologically battered women. An attempt was made to stratify the sample across demographic categories. Subjects spent six to eight hours with a trained interviewer responding to a questionnaire that collects details on historical information about the family of origin, and about a nonbattering and a battering relationship. Information about the nonviolent relationship is one form of comparison with a violent part of their lives. Subjects also complete several psychological tests to compare their responses with the standardized group. Depression is measured by the Radloff CES-D (Radloff, 1975). A general mental health index is measured by the Denver Community Mental Health Scale (Ciarlo & Reihman, 1977). Locus of control and causal attribution are measured by Levenson's Locus of Control Scale (Levenson, 1972). Traditional and feminist ideology is measured by the Spence-Helmreich Attitudes Towards Women Scale (Spence & Helmreich, 1972).

We are in the third year of this project. All data have been collected and results will soon be forthcoming. As an all-woman, feminist staff, learning to work together has been both exciting and difficult, as might be imagined when there are so many assertive and competent women

*Located at Colorado Women's College, Denver.
**NIMH Grant #R01 M #30.

researchers, interviewers, and administrative staffers. Good community relations assured a steady flow of battered women subjects from a stratified sample pool. Cancellations, crises, and ghastly horror stories plagued the interview staff. We dealt with death and mutilation, fear, minimal legal protection, and limited resources for these women. My initial hypothesis that other forms of domestic violence occur in the same home where a woman is being beaten seems to be accurate, based on the data. I am now more impressed by the strength necessary for a battered woman to escape her violent home than by the factors that keep her there.

The following conclusions can be drawn from this review:

1) The causation of violence in the home is complex and multidetermined by an interaction of many of the factors discussed. Society condones violence in general and violence against women specifically. This state of affairs has a long history and thus permeates all institutions and laws.

2) Elimination of family violence from society will probably need to take a three-pronged approach similar to the public health model for combating an epidemiological disease.

   a) Long-term preventive approaches are essential to create permanent change. This includes reassessing child-raising practices and eliminating sexism and violence from our lives. Public education is important here.

   b) Secondary level intervention is needed right now to prevent early cases from becoming worse. A free atmosphere to encourage reporting and dealing with these problems is important. Short-term approaches are most effective here.

   c) A tertiary level of care needs to be supported to help heal the victims we know about now. Shelters and safehouses are the cornerstones of effective treatment here, with psychotherapy an added benefit. Also, if the mothers are strengthened, they will have the energy to learn and to practice effective parenting skills themselves.

3) Researchers must be encouraged to study in the area of domestic violence. Basic research into areas of causation, including physiological and biochemical body changes, for example, is important. Evaluation of service programs is another form of research needed. Applications of helplessness and attribution theories can be usefully added to the treatment programs.

Until all women and children are no longer oppressed by the fear of potential violence, equality is only a dream.

REFERENCES

ABRAMSON, L., SELIGMAN, M., & TEASDALE, J. Learned helplessness in humans: Critique and reformulation. *Journal of Abnormal Psychology*, 1978, *87:* 1, 49-74.

AMIR, M. *Patterns of forcible rape.* Chicago: University of Chicago Press, 1971.

BROWNMILLER, S. *Against our will: Men, women and rape.* New York: Simon and Schuster, 1975.

BOYD, V. D. *Domestic violence: Treatment alternatives for the male batterer.* Presented at the annual meeting of the American Psychological Association, Toronto, 1978.

CHAPMAN, J., & GATES, M. (Eds.) *The victimization of women. Sage yearbooks in women policy studies. Volume 3.* Beverly Hills: Sage Publications, 1978.

CHAPPELL, D., GEIS, R., & GEIS, G. (Eds.) *Forcible rape: The crime, the victim and the offender.* New York: Columbia University Press, 1977.

CIARLO, J. A. & REIHMAN, J. The Denver community mental health questionnaire: Development of a multidimensional program evaluation instrument. In R. D. Coursey, et al. (Eds.), *Program evaluation for mental health methods, strategies, and participants.* New York: Grune & Stratton, Inc., 1977.

Colorado Association for Aid to Battered Women (CAABW) *Services to battered women in the U.S.* Monograph funded under grant from HEW. In press.

DAVIDSON, T. *Conjugal crime.* New York: Hawthorn Books, Inc., 1978.

DOBASH, R. E., DOBASH, R. P., CAVANAGH, C., & WILSON, M. Wife beating: The victims speak. *Victimology: An International Journal,* 1978, *2:* 3-4, 426-442.

DOBASH, R. E., & DOBASH, R. P. Wives: The "appropriate" victims of marital violence. *Victimology: An International Journal,* 1978, *2:* 3-4, 608-622.

FLICK, D. *Historical precedents for current attitudes regarding violence against women.* Presented at the annual meeting of the American Psychological Association, Toronto, 1978.

FIELDS, M. *Wifebeating: Government intervention policies and practices in battered women issues of public policy.* A consultation sponsored by the U.S. Commission on Civil Rights, Washington, D.C., 1978.

FRIEZE, I. H. *Social-psychological theory and problems of wifebeating.* Unpublished paper, University of Pittsburgh, 1977.

GANLEY, A. & HARRIS, L. *Domestic violence: Issues in designing and implementing programs for male batterers.* Presented at the annual meeting of the American Psychological Association, Toronto, 1978.

GARDNER, J. What is a feminist? A.P.A. Division 35 Newsletter: *Psychology of Women,* 1979, *6:* 1, 8.

GAYFORD, J. Wife battering: A preliminary review of 100 Cases. *British Medical Journal,* 1975, *1,* 94-197.

GELLES, R. *The violent home.* Beverly Hills: Sage Publications, 1974.

GROTH, G. *Sexism in psychology: Theorizing about violence against women.* Presented at the annual meeting of the American Psychological Association, Toronto, 1978.

HELFER, E. R. & KEMPE, C. H. *The battered child.* 2nd Edition. Chicago: The University of Chicago Press, 1974.

HILBERMAN, E. & MUNSON, L. Sixty battered women, *Victimology: An International Journal,* 1978, *2:* 3-4, 460-471.

HURSCH, C. J. *The trouble with rape.* Chicago: Nelson Hall, 1977.

KLINGBEIL, L. *A treatment program for male batterers.* Presented at the annual meeting of the American Psychological Association, Toronto, 1978.

KREMEN, E. *The discovery of battered wives: Consideration for the development of a social service network*. Paper presented at the annual meeting of the American Sociological Association, New York, 1976.

LEIDIG, M. *Psychology and violence against women: An overview.* Presented at the annual meeting of the American Psychological Association, Toronto, 1978.

LEVENSON, H. Distinction within the concept of internal-external control: Development of a new scale. *Proceedings of the 80th Annual Convention of the American Psychological Association,* 1972, *2,* 259-260.

MACDONALD, J. *Rape: Offenders and their victims.* Springfield, Illinois: Charles C Thomas, 1971.

MARTIN, D. *Battered wives.* San Francisco: Glide Publications, 1976.

PLECK, E., PLECK, J., GROSSMAN, M., & BART, P. The battered data syndrome: A comment on Steinmetz' article. *Victimology: An International Journal,* 1978, *2:* 3-4, 680-683.

PIZZEY, E. *Scream quietly or the neighbors will hear.* London: Penguin Books, 1974.

RADLOFF, L. Sex differences in depression: The effects of occupation and marital status. *Sex Roles,* 1975, *1:* 3, 249-265.

ROUNSAVILLE, B. J., Theories in marital violence: Evidence from a study of battered women. *Victimology: An International Journal,* 1978, *3:* 1-2, 11-31.

ROY, M. *Battered women: A psychosociological study.* New York: Van Nostrand and Co., 1978.

SCHNEIDER, E. M., & JORDAN, S. B. *Representation of women who defend themselves in response to physical or sexual assault.* New York: Center for Constitutional Rights, 1978.

SELIGMAN, M. *Helplessness: On depression, development and death.* San Francisco: Freeman, 1975.

SNELL, J., ROSENWALD, R. & ROBEY, A. The wife beater's wife: A study of family interaction. *Archives of General Psychiatry,* 1964, *11:* 2, 107-112.

SPENCE, J. & HELMREICH, R. Attitudes towards women scale. Journal Supplemental Abstracts *Catolog of Selected Documents in Psychology,* 1972, *2,* 66.

STAHLY, G. B. A review of select literature of spouse abuse. *Victimology: An International Journal,* 1978, *2:* 3-4, 591-607.

STARR, B. Comparing battered and non-battered women. *Victimology: An International Journal,* 1978, *3:* 1-2, 32-44.

STEINMETZ, S. The battered husband syndrome. *Victimology: An International Journal,* 1978, *2:* 3-4, 499-509.

STRAUS, M. Sexual inequality, cultural norms, and wife-beating. In J.R. Chapman & M. Gates (Eds.), *The victimization of women.* Beverly Hills: Sage, 1978.

STRAUS, M., GELLES, R., & STEINMETZ, S. *Violence in the american family.* New York: Doubleday, 1980.

WALKER, L. E. *The Battered Woman.* New York: Harper & Row, 1979.

WALKER, L. E. Treatment alternatives for battered women. In J.R. Chapman & M. Gates (Eds.), *The victimization of women.* Beverly Hills: Sage, 1978.(a)

WALKER, L. E. Learned helplessness and battered women. *Victimology: An International Journal,* 1978, *2:* 3-4, 525-534. (b)

WALKER, L. E. *Male batterers and their families: Treatment implications.* Presented at the annual meeting of the American Psychological Association, Toronto, 1978. (c)

WALKER, L. E. Response to Straus' paper on wife beating: Causes, treatment and research needs. In *Battered women: Issues of public policy.* Proceedings of a consultation sponsored by the U.S. Commission on Civil Rights. Washington, D.C., Jan. 30-31, 1978, pp. 160-163. (d)

WALKER, L. E. The Battered Women Syndrome Study. Grant #1-R01-MH-30147-01A1 funded by DHEW National Institute of Mental Health, 1977.

WEINER, B., FRIEZE, I., KUKLA, A., REED, L., REST, S. A., & ROSENBAUM, R. M. *Perceiving the causes of success and failure.* New York: General Learning Press, 1971.

WOLFGANG, M. E. *Patterns in criminal homicide.* Philadelphia: University of Pennsylvania Press, 1958.

6

Identifying Dangerous Child Molesters

GENE G. ABEL, JUDITH V. BECKER,
WILLIAM D. MURPHY, and BARRY FLANAGAN

INCIDENCE OF SEX CRIMES

Crimes of violence are extremely common in the United States. The
FBI reports that, in 1977, there were 466 violent crimes per 100,000
people at risk (Webster, 1978). It is difficult to determine how many
sexual crimes occur because sex crimes other than rape are not reported
by the FBI; furthermore, the reporting rate for rape is strikingly low.
Curtis (1975), for example, gathering data from a national survey, found
that 2.2 rapes are committed for each one reported. The reported rape
rate (not including attempted rapes) varies from city to city, but is approximately 57 per 100,000 females, accounting for a relatively high
percentage of violent crimes.

An even more frightening finding is that the majority of these crimes
are committed against very young females. Wells (1958), reporting on

The authors wish to thank Candi Osborn, Emily Coleman and Dr. Linda Skinner for
their assistance in collection of the data, and Drs. William Webb and Edward Sachar for
their continued support of this project. This research was supported in part by the National
Center for the Prevention and Control of Rape, Grants MH-2S051 and MH-32841.

demographic variables for almost 2,000 British rape victims, found that 84% were less than 16 years of age, and 58% were less than 13 years of age. Rape is a common crime that is usually committed against children.

If we examine the number of victims per sex offender, child molesters have many victims when compared with other sex deviates. Information on victims per offender is quite misleading when obtained from the traditional literature, which relies on arrest records and the self-report of incarcerated offenders. It is not too surprising that such sources of information would be inaccurate, since most sex offenses do not lead to convictions/incarceration and incarcerated offenders would jeopardize parole status by revealing the actual variety and frequency of their various sex crimes.

To examine this issue the authors questioned sex deviates coming for assessment/treatment in our outpatient program. Confidentiality of records was assured and subjects were aware that there would be no legal consequences of their reports. Care was taken to promote good rapport between the offender and the interviewer prior to questioning regarding the number of victims. When a range of victims was reported (which was frequently the case when there were large numbers of victims), the minimal number of victims was recorded. Table 1 indicates the average number of victims/offender by primary diagnostic classification. Heterosexual incest offenders had a relatively small number of victims (2.1), as did heterosexual rapists (5.8). Exhibitionists and frotteurs, as expected, had a very large number of victims, 199.5 and 582.8, respectively. What is surprising is that homosexual pedophiles and heterosexual pedophiles (child molesters) had an average of 31 and 62 victims, respectively, six and 12 times the number of victims for the rapists. These data were in marked contrast to those of Gebhard, Gagnon, Pomeroy, and Christenson (1965) who reported that the mean number of arrests per offender varied from 1.2 to 2.1 for each of these diagnostic categories

TABLE 1
Mean Number of Victims per Offender by Diagnosis

Diagnosis	Victims/Offender
Heterosexual incest	2.1
Heterosexual rape	5.8
Homosexual pedophilia	30.6
Heterosexual pedophilia	62.4
Exhibitionism	199.5
Frottage	582.8

listed in Table 1 (no data are available for frotteurs) and of Frisbie and Dondis (1965) who reported that homosexual pedophiles had an average of 1.3 victims and heterosexual pedophiles had 1.2 victims.

These data indicated that, unlike those who commit heterosexual incest and heterosexual rape, pedophiles involve themselves with many children. If one of society's goals is to reduce the incidence of crime against persons less capable of defending themselves against assault, and pedophiles have multiple victims, then treatment to prevent child molestation would be quite cost-efficient.

ARE CHILD MOLESTERS DANGEROUS?

Child molesters have traditionally been viewed as passive, unassertive individuals who only involve themselves with willing children and only infrequently use force during commission of the crime. Gebhard et al. (1965) report that only 12.2% of heterosexual pedophiles use significant aggression during their contact with children; however, these data rely heavily on interviews with incarcerated offenders or police records that are easily distorted by the offender or not detailed.

Christie, Marshall, and Lanthier (1978) have recently reported a study of 150 incarcerated sex offenders, 27% of which were pedophiles (victims younger than 13 years of age) and 73% heterosexual rapists. This study is unique in that, in addition to the traditional offender's self-report and arrest records, detailed information was obtained from probation officers' presentencing reports, transcripts of courtroom testimony, and reports from medical personnel examining the victims. Table 2 outlines the extent of aggression used by each category of offender.

TABLE 2
Sex Offenders' Use of Aggression
During the Offense

Type of Aggression	Child Molesters	Rapists
Used no threats	29%	7%
Used verbal threat only	12%	20%
Used physical force	59%	73%
Used excessive physical force	58%	71%
Victim sustained noticeable injury	42%	39%

Contrary to popular opinion, 58% of child molesters used excessive physical force during the crime, compared to 71% of rapists. Moreover, 42% of the child victims sustained noticeable injury, compared to 39% of the rape victims. Thus, although a smaller percentage of child molesters than rapists use physical aggression while committing the crime, the percentage of victims actually injured is slightly higher for victims of child molestation than victims of rape. This leads Christie et al. (1978) to conclude:

> Perhaps the most surprising observation of the present study concerns the degree of violence employed in the offense. It is of course not unreasonable to expect rapists to use violence, and other researchers have confirmed this expectation, but most other studies have reported pedophiles to be physically harmless individuals. For whatever reason, a substantial number of the pedophiles in our group used physical force in excess of that necessary for the commission of the crime, and this appears to be an unusual observation sufficient to warrant further examination (p. 29).

ATTEMPTS TO IDENTIFY DANGEROUS CHILD MOLESTERS AND RAPISTS

A number of authors have attempted to identify dangerous child molesters. Frisbie (1979), Kozol, Cohen, and Garofalo (1966), Cohen and Boucher (1972) and Marcus (1970) have each attempted to describe offender characteristics that are highly correlated with aggressive child molestations. Each of these scales or criteria have limited application because 1) most use ill-defined terminology that cannot be duplicated by other researchers, and 2) as Quinsey (1977) points out, the criteria are static, based on the offender's past history. It is impossible for an offender identified as dangerous to receive treatment that leads to his no longer being dangerous, since being dangerous is defined by the offender's history, and treatment will not change the history. Such static scales thus have limited applicability in dealing with child molesters.

The authors have conducted a series of psychophysiologic investigations to identify the dangerous heterosexual rapist (Abel, Barlow, Blanchard, & Guild, 1977; Abel, Becker, Blanchard, & Flanagan, in press; Abel, Blanchard, Barlow, & Mavissakalian, 1975; Abel, Blanchard, & Becker, 1978a; Abel, Blanchard, Becker, & Djenderedjian, 1978). Nonrapists, rapists, and sadistic rapists (rapists who used physical force far in excess of that necessary to complete the act of rape) were presented two-minute audiotape or videotape scenes while their erections were measured. The scenes involved a heterosexual interaction depicting a sexual act between mutually consenting adult partners, a violent rape committed upon an adult female by a male, and a physical assault (without sexual connotations) committed upon an adult female by a male.

By looking at the *relative erotic* properties of the rape scene or the assault scene versus the mutually consenting scene, it was possible to separate non-rapists from rapists, in that only rapists responded to rape stimuli. Furthermore, by an examination of rapists' erections to rape cues versus mutually consenting cues (the Rape Index), it was possible to identify those rapists who had raped at the highest frequency and those who were sadistic rapists.

DO CASES OF INCEST DIFFER FROM PEDOPHILES?

Another issue that remains unclear in the literature is whether those who commit heterosexual incest are etiologically different from heterosexual pedophiles. Quinsey (1977), in reviewing recidivism rates for these two diagnostic categories, found the recidivism rates for cases of heterosexual incest to be consistently lower than those for heterosexual pedophiles. He hypothesized that, based on this difference in recidivism rates, their etiologies may be different. Family dynamics and opportunism may account for incidents of incest, while heterosexual pedophiles may have specific sexual preferences for young females. If the causes of these two deviations vary, it follows that different treatments are needed. In the case of incest, treatment may focus on the intrafamily dynamics. The heterosexual pedophile's treatment, on the other hand, should aim at reducing his specific sexual preference for young girls.

To investigate the issue of whether pedophiles are etiologically different from incest offenders, we applied a psychophysiologic method to heterosexual pedophiles, cases of heterosexual incest, and other types of sex offenders, similar to the method the authors have used with rapists. The goals of the study were to determine: 1) if it is possible to identify offenders who involve themselves with female children from offenders who do not; 2) if the arousal pattern of heterosexual incest cases differs from that of heterosexual child molesters; and 3) if the more dangerous child molesters can be identified.

Subjects

Subjects were sexual deviates consecutively referred to the Special Problems Unit, Department of Psychiatry, University of Tennessee Center for the Health Sciences (Memphis) or to the Sexual Behavior Clinic at the New York State Psychiatric Institute (New York City). The majority of subjects volunteered and were under no coercion to participate. No subjects were severely mentally retarded or psychotic.

Each subject underwent an extensive clinical interview. All research subjects were then instructed regarding the research nature of their psychophysiologic assessment and were asked to sign informed consent statements. All participants were informed that their data were confidential and only available to the subject or the research staff. Non-research subjects underwent physiologic assessment as part of the usual assessment procedure of each clinic.

Method

Each subject then entered the laboratory where he was seated in a comfortable chair and instructed over an intercom as to how to wear the penile transducer. This small device encircles a portion of the penis and records changes in penile diameter. Any changes are then compared with the subject's full erection, so that at any one time the experimenter is able to identify exactly what percent of an erection each subject is having. Subjects were cautioned not to touch the transducer, since any manipulation of the device would immediately be noticed by the researcher.

Subjects were then presented a set of seven two-minute audiotape descriptions of various acts. The descriptions were as follows;

1) *Child initiates.* This scene describes a child eight to ten years of age initiating sexual interaction with a male. The male is described as a passive participant and it is clearly the child who is interested in the sexual activity and initiating all of it. A brief sample of such a description would be as follows: "It's in the evening and you are sitting in your car. You see an eight-year-old child waving to you. She is eight, has blonde hair, a small body and is very attractive. She is walking towards your car. She wants to talk with you and to have a sexual experience with you. She is in the car, moving right up close to you. She is putting her arms around you, feeling your body; she really enjoys it, she really likes holding you. She is unzipping your pants, she wants to feel your penis, to touch your penis and to see how big your penis is. She is eight years old; she is touching your penis and holding your penis. Now she wants to have sex with you . . ."
2) *Mutual.* This scene depicts a mutual consenting act in which both the

young child and the adult male participate equally. An excerpt would be as follows: "It's in the evening; you are in your car. You are watching a young, eight-year-old girl. She is looking over at you. She wants to meet you and you'd like to meet her. You are motioning for her to come over to the car and she is really anxious to be with you. She is sliding right into the car now; you reach your hand over and you are rubbing her skin, touching her body. She really likes that and she is coming right over next to you, putting her arms around you, holding you very tight and pressing her body close to you. You feel her body close. She is unzipping your pants; now she is feeling your penis. You really like to feel her hands on your penis . . ."

3) *Nonphysical coercion.* This scene depicts the offender using verbal coercion in order to bring about a sexual interaction with the young girl. Attempts are made to not include any references to physical force being used. A sample of the scene would be as follows: "It's late in the evening. You are in your car, watching an eight-year-old girl. She is young, has blonde hair. You want to rape her. You are telling her to come over to your car. She doesn't want to, but you threaten her. You tell her if she doesn't get over to the car, you are going to hurt her, you are going to beat her up. She is getting into the car, but quite reluctantly. You tell her to close the door or you will beat the hell out of her. She is really frightened and scared. She is eight years of age. You are looking over at her; you see her skin. She is very small. You tell her to come over close to you. She is really frightened and scared. Yo tell her to unzip your pants, to unzip them now or you are going to hurt her or her mom or dad. Now you tell her that if she doesn't touch your penis, you may kill her. She is really frightened and scared. She is unzipping your pants but she is really frightened. You've really scared her. Now you tell her to go ahead and touch your penis and feel it, to handle your penis. You feel her small hand on your penis . . ."

4) *Physical coercion.* This scene depicts the sexual assault of the young girl, using physical force to complete the act. An excerpt would be as follows: "It's in the evening and you are sitting in your car, watching an eight-year-old girl. She is young, blonde, very pretty. You want to rape her. You are getting out of the car and walking over towards her. You are grabbing her now and pulling her with you, pulling her into the car. She is fighting you, trying to get away, but it's no use, you are too strong and too powerful. You slap her across the face and tell her to be quiet. You are yanking her clothes off. She is screaming, trying to get away. She is eight years of age, blonde, very

pretty. You are going to rape her and you slap her across the face and tell her to do just what you say. You are slapping her and hitting her so that she does just what you say. You tell her to unzip your pants. She is a little hesitant, so you slap her some more. Now she is unzipping your pants and you tell her to grap your penis, to feel your penis. You have to slap her a little to get her to do that . . ."

5) *Sadism.* This scene depicts a forced sexual act involving *excess* physical coercion, more force than would be necessary to complete the sexual act. Note that an attempt is made to convey that the victim is compliant and ready to participate in the sexual act because of the physical coercion and threats used, and yet the rapist still uses more force. A sample would be as follows: "It's in the evening. You are in your car watching an eight-year-old girl. She is blonde, young, pretty. You want to rape her, have sex with her. You get out of the car. You are grabbing her, yanking her and pulling her into the car. She is fighting and trying to get away and you are really going to beat the hell out of her while you have sex with her. She says she will do anything you say, just don't hurt her, but you want to hurt her. You are slapping her across the face. She is bleeding around the face, around her mouth. She is crying, and now you force her hands into your pants. You twist and mutilate her hands. You hear her bones snapping in her hands as you force her hands into your pants. You tell her to grab hold of your penis and as she is doing that—she is doing just what you say—you slap her across the face some more so she will really hurt. Now you are forcing your penis into her mouth. She is willing to suck your penis, but you are going to shove it in deep into her until it really hurts her, until she is really frightened and scared, till she gags . . ."

6) *Physical assault.* This scene describes an assault devoid of sexual connotations. It is simply a description of the male beating up a young girl. A sample would be as follows: "It's late in the evening. You are sitting in your car watching an eight-year-old blonde girl. For some reason, you really want to beat her up—to beat her up and hit her. You don't know exactly why. You are getting out of the car and grabbing her, hitting her over the head, dragging her along to the car. You are going to beat her up in the car where she won't get loose and no one will hear her. She is eight years of age, blonde. You see her right there. You are hitting her across the face and now you are pounding on her back. She is really frightened and scared, pleading with you to stop, but it's no use. You are going to beat her up, to beat the hell out of her. She is trying to get away, but it's no use, you are

too strong. You yank her arms, pull her across the seat, slap her across the face. She is bleeding more around the mouth. You are going to just beat the hell out of her . . ."

7) *Adult mutual.* This scene is similar to Scene 2, except that the mutually consenting partner is an adult female, not a young girl. The scene would go as follows: "It's in the evening. You are sitting in your car with a woman. She is 25 or 26 years of age. You see her right there, large breasts, nice hips, she really wants to get close to you, feel you. She is reaching over for you, and you move your body over to her. You are feeling her breasts and you feel her arms around you. She is holding you very tight. Now she is reaching down and unzipping your pants. You really want her to feel your penis, to touch your penis with her hands. She is feeling your penis now. You can feel her hands on your penis . . ."

These seven scenes would constitute one set. Each set depicts the same victim (except for the last scene), but the action described varies from scene to scene. Four different sets were used. Each subject underwent two sessions of measurement. In each session, two sets were presented randomly. The subject was instructed to let himself become aroused to half of the scenes (one set) in one session, and to suppress his erections to the scenes during the other half of the presentations. Following each two-minute audiotape, the subject's maximum erection was calculated and he was asked to report the extent of sexual arousal (0 to 100%) and his percent of full erection (0 to 100%) to the preceding scene, in a way similar to the data collection methods described elsewhere (Abel & Blanchard, 1976; Abel, Barlow, Blanchard, & Guild, 1977).

Results

The subject population was composed of 27 sexual deviates, including six cases of heterosexual incest, ten heterosexual pedophiles, and 11 subjects with other sexual deviations (the latter group, some of whom had more than one diagnosis, included four homosexual pedophiles, three heterosexual adult rapists, two sadomasochists, two exhibitionists, three voyeurs, one adult homosexual, and one obscene phone caller—none of whom had histories of sexual encounters with children). Diagnostic classification was made on the basis of the subject's self-report, psychiatric records, police reports, and history from relatives *prior to* psychophysiologic measurement. One subject was classified as both incest and heterosexual pedophilia, but since 98% of his sexual contacts with children had been with relatives, he was included in the incest category.

Each subject's reported sexual arousal closely paralleled his reported degree of erection, and therefore reported degree of erection is excluded from the results section. The effect of "arouse" or "supress" instructions upon the measures is dealt with later in this chapter; unless specified, the following data are those obtained during instructions to become aroused to the various stimuli.

Figure 1 shows the mean recorded erections and reported degree of sexual arousal to each of the seven scenes for the six heterosexual incest cases. Erections varied from 11.3 to 23.8%, with lower erections to the aggressive scenes (3-6) and the adult mutual scene. The self-reported sexual arousal paralleled recorded erections to scenes 1-3, but the progressively more aggressive scenes (4-6) produced a marked disparity between the reported arousal and recorded erections. Recorded erections were much higher than reported sexual arousal for scenes 4-6. Scene 7 depicting mutually consenting intercourse with an adult female was the exception. Reported arousal was quite high (24.7%), while recorded erection was relatively low (13.6%).

It appears that socially approved sex acts are rated as quite arousing (scene 7), while erections indicate minimal sexual arousal. Socially disapproved acts such as forced sex with a child (scenes 4-6) are reported

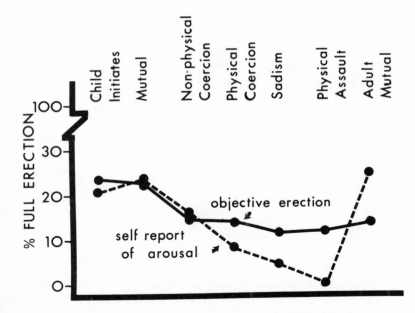

FIGURE 1. Heterosexual Incest Cases' Arousal to Pedophilic Cues

as not arousing at all, while erection measures indicate otherwise. These results lead us to conclude that sex offenders' self-reports of their erotic preferences are unreliable, a frequent finding with other types of offenders as well (Abel et al., 1975, 1978b; Abel, Barlow, Blanchard, & Guild, 1977).

As another interesting finding, it was noted that men with incest histories developed significant erections to pedophilic cues (scenes 1 and 2) that were *not* descriptions of sexual acts with their daughters or stepdaughters, but described sexual encounters with young girls who were strangers to them. If incest cases involve themselves with close relatives because of family conflicts or their mere availability, why do they get erections to scenes depicting sex with young girls not related to them? The answer may be that incest is a special subset of pedophilia.

Finally, the incest cases had minimal objective erections to scenes depicting sex with an adult female (13.7%), but relatively high arousal to sex with a child (23.8% to scene 1). Excessive sexual arousal to young unrelated females is characteristic of the diagnosis of heterosexual pedophile, not heterosexual incest. A classification system relying on recorded sexual arousal patterns would redefine heterosexual incest cases as heterosexual pedophiles.

Figure 2 shows the individual erection measures of one of the cases

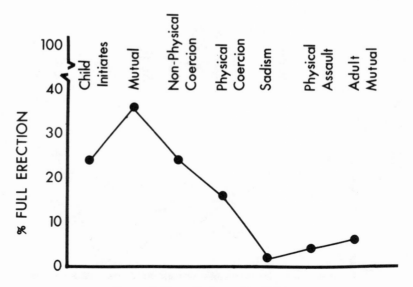

FIGURE 2. "Incest": Arousal to Children

of incest. Mr. A was a 24-year-old, three-times-married male, seeking treatment for a two-year history of incest involving his 10-year-old step-daughter. He entered assessment/treatment as a result of his wife's becoming aware of his incestuous relationship and its jeopardizing their marriage. Prior to physiologic measurement, he was questioned extensively regarding arousal to young girls other than his stepdaughter. He adamantly denied such arousal, maintaining that he was only attracted to his stepdaughter. He also reiterated that he had never used force when involving himself with her, a history consistent with his wife's report.

Figure 2 indicates that, contrary to the subject's verbal report, he showed considerable erection response to the descriptions of sexual involvements with young girls other than his stepdaughter. The subject's data also showed minimal erection response to scenes 4-6, depicting aggressive sexual interactions with the victim, which is consistent with the reports from the patient's family that he had used no physical coercion during sexual encounters with his stepdaughter.

Following completion of the study, these erection results were discussed with the subject, who shared with us that since the age of 14 he had always been attracted to young girls and that, although he had not participated in sexual involvement with young females other than his stepdaughter, he found most young girls highly erotic and was constantly fighting to control his sexual arousal to them.

The mean reported sexual arousal and recorded erections of the 10 heterosexual pedophiles are presented in Figure 3. Both arousal levels and erection records for this group are similar to those of the incest cases, with discrepancies between objective and subjective reports appearing to be related to whether the sexual activity described was socially sanctioned. Where social approval is greatest, self-reported sexual arousal is greatest (scenes 1 and 7) and objective erections are less. Where disapproval is greatest (scenes 2-6), self-reported sexual arousal is lower but recorded erections remain at or above these levels. A notable example of this finding is scene 4, a description of significant physical force used to rape a young girl. Erections to this scene were greater than erections to any other description of sexual activity with a young girl. These results indicate that heterosexual pedophiles, like rapists (Abel, Barlow, Blanchard, & Guild, 1977), are highly aroused by descriptions of physical assault of the victim.

Figure 4 reflects the individual erection measures of one of the cases of heterosexual pedophilia. Mr. B was 22 years old, unmarried and living with his family. Since age 21 he had been a frotteur, rubbing up against

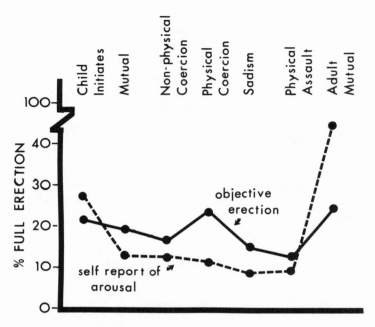

FIGURE 3. Heterosexual Pedophiles' Arousal to Pedophilic Cues

approximately 300 women in subways and buses. He had been arrested twice, once for sexual abuse (frottage) and once for jostling (pick-pocketing). During his clinical interview he reported having been arrested at age 18 for raping a six-year-old girl, but the charges were later dropped. He held the victim down, removed her clothes and had vaginal intercourse with her until he ejaculated. She subsequently was seen in a hospital emergency room, but the extent of her physical injury was unknown. He was given the clinical diagnosis of frottage and heterosexual pedophilia. He was questioned extensively as to whether he was still aroused by young girls, but he insisted that the rape of the little girl was an isolated event, and that he currently had no sexual arousal to young girls.

Erection measures in the laboratory (Figure 4), however, reflected a different picture. Scenes 1-4 generated 68, 35, 28 and 32% of a full erection, while scene 7 (adult mutual) generated only 26% of a full erection, indicating that he still had considerable arousal to young girls.

He was subsequently reinterviewed in light of these laboratory findings. Under detailed questioning he reported that "occasionally" he was

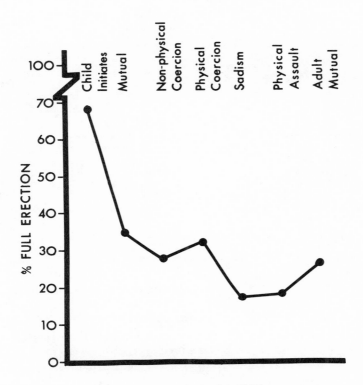

FIGURE 4. Frotteurs' Arousal to Children

still aroused to girls as young as 12 years of age, but he would give no further details. He denied arousal to females younger than 12 years old, but his report is questionable since the pedophile cues describe sexual experiences with girls 10 years of age or younger.

We next evaluated the data to determine if differences in erection responses existed between the three diagnostic categories of sex deviates. Table 3 reflects the mean erections to the seven scenes for each of the three groups. The individual data across groups showed significant variability from one subject to another, similar to that observed in our prior studies with rapists (Abel et al., 1977, 1978b). The naturally occurring differences in sexual arousability among individuals, age differences (especially an issue with cases of incest), and variations in the time of day recordings were made could all be factors contributing to this var-

TABLE 3
Erections to Heterosexual Pedophilic Cues
by Diagnosis

	Child Initiates	Mutual	Nonphysical Coercion	Physical Coercion	Sadism	Physical Assault	Adult Mutual
Diagnosis	1	2	3	4	5	6	7
Heterosexual Incest	24	23	15	14	11	12	14
Heterosexual Pedophile	22	19	16	24	15	13	24
Other	32	29	21	27	29	14	52

iability. To control for individual variability, we examined the relative arousal of the various pedophile cues *to each other*.

Each subject's arousal to descriptions of consenting sex with a child was compared to his arousal to consenting sex with an adult female by dividing the subject's erection to scenes 1 or 2 (whichever was greater) by his arousal to scene 7, a ratio we termed the Pedophile Index (PI). A major problem was what to do with erections less than 10%. Normally there is 10% "noise" in our transducer recording system, i.e., during baseline subjects may show up to 10% erection when not having sexual thoughts. Variation from 1-9% erection have limited meaning, since they fall within these noise limits. Since the validity of erection measures is greatest when comparing the presence of erection responses rather than the lack of these responses (Abel & Blanchard, 1976), we elected to take the most conservative approach and discard all erection values less than 10%.

Table 4 shows the resultant mean Pedophile Indices across the three diagnostic categories. A value greater than 1.0 would indicate that the pedophile scene generated a greater erection than the scene of sex with an adult female. Only those sexual deviates involved sexually with a child—heterosexual pedophiles (PI 1.26) or incest offenders (PI 1.57)—had indices greater than 1.0. Surprisingly, heterosexual incest cases had indices *greater than* heterosexual pedophiles, once again suggesting that, based on direct measures of sexual preference, heterosexual incest cases are actually heterosexual pedophiles.

Figure 5 displays the individual Pedophile Indices for both diagnostic

TABLE 4
Pedophile and Pedophilic Aggression Indices
by Diagnosis

Diagnosis	Pedophile Index		Pedophilic Aggression Index	
	Arouse	Suppress	Arouse	Suppress
Heterosexual Incest	1.56	1.61	.76	.77
Heterosexual Pedophile	1.26	.92	1.60	1.56
Other	.86	.99	1.21	1.02

categories, with heterosexual incest offenders' PIs well imbedded within the range of PIs for heterosexual pedophiles. Since the arousal pattern of heterosexual incest cases is similar to that of heterosexual pedophiles, treatment for heterosexual incest cases must include reduction of the patient's sexual arousal to young girls. As long as that sexual arousal is maintained, incest offenders are at risk to act on their sexual preference. Furthermore, it may be that sex with a girl relative is primarily motivated by the sexual preference for young girls, and that the reported distortion in family dynamics is the aftermath of the incestuous offender's attempts to involve himself with the most readily available young female, his own daughter, stepdaughter, etc.

We next examined the relative arousal of scenes depicting aggressive sexual acts with girls (scenes 3-6) versus scenes of sex with girls without aggressive elements (scenes 1-2). Each subject's erection to scenes 3-6

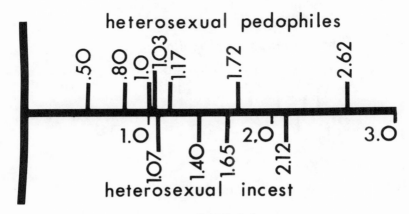

FIGURE 5. Pedophile Index

(whichever was greatest) was divided by his erection to scene 2 to calculate what we term a Pedophilic Aggression Index (PAI). For the reasons mentioned earlier, erection values less than 10% were discarded.

Table 4 shows that the PAIs for heterosexual incest cases, heterosexual pedophiles, and others are .76, 1.60 and 1.21, respectively. Examining the individual data from the "other" category of deviates revealed that aggressive deviates (three rapists, two sadomasochists) accounted for the high PAIs for this group.

Figure 6 shows the individual PAIs for heterosexual pedophiles and heterosexual incest cases. Recalling that a PAI greater than 1.0 indicates that scenes of aggressive sexual encounters with children are more erotic than non-aggressive sexual scenes, heterosexual pedophiles are far more responsive to aggressive scenes than incest offenders. Six of the eight PAIs of the heterosexual pedophiles were greater than 1.0, while none of the five cases of incest had a PAI greater than 1.0. The high PAIs for heterosexual pedophiles in the laboratory are consistent with Christie et al.'s (1978) report of their actual sexual behavior, i.e., that these individuals commit significant aggressive sexual acts against their young female victims.

Examining the clinical histories of those pedophiles with high PAIs confirms that high PAIs are indicators of the more dangerous pedophiles. The subject with a PAI of 3.85 (Figure 6) was 26 years of age, single and mildly retarded (IQ of 62). He had multiple sexual deviations, including the rape of young girls, heterosexual and homosexual pedophilia and incest, cross dressing, bestiality and voyeurism. He had been arrested once for raping a young girl and admitted to numerous other attempted and completed rapes of young girls. Furthermore, he clearly

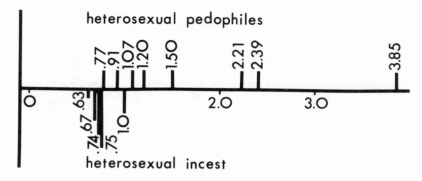

FIGURE 6. Pedophilic Aggression Index

preferred the rape of young girls as opposed to mutually consenting intercourse with them.

The pedophile whose PAI was 2.39 was a 40-year-old single male who also had multiple sexual deviations including rape (25 victims), sadism, heterosexual pedophilia, bestiality and voyeurism. His sadism was extensive and under poor control. On one occasion he shot off a teenage girl's arm with a high powered rifle for the sexual satisfaction it gave him. His poor control of his deviant urges had led to his being in psychiatric hospitals most of his life. His high PAI is obviously highly correlated with his strong preferences for aggressive sexual acts.

The pedophile whose PAI was 2.21 was single and 35 years of age. He had an IQ of 93 and evidence of brain damage. He had been raised in an institution for the retarded most of his life. His sexual deviations included homosexual and heterosexual pedophilia plus exhibitionism. Although incarcerated for "rape" on two occasions, extensive questioning failed to reveal history of rape or sadism. The rape charges apparently reflected his having a sexual interaction with young boys, but in neither case was the actual use of verbal or physical coercion documented. He was, however, preoccupied with children's bodily parts and kept extensive notebooks describing the relative erotic value of different parts of a child's body. He described wanting to cut apart various parts of a child's body to understand the body better. He also described wanting to have children naked around him and to know what it feels like to be raped.

The subject with a PAI of 1.50 was 38 years of age and sought treatment for his continuous urges to rape 13-year-old girls. In addition to heterosexual pedophilia, he had a history of sadism, window-peeping, exhibitionism, and adult homosexuality. He first became aroused to young girls at age 28, and by age 33 he regularly picked up young girls in bus stations, drove them to secluded areas, and raped them. His arousal pattern was more than simple rape. He preferred to harm, humiliate, and injure his victims during the course of the rape. He especially enjoyed anally raping them on cement floors, where the act of rape was extremely painful. He easily verbalized this sadistic arousal. By the time of his referral at age 38, he reported raping at least 50 young teenage girls.

Of the remaining four subjects with PAIs of 1.20 or less, only one had raped a child or had sadomasochistic arousal. That individual (PAI of 0.91) was the frotteur whose data were presented earlier. Of the five cases of heterosexual incest with PAI of 1.0 or less, none reported histories of rape or sadomasochism.

In summary, the PAI appears to be especially sensitive at identifying the more dangerous male who involves himself with young girls. Although the sample size is limited to 13 subjects (three subjects' data were less than 10% and consequently are not presented) who involve themselves with female children, results suggest that when the subject's PAI is 1.5 or greater, he is usually a rapist of young girls and has a history of using significant aggression to commit the rape. Equally important is that false negatives have not occurred to date. This may reflect the limited number of subjects run or the advantages of using a conservative method of calculating the PAI. One apparent false positive (heterosexual pedophile, PAI of 2.21) remains a puzzle to us. Although his history is replete with preoccupations about children's bodies and he was charged with the rape of two male children, no clear evidence of physical force during these sexual interactions could be ascertained.

Finally, we examined the effect of the subject's inhibiting his erections to the sexual stimuli. Figure 7 displays the mean erections of the pedophile and incest groups during instructions to become aroused or to suppress their erections during the stimulus presentations. For both groups, instructions to suppress generally did reduce erections to the seven descriptions, but not strikingly so.

More importantly, Table 4 indicates that instructions to become aroused or to suppress had little effect on the subjects' PIs and PAIs.

Of greatest importance was that the PAIs for the pedophile and incest groups were *not* changed by over 0.04 by the suppress instructions. The PIs for the heterosexual pedophile group was reduced from 1.26 down to .92 during suppress instructions, while the incest group's PIs increased from 1.56 to 1.61. Therefore, the incest offenders arousal to young girls remains obvious, while the pedophiles' preferences are lost. It may be that assessments using pedophilic cues must include both types of instructions to adequately assess sexual preferences for young girls.

CONCLUSIONS

FBI statistics and the psychological literature clearly indicate that rape, especially the rape of children, is common. Recent studies have pointed out that significant violence and aggression are perpetrated against child victims during rape. Our data reflect that individual child molesters have an exceedingly high number of victims. Psychophysiologic assessment of child molesters can assist in identifying 1) which deviates prefer young girls as sexual objects, and 2) which child molesters have used extensive

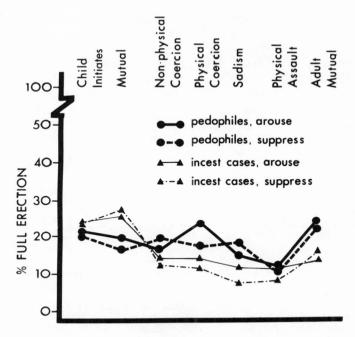

FIGURE 7. Effect of Instructions on Arousal to Pedophile Cues

violence and force while molesting young girls. Furthermore, identifying which child molesters have used extensive aggression with their victims does not rely on the subject's verbal report, which is frequently distorted.

The difficult question is whether knowing which child molesters have been aggressive in the past will identify which child molesters will be aggressive with their victims in the future. A prospective study of such individuals is needed, but the risks to society's children is high for such a project. Two studies indicate that the best predictor of future acts of violence is a high frequency of past acts of violence. Wolfgang, Figlio and Sellin (1972) found that, of a group of 10,000 boys in Philadelphia, 6% were chronic offenders and were accountable for 71% of the homicides, 77% of the rapes, 70% of the robberies, and 69% of the aggravated assaults committed by the entire group of 10,000. The PROMIS Research Project (1977) found that when the number of arrests of an offender for street crimes exceeded four, the probability of subsequent arrests for street crimes approached certainty. A first step in identifying those child molesters who will be dangerous thus appears to be the identification of those who have been dangerous in the past. Psycho-physiologic assessment using this type of pedophilic cues appears to be able to identify such child molesters.

A final conclusion from these studies is that the so-called cases of heterosexual incest are not different in their sexual preferences from heterosexual pedophiles, since both groups are highly aroused by young children other than their female relatives. Treatment for both groups must therefore include reduction of the child molester's sexual preference for young girls.

REFERENCES

ABEL, G. G., BARLOW, D. H., BLANCHARD, E. B., & GUILD, D. The components of rapists' sexual arousal. *Archives of General Psychiatry*, 1977, *34*, 895-903.

ABEL, G. G., BECKER, J. V., BLANCHARD, E., & FLANAGAN, B. The behavioral assessment of rapists. In J. R. Hays, J. K. Roberts, & K. S. Solway (Eds.), *Violence and the violent individual*. Halliswood, N.Y.: Spectrum Publications, in press.

ABEL, G. G., & BLANCHARD, E. B. The measurement and generation of sexual arousal. In M. Hersen, R. Eisler, & P. M. Miller (Eds.), *Progress in behavior modification* (Vol. II). New York: Academic Press, 1976.

ABEL, G. G., BLANCHARD, E. B., BARLOW, D. H., & MAVISSAKALIAN, M. Identifying specific erotic cues in sexual deviation by audiotaped descriptions. *Journal of Applied Behavior Analysis*, 1975, *8*, 247-260.

ABEL, G. G., BLANCHARD, E. B., & BECKER, J. V. An integrated treatment program for rapists. In R. Rada (Ed.), *Clinical aspects of the rapist*. New York: Grune & Stratton, 1978a.

ABEL, G. G., BLANCHARD, E. B., BECKER, J. V., & DJENDEREDJIAN, A. Differentiating sexual aggressives with penile measures. *Criminal Justice and Behavior*, 1978b, *5*, 315-332.

CHRISTIE, M., MARSHALL, W., & LANTHIER, R. *A descriptive study of incarcerated rapists and pedophiles*. Unpublished manuscript, 1978.

COHEN, M. L., & BOUCHER, R. J. Misunderstanding about sex criminals. *Sexual Behavior*, 1972, *2*, 56-62.

CURTIS, L. A. Present and future measures of victimization in forcible rape. In M. Walker (Ed.), *Rape: Research, action, prevention*. Report #29. Tuscaloosa, Alabama: Center for Correctional Psychology, Department of Psychology, University of Alabama, 1975.

FRISBIE, L. V. *Another look at sex offenders in California*. California Mental Health Research Monograph No. 12, 1969.

FRISBIE, L. V., & DONDIS, E. H. *Recidivism among treated sex offenders*. California Mental Health Research Monograph No. 5, 1965.

GEBHARD, P. H., GAGNON, J. H., POMEROY, W. B., & CHRISTENSON, C. U. *Sex offenders*. New York: Harper & Row, 1965.

KOZOL, H. L. COHEN, M. L., & GAROFALO, R. F. The criminally dangerous sex offender. *The New England Journal of Medicine*, 1966, *275*, 79-84.

MARCUS, A. M. Encounters with the dangerous sexual offender. *Canada's Mental Health*, 1970, *18*, 9-14.

PROMIS Research Project. *Highlights of interim findings and implications (Publication 1)*. Washington, D.C.: Institute for Law and Social Research, 1977.

QUINSEY, V. L. The assessment and treatment of child molesters: A review. *Canadian Psychological Review*, 1977, *18*, 204-220.

WEBSTER, W. H. *Crime in the United States-1977* (Uniform Crime Reports). Washington, D.C.: U.S. Government Printing Office, 1978.

WELLS, N. H. Sexual offenses as seen by a woman police surgeon. *British Medical Journal*, 1958, *5109*, 1404-1408.

WOLFGANG, M. E., FIGLIO, R. M., & SELLIN, T. *Delinquency in a birth cohort.* Chicago: University of Chicago, Press, 1972.

7

Effects of Victim Resistance Strategies on the Sexual Arousal and Attitudes of Violent Rapists

JANICE K. MARQUES

" 'If a guy grabs you, scream,' says (Chicago Police Sergeant) Sandburg. 'If he's got a knife at your throat or a gun at your head, relax and enjoy it' " (Schultz, 1972, p. 62). While the notion that victimization can be fun for women has survived only in fictional accounts of rape, suggestions for avoiding or reacting to sexual assaults continue to thrive and multiply in the literature. Women are urged to secure their homes, avoid dark or lonely streets, and to take heed from grisly stories about brutal assaults on Good Samaritans (Csida & Csida, 1974; Gager & Schurr, 1976; Horos, 1974). Although most writers agree on avoidance

This paper is based on a doctoral dissertation submitted by the author, under the supervision of G. Alan Marlatt, to the Department of Psychology, University of Washington.

The author wishes to thank D. R. Laws, Director of the Sexual Behavior Laboratory at Atascadero State Hospital, for the use of his facility, as well as for his technical consultation and his helpful comments on an earlier version of this paper.

tactics, considerable controversy surrounds the issue of rape resistance. Suggestions for reacting to an attack range from vigorous self-defense, screams, and verbal aggression to flattery, humor, and fainting (Foote, 1978; Hyde, 1976; Manville, 1974). Contradictions flourish in the popular literature on rape resistance, and it is not uncommon to find one expert's strategy described as a potential invitation to murder in the next "how to" piece (Selkin, 1975; Storaska, 1975).

There appear to be two primary reasons for the development and popularity of this controversy. The first is the dramatic growth of interest in rape during the 1970s. Previously, public concern and outrage about rape were intermittent, with peaks following reports of particularly savage or bizarre crimes, and with "troughs of public indifference in between" (Rada, 1978, p. 2). During this decade, however, rape has found a place in the national consciousness as a major social issue. This sustained interest is due in part to the alarming increases reported each year in the incidence of rape and its continued status as the fastest growing violent crime in the United States. The *Uniform Crime Reports* for 1977, for example, showed a 99% increase in reported rapes over 1968 and an 11% increase over 1976 (FBI, 1978). Although such figures may partially reflect higher rates of reporting, the fact remains that rape is an increasingly visible problem.

As startling as they are, statistics alone cannot explain the promotion of rape from a street crime to an issue of widespread concern in a society constantly bombarded with alarming figures and sensational news. More importantly, rape became a major focus of the women's movement in the 1970s. In speak-outs, conferences, and feminist writings, rape was exposed as a pervasive threat to all women, an act of oppression which represented not so much deviance as overconformity to the aggressive male role in our society (Connell & Wilson, 1974; Russell, 1975). Since the first widely read analysis of the "all-American crime" was published 10 years ago (Griffin, 1971), dozens of writers have added embellishments and further demands for legal, social, and political reform (e.g., Brownmiller, 1975; Clark & Lewis, 1977; Davis, 1975; Greer, 1973). The feminist appraisal of most men as potential rapists and all women as conceivable targets (Medea & Thompson, 1974) stimulated not only widespread interest in rape, but also public demand for information on how to avoid, resist, or cope with its occurrence. A host of experts soon emerged from the ranks of radical feminists, law and order enthusiasts, rapists, martial arts instructors, and social scientists, offering bits of advice as varied as their backgrounds.

The second major reason for the continuing controversy surrounding rape resistance is that the accumulation of knowledge has not kept pace with the interest and demand. The war on rape began as a social movement, not as an academic endeavor; at best it has since moved to the border between politics and science, where ideological concerns and opinions merge with empirical methods. Many social scientists have now focused their research efforts on rape and its victims, but straightforward, empirically derived answers to the concerned public's questions about rape resistance have not resulted.

Most of the available information on rape resistance has come from survey research involving victims, offenders, or police records, in which definitions of resistance and measures of its effectiveness have varied considerably. In Amir's (1971) study of Philadelphia rape cases, the victim's response was "submissive" in 55% of the assaults, "resistant" in almost 27%, and "fighting" in 18%. Verbal protests were included in the "submissive" category by this author, who noted that, consistent with assumptions of female masochism, many women will submit without any "genuine" resistance (p. 173). In contrast to Amir's (1971) figures, Hindelang and Davis (1977) reported victimization data from 13 cities indicating that half of the rape victims and four out of five of the attempted rape victims took some measures to protect themselves from, or to ward off, their attackers. While victims of both attempted and completed assaults in this study often screamed or hit their assailants, running away was much more common in attempted than in completed rapes. Similar results were reported by Giacinti and Tjaden (Note 1), who found that 66% of the 319 interrupted rapes they studied in Denver were prevented by the victim's active resistance. The most successful tactics were fleeing, physical resistance, crying aloud, and verbal refusal.

Results of a U.S. Department of Justice study conducted by the Battelle Law and Justice Study Center (1978), which included data on 1,260 rape complaints in five cities, also indicated that the majority of rape victims resisted. Initial resistance efforts were usually verbal attempts by the victim to: a) make herself unattractive to the assailant or elicit his sympathy; b) threaten retaliation; or c) feign stipulated consent, communicating a willingness to submit after using the restroom, changing clothes, etc. In evaluating the effectiveness of these tactics, the Battelle researchers concluded that, "although these latter ruses sometimes allowed a victim to escape the situation, verbal resistance was singularly ineffective in thwarting sexual assaults" (p. 18). Screaming was found to be the most effective method of terminating an assault, although it caused some offenders to become more violent in order to silence their victims.

Two California studies (Chappell & James, Note 2; Queen's Bench Foundation, 1976) yielded conflicting evidence on the relative effects of various resistance strategies. Chappell and James' interviews with 50 convicted rapists at Atascadero State Hospital indicated that: a) Passivity or compliance was the victim reaction most rapists preferred; b) physical resistance (including screaming) was more likely to provoke harm to the victim than was verbal resistance; and c) convincing the offender of a victim's altered state of health or eliciting his sympathy "might terminate the attack or minimize injury" (p. 29). The Queen's Bench Foundation (1976), however, found that pleas for sympathy appeared to encourage rapists to complete the assault, and that the most effective resistance was aggressive victim refusal to be raped. Their data from 73 violent offenders and 108 victims of rape or attempted rape indicated that: a) Rapists, more often than deterred assailants, perceived their victims as frightened; b) attempted rape victims tended to be more suspicious than rape victims, and more often responded in a hostile manner prior to the signal of the attack; and c) victims of attempted rape used a greater variety of tactics and produced more immediate, forceful, and determined resistance efforts than did victims of completed assaults. Consistent with Chappell and James' (Note 2) findings, these authors reported that screaming, physical resistance, and victim anger incurred greater risk of injury to the victim; however, victim calmness and passivity were also correlated with the intensification of violence during assaults.

Although both Chappell and James (Note 2) and the Queen's Bench Foundation (1976) found evidence that verbal resistance may be effective in rape deterrence, there was no consensus regarding which tactic was most successful. Brodsky (1976a) addressed this issue experimentally by presenting videotape depictions of nine verbal resistance strategies to rape conferees, forensic treatment personnel, and rapists. The conferees rated verbal attacks by potential victims as the most effective response, while the treatment personnel's ratings favored both the development of a personal relationship with the rapist and verbal attacks as deterrence measures. In the rapist sample, a plea based on body weakness (recent hospital release) received the highest rating, followed by acquiescence and moral appeals. When asked for suggestions on rape resistance, however, the rapists tended to advocate either the development of a relationship or verbal attacks and refusals.

Thus, research has begun to test the popular advice for potential victims, but as yet there is little agreement concerning the effectiveness of the various tactics. Although further studies may provide the answers, it is also possible that plain and simple solutions for women facing rape will not be forthcoming. The convergence of social scientists on a problem typically serves to complicate it rather than simplify it, and rape is unlikely to be an exception. While simple models have been proposed, there is increasing evidence that the prediction and control of rape will require the understanding of a multidetermined social behavior.

As previous authors (Brodsky, 1976b; Feldman-Summers, 1976) have noted, efforts to understand rape and its prevention have traditionally emphasized one of the following factors: a) victim characteristics; b) traits of the rapist; c) situational determinants; or d) societal influences. Blaming the victim, a stance which often characterizes the average citizen's view of social problems (Ryan, 1974), has been particularly common in rape. Despite the fact that rape has the lowest victim-precipitation rate of the major violent crimes (Curtis, 1974), recent studies have found the public quite willing to attribute responsibility to rape victims (Feild, 1978) and to believe that conscious or unconscious rape wishes contribute to their victimization (Hotchkiss, 1978). Although some suggestions for avoiding and resisting rape still imply that sexual assaults result from women's lack of vigilance or assertiveness, the victim-blame perspective has found little empirical support and is now under fire in the literature (e.g., Weis & Borges, 1973).

Evidence supporting the models which attribute rape to offender traits or to provocative situations is also relatively weak. While some researchers have found personality differences between rapists and other groups (Fisher & Rivlin, 1971; Rader, 1977), most find a wide variety of personalities represented and fail to draw a consistent picture of the rapist's character (Battelle Center, 1978; Rada, 1977). Notions that rape is caused by mental illness or overwhelming sexual desire have also fared poorly; for example, clinical findings have suggested that the incidence of psychosis may be lower in rapist samples than in the general population (Henn, Herjanic, & Vanderpearl, 1976), and that few offenders are motivated by sexual needs (Groth & Burgess, 1977). Similarly, although some situations conducive to sexual assaults have been identified (e.g., hitchhiking), and although campaigns for improving home security or avoiding high-risk areas are popular, there is as yet little evidence on the extent to which rape is situationally determined or is affected by environmental modifications (Feldman-Summers, 1976).

The fourth model of rape emphasizes the role of societal variables, from broad cultural values to specific police and court procedures, in encouraging the victimization of women. This orientation has been the driving force of the feminist protest, as well as the stimulus for many recent investigations by social scientists. Although its broad causal hypotheses are difficult to test, support has been found for some of the model's assumptions, including: a) the wide cross-cultural variance in rape rates (Chappell & Fogarty, 1978); b) the criminal justice system's leniency toward rapists (Gillam, 1978; Robin, 1977); and c) the similarity of attitudes toward rape among male citizens, police officers, and convicted rapists (Feild, 1978). In one recent study (Malamuth, Haber, & Feshbach, 1980), over half of the male college students sampled indicated some likelihood that they would be inclined to rape if assured they would not be caught. Although there is increasing evidence that American society condones forceful sexual coercion (Dietz, 1978), the social perspective fails to answer the crucial questions of which members of the culture will rape and why some will commit bizarre or particularly violent crimes.

Thus, while blaming society appears to be more defensible than blaming the victim, each of the popular models is incomplete. In practice, few authors work from a singular version of why rape occurs or propose interventions which follow directly from a clearly stated model. More commonly, rape prevention plans include multiple targets and are at least implicitly based on a model of rape as determined by individual and situational, as well as cultural, factors.

Although it has not been well articulated in the specific case of rape, Bandura's (1973) social learning theory of aggression offers a framework for understanding the process by which individual rapists are carved from the violence-promoting conditions of our society. From this perspective, ingredients from each of the four single-factor models play a role in the making of a rapist. The sociocultural context is critical in providing opportunities to learn sexually aggressive behavior; successful violent models permeate the mass media, and punishment rarely befalls those who follow suit. Within this cultural milieu, performances of sexually assaultive acts are determined both by environmental conditions and a host of person variables. The behavior of rapists is not capricious, and even the repetitive offender is likely to be influenced by a variety of situational factors, including such victim characteristics as availability, isolation, and apparent vulnerability. Similarly, offender characteristics will determine how the rapist interprets, and at times creates, the conditions surrounding a potential assault.

If sexual assaults are determined by multiple contextual and person variables, the effects of a given resistance tactic are likely to be moderated by characteristics of the offender, the victim, and the situation. There is, for example, some evidence that the outcome of a victim's resistance strategy depends on the type of offender she is facing (Brodsky, 1976a;

Cohen, Garofalo, Boucher, & Seghorn, 1971) and on the social conditions of the assault (Queen's Bench Foundation, 1976). Thus, the simple question of whether resistance works might well be unanswerable, even by the grandest of surveys. A more useful approach may be to ask, "What are the effects of this type of resistance, under these conditions, with this type of assailant?" Similarly, the question of how resistance works needs attention. For example, was an assailant deterred because the victim's behavior frightened him, dampened his anger or sexual arousal, elicited his sympathy, or simply bought time for the victim to escape?

The present study was designed to address these questions. The primary research question concerned how several verbal resistance strategies affect the behaviors of violent rapists. In addition to assessing the effects of resistance on the rapist's inclinations toward completing the rape or harming his victim, measures of sexual arousal and feelings toward the victim were also included in an attempt to explore the process by which resistance succeeds or fails. The three strategies selected for the study were those most often recommended in the literature: assertive refusal, plea for sympathy, and establishing a relationship with the rapist. Advocates of the assertive strategy suggest that a clear, unyielding refusal may startle the assailant and interrupt his plan, since he expects a fearful and passive victim (Selkin, 1975). Pleas for sympathy and efforts to establish a relationship with the rapist are also designed to catch the assailant off guard, by forcing him out of his fantasy and into a personal encounter. The pleading victim attempts to get the rapist to see her as a human being with feelings and problems of her own (Horos, 1974), while the woman using a relationship strategy emphasizes her concern for the rapist's feelings and problems (Manville, 1974).

The effects of physical resistance were not addressed in the study, primarily due to the methodological problems involved in presenting such stimuli. Verbal responses, however, were easily incorporated into an already established methodology for assessing rapists' behavior under controlled laboratory conditions (Abel, Barlow, Blanchard, & Guild, 1977). Audiotape descriptions of sexual assault scenes were presented, each of which described the rapist interacting with a potential victim whose response to the attack varied. Two series of tapes were constructed which differed in terms of the scene of the assault, but situational variables and victim characteristics were not systematically manipulated in the study.

Although a number of offender variables need to be studied in rape resistance, previous researchers (Queen's Bench Foundation, 1976) have suggested that initial research focus on the crucial question of what deters the most dangerous assailants. The research subjects chosen for this study were convicted violent rapists at Atascadero State Hospital, a maximum security facility in California specializing in the treatment of mentally disordered offenders. At the time of the study, approximately 200 rapists were confined at the hospital, many of whom had committed multiple or violent offenses. To minimize sampling bias, only patients with nonpsychotic diagnoses and with patterns of sexual arousal similar to those found in laboratory studies of unincarcerated rapists were included.

The lack of previous research on how victim responses affect rapists' sexual arousal and the contradictory evidence regarding the behavioral effects of resistance encouraged an exploratory approach in this study. Several broad formulations, however, were tested. It was hypothesized that:

1) The resistance strategies would differ in their effects on rapists' levels of sexual arousal.
2) The resistance strategies would differ in their effects on rapists' self-reports of sexual arousal and attitudes (feelings toward the victim and probabilities of raping or harming her).
3) A rapist's inclination toward completing a rape would be stronger if he were sexually aroused by the interaction with his victim than if he were not.
4) A rapist's inclination toward harming a victim would be stronger if he were angered by the interaction with her than if he were not.

METHOD

Subjects

Sample selection. Following approval from the Hospital Research Committee, administration, and Committee for the Protection of Human Subjects, volunteers were recruited by announcing the study in patient groups, program staff meetings, and the patient newspaper. A three-stage screening process was then used to select a sample of violent rapists who were sexually responsive to rape cues. First, individual interviews were conducted by the experimenter (a female clinical psychology intern) to explain the procedures of the study and to determine which of the volunteers met the following criteria: a) commission of a rape offense against a female over 13 years old (to avoid pedophilia as a confounding

factor); b) ability to read and write; c) no history of assault in the institution; d) prior exposure to pornography; e) taking no medications
known to inhibit erections; f) no history of untreated venereal disease;
and g) no evidence of psychosis, retardation, or other condition which
would impair ability to give informed consent. Issues of confidentiality,
possible coercion, rights to privacy, and potential risks and benefits were
also discussed during this initial contact. A detailed consent form was
reviewed with the patient, which emphasized that his participation was
voluntary and that no negative consequences would result from declining
or discontinuing at any point. Assurance was also given that his results
would be strictly confidential and would not affect the length of his
commitment.

Since the patients had been institutionalized and in treatment for
varying amounts of time, a second screening process was designed to
eliminate those who were no longer responsive to rape cues. Each of the
30 volunteers who met the initial interview criteria was given a code
number and an appointment with a male research associate for a laboratory session in which: a) The patient was introduced to the experimental setting and instructed in the proper handling and placement of
the penile strain gauge; b) the polygraph was specifically calibrated for
his range of response, so that self-reported and recorded maximum
erections coincided; and c) his arousal pattern was assessed using the
"rape index" procedure developed and described by Abel and his associates (Abel et al., 1977; Abel, Blanchard, & Becker, 1978). In this
procedure, a series of videotape scenes depicting either mutually consenting intercourse or rape was presented. As recommended by Abel et
al. (1978), both the patient's arousal and his ability to inhibit arousal
were assessed by presenting two of each type of scene under instructions
to become aroused, and two under instructions to suppress arousal. A
pair of rape indices (average penile response to rape scenes divided by
average penile response to consenting intercourse scenes) was then computed for each individual, one for the "arouse" condition and one for
the "suppress" condition. Although Abel et al. (1977) initially found that
an index value of .50 tended to discriminate between rapists (>.50) and
nonrapists (<.50), more recent work has suggested that a higher value
is needed for this discrimination when videotape stimuli are used (Abel,
Note 3). In the present study, only the 25 patients with one or both
indices above .80 were asked to participate in subsequent procedures.

The third screening procedure was a review of the patients' records
to eliminate those who: a) were diagnosed as psychotic, either in the
hospital or at the time of their offenses; or b) did not commit violent

crimes as determined by police and probation reports. The criterion for violence was "force or threat of force excessive of that necessary to accomplish a rape and exceeding the violence of rape itself" (Queen's Bench Foundation, 1976, p. 60). Four of the 25 volunteers were eliminated; of the remaining 21 potential subjects, three served as pilot subjects and consultants, one returned to court, and one declined to continue. Thus, 16 subjects began the study. Of these, three were dropped because of relative unresponsiveness to the audiotape stimuli, and one discontinued because he did not want further exposure to rape themes. Individuals not completing the experiment were later debriefed and given the same treatment option (a behavior therapy program designed to alter deviant sexual arousal patterns) as those completing it.

Sample characteristics. The 12 subjects who completed the study were predominantly young, white, high-school graduates with varied criminal backgrounds (see Table 1). Ages ranged from 20-39, with a mean t of 24.5; at the time of their committing offenses, the mean age was 22.7. Ethnic composition of the sample was: eight Caucasion, two Hispanic, and two Black. All 12 had primary hospital diagnoses of "sexual deviation, aggressive sexuality"; half had secondary diagnoses of personality disorder, alcoholism, or drug dependence. Most had no previous psychiatric care, although three had been evaluated or counseled in correctional settings and two had been hospitalized following previous offenses. Seven of the subjects had prior felony convictions, five of whom had been convicted of assaultive, nonsexual crimes. Half had prior sexual offenses, ranging from exhibitionism to rape. The subjects reported having committed a range of 1-40 rapes each, with a mean of 9.6. In their committing offenses, seven used lethal weapons, and five were under the influence of alcohol or other drugs. Victims of three subjects were hospitalized as a result of the assaults.

Apparatus and Setting

Changes in penile circumference were detected by a digital pulse volume strain gauge, which was used as a penile transducer in the manner described by Bancroft, Jones, and Pullan (1966), and which has been recommended as the most suitable circumferential device currently available (Laws, 1977). A Beckman RM Dynograph recorded the penile circumference changes and stimulus events. The study was conducted in the interview and experimental rooms of the Sexual Behavior Laboratory, a supplemental treatment unit located in the limited-access clinical laboratory area of the hospital. Half of the laboratory's experimental

TABLE 1
Summary of Subject Characteristics

Characteristic	\underline{1}	\underline{2}	\underline{3}	\underline{4}	\underline{5}	\underline{6}	\underline{7}	\underline{8}	\underline{9}	\underline{10}	\underline{11}	\underline{12}
Age at time of participation (years)	27	20	20	20	27	32	39	22	23	21	20	23
Age at time of offense (years)	21	19	19	19	25	31	38	21	23	20	18	19
Ethnic identification (C=Caucasian; H=Hispanic; B=Black)	C	C	H	H	C	C	C	B	C	B	C	C
Marital status (S=single; M=married)	S	M	S	M	M	S	S	S	S	S	S	S
Years of education (G.E.D.=12)	13	11	14	12	14	15	13	11	12	14	11	10
Previous psychiatric care (0=none; 1=evaluation/counseling; 2=hospitalization)	0	0	0	1	0	1	2	0	2	1	0	0
Length of current incarceration (months)	60	16	15	5	23	4	10	17	2	5	1	36
Number of prior sexual offense convictions	0	1	0	4	0	3	4	1	2	0	0	0
Number of prior convictions for violent, non-sexual crimes	0	1	0	1	0	2	4	0	2	0	0	0
Number of rapes committed (self-report)	22	11	3	10	3	7	40	2	3	9	1	4
Approach toward victims (D=dominant or aggressive; T=tentative or polite)	D	D	D	T	D	T	D	D	T	T	D	D
Weapon used in offense (W=yes; NW=no)	NW	W	NW	W	NW	W	W	NW	W	W	NW	W

Subject

room contained the programming and recording equipment, and half was a sound-attenuated subject room. The two areas were divided by a wall containing a subject console, into which the penile transducer leads and the subject's headset and microphone were plugged. The subject sat in a comfortable reclining chair facing the console, and communicated with the experimenter through a two-way intercom. Videotapes used in the screening sessions were presented on a monitor in the subject room; audiotapes were presented through the subject's headphones.

Treatment Conditions

The resistance strategies were presented in the context of 4½-minute audiotape descriptions of sexual assault scenes. Although presented to the subject as a continuous narrative, each tape was divided into two distinct parts. The first two-thirds of the tape (Part 1) described the setting, the assailant's initial interaction with his potential victim, and the development of his conviction to rape her; it ended as the attack was initiated. The last one-third (Part 2) began with the victim's response to the attack and contained all of the verbal resistance material. The tapes uniformly ended on an ambiguous note; the assailant was still feeling an urge to rape, but had not achieved penetration.

Pilot work was conducted to: a) determine common elements in rapists' fantasies; b) develop settings and themes with relatively wide appeal; c) select voices for the recordings; and d) evaluate the credibility of the victims' statements. Two series of tapes were constructed, both of which emphasized themes of control and dominance. In one (Series A), the assault was a premeditated act of vengeance against women in general and involved a hitchhiking victim; in the other (Series B), the assault followed a brief attempt to seduce the victim and took place in the assailant's apartment. Scripts were written in second person and were recorded in a male staff psychologist's voice, with a predominant tone of controlled determination. The victim's reactions broke into the narrative in Part 2, and were presented in a female college student's voice, with affect appropriate to the content of her strategy. Number of words in the resistance strategies were matched, as was the modest degree of physical resistance described in all scenes. Within each of the two series, four tapes were constructed which were identical except for the victim's reaction, which was one of the following:

> *Assertive refusal.* Victim strongly and repeatedly confronts her attacker with firm refusals to be raped, intimidated, or even

touched. Her tone is angry throughout the interaction; both series end with the victim's assertion that she is leaving and he cannot stop her.

Plea for sympathy. Victim tearfully pleads with her assailant, begging him to let her go and not harm her. In one series, the plea is based on body weakness (recent hospital release); in the other, the victim focuses on her fear that her fiance will find out and leave her.

Establishing a relationship. Victim calmly attempts to engage her attacker in a conversation. She suggests they get to know each other, then tries to draw him out by noting that he seems upset and by emphasizing her concern and willingness to talk to him about it.

No-resistance control. As in all conditions, the victim is physically uncooperative, but in this case she does not verbalize her objections. The narrative elaborates somewhat on the victim's failure to "try talking her way out of it" in order to match the length of tapes in other conditions.

Procedure

Following the screening procedures, subjects were individually scheduled for the laboratory sessions of the study proper. In order to learn about individual response patterns, as well as about the composite group results, a repeated measures design was used, which exposed each subject to both series of tapes and all treatment conditions. All eight tapes were presented twice to the subject; order of presentation was independently randomized for each individual to control for order effects of the series. The subject's participation consisted of four half-hour sessions, which were scheduled over a period of one week to 10 days. Four audiotapes were presented in each session.

The procedure for each laboratory session was as follows: The experimenter met the subject, explained the general procedure for the session, gave him the self-report forms on a clipboard, then asked him to go into the subject room and to report when the headset and penile strain gauge were in place. After a stable zero baseline was displayed on the polygraph, a recorded set of instructions asked the subject to "imagine himself as the man involved in each of the scenes," and to "form a mental image of the action being described." He was also instructed to number and complete one of the self-report forms immediately after each tape. After the subject was asked if he had any questions, the first audiotape was played. Each of the remaining three tapes was presented following completion of the self-report form and return to baseline on the polygraph. It should be noted that the instructional set was not varied in this procedure, since pilot data indicated that the audiotapes yielded insignificant levels of arousal (less than 20% of maximum erection) under "suppress" instructions.

After completion of the laboratory sessions, each subject was scheduled for a 90-minute debriefing interview with the experimenter, which included: a) discussion of the subject's reactions to the study; b) questions about his history, offenses, and opinions regarding victim resistance; c) a presentation of his results and a summary of group results; and d) assessment of the subject's interest in modifying any deviant sexual arousal patterns evidenced by his laboratory responses or by his own personal concerns. Subjects requesting treatment were seen subsequently by the experimenter and a member of the Sexual Behavior Laboratory staff to develop their individualized treatment plans.

Dependent Measures

Physiological measures. Pre- and postresistance measures of penile circumference were used to assess the effects of the strategies on sexual arousal. Although the polygraph continually recorded the subject's response, readings at two critical points in each stimulus presentation served as the primary data points: a) at the transition between Parts 1 and 2 on the tape (just before the victim verbally resisted the attack); and b) at the end of the tape (just after presentation of the victim's last statement). Maximum erection achieved during the stimulus presentation was also recorded. Since the equipment was specifically calibrated for each subject's range of response, the polygraph readings were consistently between 0-100% of maximum erection.

Self-reports. Attitudinal effects of the resistance strategies were measured by an 11-item self-report form which was completed after each tape presentation. The first 10 items required responses on a four-point scale (ranging from "not at all" to "very much so") to questions regarding: a) clarity of the scene; b) sexual arousal; c) feelings toward the victim (anger, fear, and sympathy); and d) likelihood of completing the rape, hurting the victim, using a weapon, or letting the victim escape, if the subject were "on the street" and alone with her. The final item, which required a brief written description of what the victim on the tape was feeling, was used to check experimental conditions and to identify possible inattentiveness or perceptual distortions by the subjects.

RESULTS

Physiological Measures: Hypothesis 1

Polygraph recordings of erection responses (changes in penile circumference) were used to test the hypothesis that the resistance strategies would differ in their effects on rapists' levels of sexual arousal. The analyses focused on the erection measures obtained at the transition between Parts 1 and 2 on each tape presentation (preresistance), and those obtained at the end of each presentation (postresistance). Means and standard deviations of these pre and post measures, as well as the pre-post changes in penile erection across the four treatment conditions and two tape series are presented in Table 2. The means for each treatment condition are also presented graphically in Figure 1. Figure 2 shows each subject's mean erection response to the four tape presentations in each condition. Since Part 2 of each audiotape contained ongoing references to rape cues as well as the victim's resistance strategy, it should be emphasized that the pre-post erection changes reflect relative, not absolute, effects of the strategies. The rape cues were, however, identical across the four conditions, enabling valid comparisons of these relative effects to be made.

The pre, post, and change measures were analyzed in separate two-factor (treatments X series) analyses of variance (ANOVAs), with repeated measures on both factors and on subjects. Results of these analyses are summarized in Table 3. Since departures from homogeneity of the variance-covariance matrices in repeated measures analyses yield positively biased F ratios, reduced degrees of freedom were used to provide conservative tests of the obtained ratios (Edwards, 1972). The preresistance ANOVA found that the erection measures did not differ significantly across the four treatment conditions, although the Series B tapes produced greater erection responses than did the Series A tapes. The postresistance analysis revealed a significant main effect for treatment conditions, but neither the series effect nor the treatments X series interaction was significant. The same result was obtained in the ANOVA of the pre-post changes.

Planned comparisons of pre-post changes among the six treatment condition pairs were performed using the Bonferroni test of significant differences (Neter & Wasserman, 1974). This procedure was chosen in order to maintain a constant α level (.05, two-tailed) across the multiple comparisons. The results indicated that the plea for sympathy (PS) condition accounted for the treatments effect; the PS changes were signif-

TABLE 2

Means and Standard Deviations for Penile Erection Measures (by Treatment Conditions and Tape Series)

Measure and series	Condition							
	Assertive refusal		Plea for sympathy		Establishing relationship		No-resistance control	
	M	SD	M	SD	M	SD	M	SD
Pre-resistance[a]	42.65	29.64	40.77	29.46	43.19	30.51	38.83	29.45
Series A[b]	37.08	27.96	39.54	30.65	39.04	28.94	37.54	31.01
Series B[b]	48.21	30.79	42.00	28.82	47.33	32.08	40.13	28.40
Post-resistance[a]	33.02	24.30	69.52	21.65	38.17	25.30	34.27	24.79
Series A[b]	29.38	21.74	68.13	22.39	34.63	26.27	34.25	27.77
Series B[b]	36.67	26.58	70.92	21.27	41.71	24.34	34.29	22.02
Pre-post change[a]	-9.63	22.25	28.75	24.78	-5.02	33.44	-4.56	17.20
Series A[b]	-7.71	16.92	28.58	26.42	-4.42	37.54	-3.29	18.76
Series B[b]	-11.54	26.78	28.92	23.58	-5.63	29.59	-5.83	15.79

Note. Scores represent percentages of maximum erection.
[a] Based on n = 48 trials per condition
[b] Based on n = 24 trials per condition

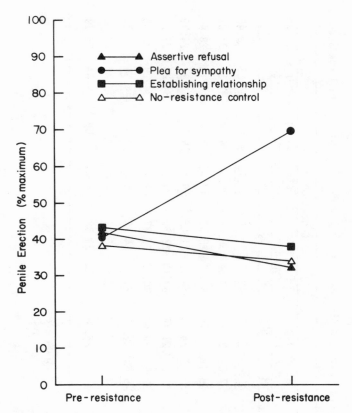

FIGURE 1. Mean pre-resistance and post-resistance penile erections for all 12 subjects across the four treatment conditions.

icantly different from those in the assertive refusal (AR), establishing a relationship (ER), and no-resistance control (NC) conditions, but the latter three conditions did not differ from each other. Thus, Hypothesis 1 was corroborated for comparisons involving the PS strategy; as Figures 1 and 2 demonstrate, the plea tended to enhance the rapists' sexual arousal, while the other strategies did not.

Self-reports: Hypothesis 2

Data from the self-report form which was completed after each tape presentation were used to test the hypothesis that the resistance strategies would differ in their effects on rapists' self-reported levels of sexual arousal, feelings toward the victim, and probabilities of raping or harm-

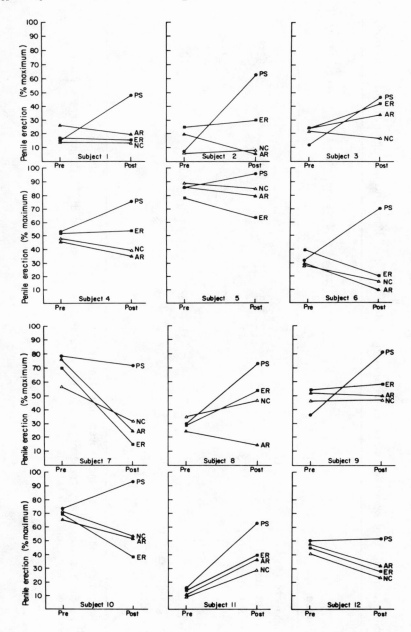

FIGURE 2. Mean pre-resistance and post-resistance penile erections for Subjects 1-12 across the four treatment conditions.

TABLE 3

Summary of Analyses of Variance on Physiological Measures (Pre, Post, and Change in Penile Erection)

Source	df^a	Pre-resistance F^b	Post-resistance F^b	Pre-post change F^b
Subjects (S)	11			
Treatments (A)	3	1.30	32.98**	36.98**
SxA: Error (a)	33			
Series (B)	1	7.32*	4.32	.67
SxB: Error (b)	11			
AxB	3	.62	.43	.20
SxAxB: Error (c)	33			
Residual error	96			
Total	191			

^{a} Not corrected for variance-covariance violations.

^{b} Fs for treatments and treatments x series were tested with reduced df (1,11) to correct for variance-covariance violations.

* $p<.05$.

** $p<.001$.

ing her. Mean scores for Items 1-10 across the four treatment conditions and two tape series are presented in Table 4. Item 1, while not bearing directly on Hypothesis 2, was included in the analysis to determine whether the scenes in all conditions were equally clear to the subjects. Item 11, however, was used during the experiment to monitor the subjects' attentiveness and accuracy of perception, and was not included. Separate two-factor ANOVAs with repeated measures were used to assess the effects of treatment conditions and tape series on each of the self-report items (see Table 5). Treatments X series interactions were also tested, but none reached significance. As in the previous analyses, all Fs were tested conservatively, and all pairwise comparisons were performed using the Bonferroni procedure at a constant .05 level of significance (two-tailed).

A significant series effect was found only on Item 1, which asked the subject whether he was "able to imagine actually being in the situation" presented on the tape, and to rate how clear it was to him. While the Series B tapes produced clearer images than the Series A tapes, there were no differences among the four treatment conditions on this item. Significant treatments effects were, however, found on Items 2 and 3, which asked the subject to rate "How sexually excited or aroused did you get during the scene?" and "How sexually excited were you at the end of the tape?" Again, pairwise comparisons indicated that the PS condition tended to produce higher levels of sexual arousal than did other conditions.

Items 4, 5, and 6 asked the subject to rate his feelings toward the victim on the tape. Item 4 asked if he felt "angry" toward her, Item 5 if he felt "afraid" of her, and Item 6 if he felt "sympathetic or sorry" for her. Significant treatments effects were found on Items 4 and 6; pairwise tests, however, revealed significance only in comparisons involving the AR condition, which produced higher anger ratings than the NC condition and lower sympathy ratings than the PS condition.

Items 7-10 asked the subject to predict how he would behave if he were alone with the victim "on the street." Item 7 asked if he would be "likely to rape her," Item 8 if he would be "likely to hurt her," Item 9 if he would be "likely to use a weapon on her," and Item 10 if he would "feel like letting her go" if she tried to escape. A significant treatments effect was found only on Item 8, with the subjects reporting a higher likelihood of hurting the AR victim than the other three. The means for Item 9 showed a similar pattern, although half of the subjects indicated that they were "not at all" likely to use a weapon on any of the victims. Inspection of the data revealed that five of the six subjects who

TABLE 4

Self-Report Means by Treatment Conditions and Tape Series

	Assertive refusal			Plea for sympathy			Establishing relationship			No-resistance control		
Item	A^a	B^a	M^b	A^a	B^a	M^b	A^a	B^a	M^b	A^a	B^a	M^b
1. Clarity of scene	3.00	3.25	3.13	3.17	3.29	3.23	3.25	3.42	3.33	2.88	3.08	2.98
2. Arousal during scene	2.38	2.75	2.56	2.96	2.83	2.90	2.54	2.75	2.65	2.25	2.46	2.35
3. Arousal at end of tape	2.17	2.58	2.38	2.94	2.92	2.93	2.08	2.15	2.12	2.04	2.21	2.13
4. Anger toward victim	2.13	2.08	2.10	1.46	1.54	1.50	1.33	1.67	1.50	1.33	1.33	1.33
5. Fear of victim	1.42	1.38	1.40	1.17	1.08	1.13	1.29	1.25	1.27	1.17	1.17	1.17
6. Sympathy for victim	1.42	1.46	1.44	2.33	2.00	2.17	1.81	1.92	1.87	1.71	1.83	1.77
7. Likely to rape victim	2.17	2.13	2.15	2.17	2.29	2.23	2.00	2.02	2.01	2.04	2.04	2.04
8. Likely to hurt victim	1.83	1.71	1.77	1.25	1.25	1.25	1.13	1.25	1.19	1.13	1.13	1.13
9. Likely to use weapon	1.48	1.48	1.48	1.15	1.21	1.18	1.19	1.13	1.16	1.06	1.10	1.08
10. Likely to allow escape	1.94	2.06	2.00	2.08	2.13	2.10	2.46	2.13	2.29	2.42	2.33	2.38

Note. Scores represent ratings on a 4-point scale (1=not at all; 2=somewhat; 3=moderately so; 4=very much so).

[a] Based on n=24 trials.
[b] Based on n=48 trials.

TABLE 5

Summary of Treatment and Series Effects in Analyses
of Variance on Self-reports

Item	Treatment $\underline{F}^a$	Series $\underline{F}^b$
1. Clarity of scene	3.16	6.07*
2. Arousal during scene	5.53*	1.04
3. Arousal at end of tape	10.80**	1.26
4. Anger toward victim	6.20*	4.07
5. Fear of victim	3.69	.87
6. Sympathy for victim	6.46*	.02
7. Likely to rape victim	.59	.04
8. Likely to hurt victim	5.96*	.13
9. Likely to use weapon	3.95	.15
10. Likely to allow escape	1.59	2.20

[a]Treatment $\underline{F}$s were tested with reduced $\underline{df}$ (1,11) to correct for variance-covariance violations.

[b]$\underline{df}$=1,11.

*$\underline{p}$<.05.

**$\underline{p}$<.01.

reported some inclincation to use a weapon were most likely to do so with the AR victim. Despite this trend, the treatments effect on Item 9 did not reach significance. On Items 7 and 10, the treatments effects were far from significant, and no clear trends were identified.

Thus, the analyses corroborated parts of Hypothesis 2. The resistance strategies differed in their effects on rapists' self-reports of sexual arousal, feelings of anger and sympathy, and inclinations toward hurting the victim. There were, however, no significant differences among the conditions on three of the last four items, which addressed the most crucial effects.

Relationships Among the Measures: Hypotheses 3 and 4

Hypothesis 3. Two tests of the hypothesis that the inclination toward completing a rape would be stronger if the rapist were sexually aroused than if he were not were performed, one using the physiological measures and one using the self-report arousal measures. First, the 192 trials were divided into low arousal (postresistance scores <50% of maximum erection) and high arousal (postresistance scores ≥50% of maximum erection) groups, and the Item 7 (likely to rape victim) scores for these two groups were compared. The mean score on Item 7 for the low arousal group ($n = 120$ trials) was 1.90; the mean for the high arousal group ($n = 72$ trials) was 2.46. Since the groups were independent samples of trials but not of subjects, an approximate t was calculated and a two-tailed test was used to provide a conservative estimate of significance. The test revealed that the "likely to rape victim" mean was significantly higher for the high arousal trials than for the low arousal trials, $t(190) = 3.68$, $p < .001$, as predicted by the hypothesis.

This finding was supported by the second test, which defined the low arousal group ($n = 106$) as those trials with scores of 1 or 2 on Item 3 (ratings of "not at all" or "somewhat" aroused at the end of the tape) and the high arousal group ($n = 86$) as those trials with scores of 3 or 4 on Item 3 (ratings of "moderately" or "very much" aroused). The mean "likely to rape victim" score was 1.74 for the low arousal group and 2.58 for the high arousal group. Since the variances of the two samples differed, the approximate t was calculated using separate variance estimates and was tested with reduced df, but was again significant, $t(160) = 5.90$, $p < .0001$ (two-tailed), suggesting that the subjects were more inclined to rape when they felt sexually aroused.

Hypothesis 4. The prediction that a rapist's inclination toward harming a victim would be stronger if he were angered than if he were not was tested by comparing the Item 8 (likely to hurt victim) responses given when subjects reported feeling some anger with those given when the subjects were not angry. The trials were divided into an angered group (ratings of "somewhat," "moderately so," or "very much so" on Item 4) and a non-angered group (ratings of "not at all" on Item 4). The mean Item 8 score for the angered group ($n = 77$ trials) was 1.75; the mean score for the non-angered group ($n = 113$ trials) was 1.06. Again, separate variance estimates and reduced df were used in the test because the sample variances were unequal. The mean "likely to hurt victim" rating was found to be significantly higher on the angered trials than on the non-angered trials, $t(88) = 7.21$, $p < .0001$ (two-tailed). Although this result was consistent with Hypothesis 4, inspection of the data revealed that the modal score on both Items 4 and 8 was the lowest rating (1), suggesting that there were too few scores of 2, 3, or 4 on either measure to adequately evaluate the hypothesis, except for cases of "not at all angry" rapists.

Other relationships. Although no other hypotheses were tested regarding the relationships among measures, some of these were explored for descriptive purposes. First, significant correlations were found between the polygraph measures of maximum erection and Item 2 (arousal during scene) scores, and between postresistance erection measures and Item 3 (arousal at end of tape) scores, $rs = .67$ and .68. (Computation of the Kendall rank coefficients of correlation supported the findings of the parametric procedure.) When these correlations were calculated separately for each subject, however, they ranged from $-.27$ to .90 for the first pair of measures and from $-.07$ to .94 for the second, indicating a wide range of individual differences in the extent to which erection and self-report measures coincided.

Second, correlation coefficients between all pairs of self-report items were calculated to explore further the relationships among rapists' self-reported levels of sexual arousal, feelings toward the victim, and predicted actions (see Table 6). A similar pattern of significance was again obtained using the Kendall rank correlation procedure. It should be noted that, since "not at all" response tendencies were found on Items 4, 5, 8, and 9, the correlations between pairs of these items may be inflated.

As can be seen in Table 6, Item 7 (likely to rape victim) ratings were most closely associated with Item 3 (arousal at end of tape) scores, but were also highly related to anger ratings (Item 4). The possibility that the sum of scores on Items 3 and 4 would be even more highly correlated with Item 7 scores was explored and confirmed, $r = .59$, suggesting that the combination of anger and sexual arousal experienced by the rapist was more closely associated with his inclination toward rape than was either factor alone. The likelihood of hurting or using a weapon on the victim (Items 8 and 9) was most closely related to the anger scores. Again, the extent to which the correlations between anger and the victim injury items was due to shared response biases were not determined. The fact that Item 5 had considerably lower correlations with these items, however, despite sharing the same bias, suggests that the relationships between anger and harming or using a weapon on the victim were not simply spurious. The rated likelihood of allowing the victim to escape (Item 10) was most closely associated with the rapists' feelings of sym-

TABLE 6
Intercorrelation Matrix for Self-report Items

Item	2	3	4	5	6	7	8	9	10
1. Clarity of scene	.44**	.37**	.29**	.00	.22*	.27*	.19	.21	.08
2. Arousal during scene		.69**	.38**	.19	.07	.48**	.35**	.31**	-.21
3. Arousal at end of tape			.31**	.06	.01	.53**	.36**	.24*	-.31**
4. Anger toward victim				.30**	-.26*	.44**	.62**	.48**	-.42**
5. Fear of victim					.16	.13	.27*	.13	-.07
6. Sympathy for victim						-.21	-.20	-.11	.47**
7. Likely to rape victim							.42**	.21	-.35**
8. Likely to hurt victim								.72**	-.28**
9. Likely to use weapon									-.07
10. Likely to allow escape									

Note. n=192.

  * p<.001.

  ** p<.0001.

pathy for the victim (Item 6), although the subjects also appeared less inclined to allow a victim to escape when they felt sexually aroused or felt angry toward her.

DISCUSSION

The results were consistent with all or part of each of the four hypotheses. As predicted by Hypothesis 1, a significant difference was found among the effects of the resistance strategies on the physiological measures of sexual arousal. Significant effects of the strategies were also found on half of the self-report items, corroborating Hypothesis 2 for the cases of self-reported sexual arousal, feelings of anger and sympathy toward the victim, and likelihood of hurting the victim. There were, however, no differences among the four conditions on two of the most crucial items, "likely to rape victim" and "likely to allow escape." Consistent with Hypothesis 3, subjects were more inclined to rape a victim when they were sexually aroused than when they were not. Similarly, when subjects were angry, they were more likely to hurt the victim than when they were not, as predicted by Hypothesis 4. After a brief review of factors affecting the validity of this study, these results will be discussed in the context of current theoretical and practical issues in the study of rape.

The primary threat to the internal validity of this study is the question of whether incarcerated felons can be trusted to give honest answers. Since males possess considerable inhibitory control over erection responses (Laws & Rubin, 1969), this question applies to both the physiological and self-report findings (Farkas, 1978). Despite the assurances of confidentiality, some subjects may have suspected that their results would affect the length of their incarceration, and thus may have been unwilling to report a high likelihood of raping or harming a victim. It is less apparent how the erection measures may have reflected this concern, since the participants had demonstrated their arousal to rape cues in the screening sessions and were not expected to "improve" in the experiment but to use the study as an opportunity to learn about themselves.

The extent to which experimenter effects influenced the results is difficult to determine. There is evidence, for example, that informal experimenters (as in the present study) permit less socially desirable responses to explicitly sexual material than do formal experimenters (Abramson, Goldberg, Mosher, Abramson, & Gottesdiener, 1975). Also, bias may have been introduced by the experimenter's hypotheses; although the debriefing data confirmed that the subjects believed the study to be exploratory, the fact that their erection responses were measured in conjunction with the self-reports may have induced the expectancy that arousal was associated with other measures.

The key threat to the external validity of the study again involves the use of incarcerated offenders. Considerable controversy surrounds the question of whether small groups of convicted rapists resemble the larger population of assailants-at-large or whether they represent only the "lunatic fringe" (Hotchkiss, 1978, p. 23). Clearly, incarcerated rapists are a select group. In California, for example, over 7,000 forcible rapes were reported in 1977, but only 389 rapists were convicted, one-third of whom received some form of probation (California Department of Justice, 1978; Gillam, 1978). Previous researchers using the Atascadero population have cautioned that their results may apply only to that small percentage of rapists who resort to substantial violence or repetitive attacks (Chappell & James, Note 2; Queen's Bench Foundation, 1976). The same caution is urged in regard to the present findings. The inclusion of only violent rapists was intentional; whether those who volunteered were "typical" violent rapists, however, is unknown.

The external validity of the study is also limited to the extent that the results were obtained under conditions which differed from those under which rape naturally occurs. Since the audiotapes were weak representations of actual assault scenes, the possibility exists that the strategies would have different or more powerful effects outside the laboratory. A number of factors which are likely to affect the outcomes of naturally occurring assaults were ignored or held constant in this research. For example, the study did not include intoxicated, outraged, or paired assailants. Effects of the victim's size, age, and body language were not assessed, nor was her skill, timing of the resistance, or ability to convince the assailant of her credibility. Finally, since the strategies were presented in two specific contexts, the findings may not represent the effects of similar strategies in the thousands of other rape situations which occur.

Despite the above limitations, the present findings relate directly to several controversies in the rape literature. First, although the violent nature of rape is currently emphasized, there is some disagreement regarding the extent to which rape involves a sexual, as well as an aggressive, component (Geis, 1977). The sexual arousal data will now be discussed as they contribute to our understanding of the sexual component of rape.

The most striking result in this study was the dramatically higher levels of sexual arousal produced by the plea for sympathy (PS) presentation compared to the assertive refusal (AR), establishing a relationship (ER), or non-resistance control (NC) presentations. All 12 subjects were most aroused by the pleading victim, and only one failed to show a mean pre-post increase in penile circumference for the PS condition. By contrast, the AR condition produced arousal decrements in 10 of the 12 subjects, while the other two conditions had highly variable effects.

Several previous authors have ventured predictions about the effects of resistance on rapists' sexual arousal. For example, Brodsky (1976a) observed that, while crying and signs of personal weakness on the part of the victim might deter the dominant, aggressive rapist, such tactics were likely to increase the sexual excitement of the rapist who is more tentative in his approach. In the present study, however, all four of the subjects who described their approaches as "tentative or polite" and seven of the eight "dominant or aggressive" subjects showed increased arousal during the PS presentation. Feminists (e.g., Horos, 1974), emphasizing the rapist's desire for power and dominance, have often predicted that a fearfully pleading victim is just what the rapist wants. To the extent that getting what one wants produces erections, the results of this study agree with this assertion.

In the debriefing sessions, when subjects were shown graphs of their erection responses across the four conditions, two were surprised by their responses to the PS victim, but most were not; consistent with Horos' (1974) prediction, a typical comment was, "She's showing fear, and that's what I like." Earlier in the same interview, however, when asked what reactions they wanted from the victims of their committing offenses, most had indicated a desire for compliance or submission (as did the rapists interviewed by Chappell and James, Note 2). Although some subjects perceived the NC victim's silence as an indication of consent, this perception was not consistent; thus, the possibility remains that a purely submissive response would be more arousing than a plea. Another interpretation, however, is that rapists may consider a pleading victim to be "submissive," as did a previous rape researcher (Amir, 1971).

When asked what they wanted from rape, only one of the subjects reported that his motive was sexual, while seven said they were motivated by needs for power, control, recognition, or affirmation of their masculinity, and four sought revenge or wanted to express anger. Given this preponderance of power and anger motives, the PS effect may indicate that these rapists, while not wanting vigorous or aggressive resistance, find a "submissive" victim who pleads and shows fear more arousing than one who calmly submits and offers less visible confirmation of the assailant's powerful impact on her.

One reason for the inclusion of sexual arousal measures in this study was to explore the possibility that this variable mediates the behavioral effects of victim resistance. As predicted, the subjects indicated they were more likely to rape when they were moderately or highly aroused than when they were somewhat or not at all sexually aroused. These results are consistent with Abel et al.'s (1977) finding that high arousal to rape cues identified subjects who had been inclined to rape, and also with their conclusion that measures of sexual arousal can provide useful information on subjects' current "urges to rape." Although a moderately high correlation was found between arousal (Item 3) and inclination toward rape (Item 7), the extent to which arousal mediated the different effects of the individual strategies could not be assessed, since there were no significant differences among the conditions on Item 7. Thus, while the PS condition yielded the highest arousal ratings, it had approximately the same "likely to rape" scores as did conditions yielding lower arousal.

Further inspection of the data revealed clear individual differences in the extent to which sexual arousal was associated with the likelihood of raping a victim. For half the subjects, anger was more highly correlated with the inclination toward rape than was sexual arousal. Overall, the combination of anger and sexual arousal was more closely related to the probability of raping a victim than was either factor alone. It appears, then, that a rapist may be most likely to rape a victim whose behavior enhances both his sexual arousal and anger. For some, the arousal component would be more important; for others, the anger component would be more closely related to the desire to rape.

Although this study did not seek an answer to the question of whether rape is essentially a sexual or an aggressive act, these results suggest that both components are important, at least in the offender's experience of sexual assault. They do not, however, indicate that the rapist's motive is the same blend of sexual and aggressive components. Eleven of the subjects, in fact, described their motivation as nonsexual. Similarly, pilot work on the audiotape scripts suggested that themes of control, dominance, and revenge had wider appeal than did erotic themes which emphasized the rapist's sexual interest in the victim. Groth and Burgess' (1977) definition of rape as a sexual deviation, a "behavior directed toward the sexual expression and gratification of needs that are not basically sexual" (p. 400), appears consistent with the responses of the rapists in this study. For these men, anger and power motives were clearly cast in the sexual arena; thus, victim responses which made them feel feared, respected, and powerful were also sexually arousing. How the rapists learned to express their needs for power, control, and revenge in sexual behavior, however, was not explored.

A second issue in rape which is addressed by the present findings concerns the role of the victim in preventing sexual assaults. Overall, the effects of the resistance strategies on the rapists' self-reports appear quite modest in view of the diversity of victim responses presented. When asked if they would be likely to rape the victim described, the subjects reported an almost equal probability of raping all four victims. The likelihood of allowing a victim to escape was also remarkably similar across the conditions. The subjects were, however, more likely to hurt the AR victim than the other three, and five of the six subjects who considered using a weapon were most inclined to do so with the AR victim.

Thus, the self-report results suggest that the AR strategy carries with it a greater risk of harm to the victim. Since this strategy was the most aggressive victim response studied, this finding is consistent with the belief that "vigorous" resistance incurs a substantial risk of victim injury (Hilberman, 1976; Queen's Bench Foundation, 1976; Robin, 1977). The subjects agreed on this point as well; 10 believed that active victim resistance will provoke injury, and two believed that it may deter rapists in populated areas but will incite violence in isolated settings. There were, unfortunately, no identifiable trends regarding which strategy was least likely to result in victim injury; nor was there evidence consistent with Medea and Thompson's (1974) contention that signs of pain or weakness "will only make the rapist more violent" (p. 95), or with the Queen's Bench Foundation's (1976) finding that victim calmness was associated with increased violence.

Unlike previous studies (e.g., Chappell & James, Note 2; Queen's Bench Foundation, 1976), this investigation did not find any of the verbal strategies to be potentially more effective in deterring rape than the others, or even more effective than saying nothing. Similarly, the data yielded only partial support for Brodsky's (1976a) predictions that: a) Dominant, aggressive rapists will be deterred by pleas but encouraged by verbal refusals; and b) rapists with tentative approaches will be deterred by refusals but encouraged by pleas. The eight "dominant or aggressive" subjects did not tend to identify the AR victim as most likely to get raped; all four victims, in fact, appeared to have about the same chance with these men. Two of the four "tentative or polite" subjects were, however, most likely to rape the PS victim, while the third was inclined to rape the AR victim, and the fourth was "very much inclined" to rape all four of the victims.

Although the failure to find significance on the "likely to rape victim" and "likely to allow escape" items may have been partly due to weaknesses in the stimuli or to the subjects' unwillingness to report their inclinations, it may also reflect truly insignificant effects. That is, as suggested by the Battelle (1978) researchers, verbal resistance may be "singularly ineffective in thwarting sexual assaults" (p. 18). Or the findings may be viewed as another triumph for individual differences, with each of the strategies succeeding with one rapist but failing with another. Ten of the 12 subjects did, after all, identify some of the victims as more likely to get raped than others. Whether these slight differences in ratings translate to different behaviors in actual rape situations, however, is unknown. Data from the debriefing interviews suggest they may not. When asked if there were "anything your most recent victim could have said to stop you," only two of the subjects said "yes," while eight said "no" and two were unsure.

Despite the fact that the victim-blame model of rape is currently the target of substantial criticism, "What did she do to deserve this?" remains a popular question in rape. In this study, however, victim responses were explored in order to determine, "What, if anything, can she do to prevent this?" The distinction between these two questions is a crucial one. The present research was an attempt not to blame the victim, but to learn how rapists may respond if she uses the resistance strategies currently recommended. Its theoretical perspective was a view of rape as a socially learned behavior, a function of multiple contextual and personal variables. The potential victim's response was seen as only one of many conditions whose behavioral impact depends on how they are interpreted by the rapist.

The present findings appear more consistent with this model of rape than with the victim-blame model. For these violent offenders, the victim's responses were not powerful determinants of their predicted actions. Although the strategies did influence the rapists in some ways, the offender's emotional responses and likely actions were not simply a function of the victim's behavior. For example, the likelihood of allowing a victim to escape was most closely related to the rapist's feeling of sympathy toward her. The PS victim, however, did not get a more sympathetic response than did the victim who calmly talked to the rapist or the one who said nothing, nor were her chances for escape greater than those of the other victims. While the AR victim generally tended to anger the subjects and was also the most likely to get hurt, one of the subjects was more inclined to hurt the PS victim. In the debriefing interview, he explained that he saw the plea as an attempt to "con" or manipulate him. Thus, it was not the victim's response but the offender's perception of her motives and credibility that determined his reaction.

The present findings are a richer source of theoretical implications than of simple answers for potential rape victims. While the AR strategy angered the rapists and incurred a greater risk of harm to the victim, it did not yield an increased probability of rape, perhaps because it tended to quell the sexual arousal of the rapists. The effects of the PS tactic were in some ways complementary to those of the AR strategy: It enhanced the sexual arousal of the rapists but did not tend to produce the anger component of the urge to rape. The ER strategy, by comparison, had relatively weak effects on both the sexual arousal and anger components, and failed to distinguish itself from the NC response on any of the dependent measures. These results appeared to suggest that a calm, sympathetic attempt to relate to the rapist was tantamount to saying nothing. Oddly enough, when asked for their recommendations on verbal resistance, nine of the subjects described an ER strategy, while one suggested trying the AR tactic first and then the ER approach if the refusal fails, one recommended compliance, and one suggested laughing. "Showing concern" and "talking calmly" were the most common elements in the subjects' advice for victims attempting to verbally resist an attack. Thus, the subjects tended to agree with Medea and Thompson's (1974) recommendation of staying calm and talking "sanely" as a conservative strategy for victims. Although they did not see verbal resistance as an effective deterrent, these violent offenders believed that a victim who calmly showed concern for the assailant could at least avoid making things worse for herself.

Overall, the results are not encouraging for women facing rape, at least for those who would hope to verbally dissuade a violent assailant after his initiation of the attack. On the brighter side, victims in actual rape encounters have a number of resources which were not considered in this study. For example, several subjects indicated that physical resistance or screaming may deter a rapist when there are other people near who could intervene. Few rapists appear willing to risk being caught in order to complete an assault. Also, women are not limited to one strategy, as were the victims in this study. They can resist earlier in the encounter, try a number of tactics, and revise their approaches based on the assailant's response. In this regard, the present findings suggest that if one's initial resistance strategy appears to enhance the rapist's sexual arousal or anger, it may be wise to try something else. If the victim's response appears to calm the rapist or elicit his sympathy, however, staying with this tactic may increase her chances of escape.

In considering these implications, it is important to remember that the responses of a dozen violent offenders who had a considerable amount

of experience with victim reactions may not represent those of less sea-
soned or aggressive rapists. It should also be emphasized that the findings reflect the subjects' inclinations toward sexual aggression, not their
actual performances of the behavior. The fact that the urge to rape
appeared stronger when the subjects were both sexually and emotionally
aroused does not imply that rape is likely to occur whenever a rapist is
excited during his interaction with a woman. Consistent with Bandura's
(1973) view, arousal tended to augment the probability of aggression in
this study, but was not a prerequisite for its occurrence.

There is little evidence that rape is an explosive act of passion. In fact,
rapists often carefully plan their attacks, seek out victims who are isolated
or vulnerable, and evaluate the probable consequences of their actions
before initiating assaults. Research is needed to determine how situational variables and the offender's cognitive appraisals affect whether
he will act on the inclinations measured in this experiment. In addition
to contributing to our ability to predict rapists' behavior, such studies
would offer opportunities to test the value of social learning theory as
a framework for understanding rape.

Additional studies of rape resistance are also needed to better advise
women regarding the benefits and risks associated with the tactics which
are currently recommended for potential victims. The extent to which
the effects of resistance are moderated by observable characteristics of
the offender, victim, and conditions of the assault must be explored.
Although data from actual sexual assaults will provide the most important tests of these effects, the results of the present study suggest that
controlled laboratory investigation can be useful both in supplementing
field research and in exploring the rapist's reactions in more depth.

REFERENCE NOTES

1. Giacinti, T. A., & Tjaden, C. *The crime of rape in Denver.* Report submitted to the Denver
   High Impact Anti-Crime Council, 1973.
2. Chappell, D., & James, J. *Victim selection and apprehension from the rapist's perspective: A
   preliminary investigation.* Paper presented at the Second International Symposium on
   Victimology, Boston, September 1976.
3. Abel, G. G. *Identifying the dangerous rapist.* Colloquium presented at Atascadero State
   Hospital, Atascadero, California, October 1977.

REFERENCES

ABEL, G. G., BARLOW, D. H., BLANCHARD, E. B., & GUILD, D. The components of rapists' sexual arousal. *Archives of General Psychiatry,* 1977, *34,* 895-903.

ABEL, G. G., BLANCHARD, E. B., & BECKER, J. V. An integrated treatment program for rapists. In R. Rada (Ed.), *Clinical aspects of the rapist.* New York: Grune and Stratton, 1978.

ABRAMSON, P., GOLDBERG, P., MOSHER, D., ABRAMSON, L., & GOTTESDIENER, M. Experimenter effects on responses to explicitly erotic stimuli. *Journal of Research in Personality,* 1975, *9,* 136-146.

AMIR, M. *Patterns of forcible rape.* Chicago: University of Chicago Press, 1971.

BANCROFT, J., JONES, H. G., & PULLAN, B. R. A simple transducer for measuring penile erection, with comments on its use in the treatment of sexual disorders. *Behaviour Research and Therapy,* 1966, *4,* 239-241.

BANDURA, A. *Aggression: A social learning analysis.* Englewood Cliffs, N. J.: Prentice-Hall, 1973.

BATTELLE LAW & JUSTICE STUDY CENTER. *Forcible rape: Final project report.* Washington, D. C.: U. S. Government Printing Office, 1978.

BRODSKY, S. L. Prevention of rape: Deterrence by the potential victim. In M. J. Walker & S. L. Brodsky (Eds.), *Sexual assault: The victim and the rapist.* Lexington, Mass.: Lexington Books, 1976.(a)

BRODSKY, S. L. Sexual assault: Perspectives on prevention and assailants. In M. J. Walker & S. L. Brodsky (Eds.), *Sexual assault: The victim and the rapist.* Lexington, Mass.: Lexington Books, 1976.(b)

BROWNMILLER, S. *Against our will: Men, women and rape.* New York: Simon and Schuster, 1975.

California Department of Justice, Bureau of Criminal Statistics. *Crime and delinquency in California, 1977—Part I.* Sacramento, Calif.: Author, 1978.

CHAPPELL , D., & FOGARTY, F. *Forcible rape: A literature review and annotated bibliography.* Washington, D. C.: U. S. Government Printing Office, 1978.

CLARK, L., & LEWIS, D. *Rape: The price of coercive sexuality.* Toronto: Women's Press, 1977.

COHEN, M. L., GAROFALO, R., BOUCHER, R., & SEGHORN, T. The psychology of rapists. *Seminars in Psychiatry,* 1971, *3,* 307-327.

CONNELL, N., & WILSON, C. (Eds.) *Rape: The first sourcebook for women.* New York: New American Library, 1974.

CSIDA, J. B. & CSIDA, J. *Rape: How to avoid it and what to do about it if you can't.* Chatsworth, Ca.: Books for Better Living, 1974.

CURTIS, L. Victim precipitation and violent crime. *Social problems,* 1974, *21,* 594-605.

DAVIS, A. JoAnne Little: The dialectics of rape. *Ms.,* June 1975, pp. 74-77; 106-108.

DIETZ, P. E. Social factors in rapist behavior. In R. T. Rada (Ed.), *Clinical aspects of the rapist.* New York: Grune & Stratton, 1978.

EDWARDS, A. L. *Experimental design in psychological research* (4th ed.). New York: Holt, Rinehart and Winston, 1972.

FARKAS, G. M. Comments on Levin et al. and Rosen and Kopel: Internal and external validity issues. *Journal of Consulting and Clinical Psychology,* 1978, *46,* 1515-1516.

Federal Bureau of Investigation, Department of Justice. *Crime in the United States: Uniform Crime Reports, 1977.* Washington, D. C.: U. S. Government Printing Office, 1978.

FEILD, H. S. Attitudes toward rape: A comparative analysis of police, rapists, crisis counselors, and citizens. *Journal of Personality and Social Psychology,* 1978, *36,* 156-179.

FELDMAN-SUMMERS, S. Conceptual and empirical issues associated with rape. In E. C. Viano (Ed.), *Victimology: Victims and society.* Washington, D. C.: Visage Press, 1976.

FISHER, G., & RIVLIN, E. Psychological needs of rapists. *British Journal of Criminology,* 1971, *11,* 182-185.

FOOTE, C. Getting tough about rape. *Human Behavior,* December 1978, pp. 24-26.
GAGER, N., & SCHURR, C. *Sexual assault: Confronting rape in America.* New York: Grosset & Dunlap, 1976.
GEIS, G. Forcible rape: An introduction. In D. Chappell, R. Geis, & G. Geis (Eds.), *Forcible rape: The crime, the victim, and the offender.* New York: Columbia University Press, 1977.
GILLAM, J. Mandatory prison term for rape OK'd. *Los Angeles Times,* September 29, 1978, p. 22.
GREER, G. Seduction is a four-letter word. *Playboy,* January 1973, pp. 80-82; 164; 178; 224-228.
GRIFFIN, S. Rape: The all-American crime. *Ramparts,* September 1971, pp. 26-35.
GROTH, A. N., & BURGESS, A. W. Rape: A sexual deviation. *American Journal of Orthopsychiatry,* 1977, *47,* 400-406.
HENN, F. A., HERJANIC, M., & VANDERPEARL, R. H. Forensic psychiatry: Profiles of two types of sex offenders. *American Journal of Psychiatry,* 1976, *133,* 694-696.
HILBERMAN, E. *The rape victim.* New York: Basic Books, 1976.
HINDELANG, M. J., & DAVIS, B. L. Forcible rape in the United States: A statistical profile. In D. Chappell, R. Geis, & G. Geis (Eds.), *Forcible rape: The crime, the victim, and the offender.* New York: Columbia University Press, 1977.
HOROS, C. V. *Rape.* New Canaan, Conn.: Tobey Publishing, 1974.
HOTCHKISS, S. The realities of rape. *Human Behavior,* December, 1978, pp. 18-23.
HYDE, M. O. *Speak out on rape!* New York: McGraw-Hill, 1976.
LAWS, D. R. A comparison of the measurement characteristics of two circumferential penile transducers. *Archives of Sexual Behavior,* 1977, *6,* 45-51.
LAWS, D. R. & RUBIN, H. H. Instructional control of an autonomic sexual response. *Journal of Applied Behavior Analysis,* 1969, *2,* 93-99.
MALAMUTH, N. M., HABER, S., and FESHBACH, S. Testing hypotheses regarding rape: Exposure to sexual violence, sex differences, and the "normality" of rapists. *Journal of Research in Personality,* 1980, *14,* 121-137.
MANVILLE, W. H. Mind of the rapist. *Cosmopolitan,* July 1974, pp. 74-77; 87.
MEDEA, A., & THOMPSON, K. *Against rape.* New York: Farrar, Straus and Giroux, 1974.
NETER, J., & WASSERMAN, W. *Applied linear statistical models.* Homewood, Ill.: Richard D. Irwin, 1974.
Queen's Bench Foundation. *Rape: Prevention and resistance.* San Francisco: Author, 1976.
RADA, R. T. Commonly asked questions about the rapist. *Medical Aspects of Human Sexuality,* January 1977, pp. 47; 51-53; 56.
RADA, R. T. (Ed.) *Clinical aspects of the rapist.* New York: Grune & Stratton, 1978.
RADER, C. MMPI profile types of exposers, rapists, and assaulters in a court services population. *Journal of Consulting and Clinical Psychology,* 1977, *45,* 61-69.
ROBIN, G. D. Forcible rape: Institutionalized sexism in the criminal justice system. *Crime and Delinquency,* 1977, *23,* 136-153.
RUSSELL, D. *The politics of rape: The victim's perspective.* New York: Stein & Day, 1975.
RYAN, W. *Blaming the victim.* New York: Pantheon, 1974.
SCHULTZ, T. Rape, fear, and the law. *The Chicago Guide,* November 1972, pp. 56-62.
SELKIN, J. Rape. *Psychology Today,* January 1975, pp. 71-76.
STORASKA, F. *How to say no to a rapist and survive.* New York: Random House, 1975.
WEIS, K., & BORGES, S. S. Victimology and rape: The case of the legitimate victim. *Issues in Criminology,* 1973, *8,* 71-115.

8

Training Police Officers to Intervene in Domestic Violence

Donald G. Dutton

Introduction and Background to Interpersonal Conflict-Management Training

When Robert Peel presented his "Bill for improving Police in and near the Metropolis" to the British parliament in 1829, he faced considerable opposition, based somewhat on fear that the notorious activities of the pre-Revolutionary French police would be duplicated in England. Indeed, a parliamentary report in 1818 recommended against the establishment of a police force, arguing that rational and humane laws, an enlightened magistracy, and "above all, the moral habits and opinions of the people" (Reith, 1938) were sufficient to ensure both the maintenance of order and protection of individual rights.

Peel's strategy for countering such opposition was to present a modified proposal (he initially wanted a national police force), buttressed by impressive data on increases in criminal committals, for a force to *preserve the public order*. The initial emphasis, therefore, was on the police force's function of maintaining peace, rather than on its "law enforcement" function. To this day, order maintenance and service functions comprise over 80% of a police officer's time, while law enforcement duties take up only about 10-15% (Wilson, 1969).

173

Despite the historical antecedents and present-day realities, the emphasis of police department training, policy, orientation, and data collection is on the law enforcement aspect of the police role, perhaps because this aspect lends itself more readily to the collection of statistics which can be used to demonstrate police productivity. Since 1966, however, most major police departments in North America have begun to shift from the traditional, authoritarian, law-enforcement-oriented police model toward a more expanded, professional, service-oriented conceptualization of the police role. One of the catalysts (and consequences) of this shift has been an increasing emphasis on the responsibility of the police in the area known as "conflict management." This term applies, in its narrowest sense, to the management of domestic disputes between persons connected through either affection or housing location or both, and in its broadest sense, to the entire range of conflict situations which occur where two citizens experience a conflict of interest (real or imagined), such as in landlord-tenant disputes or merchant-customer disputes.

In a sense, conflict-management situations straddle the police responses of order maintenance and law enforcement. Initially, it is usually unclear to a police officer answering a neighborhood conflict call whether or not there is evidence of a clear-cut violation of a well-defined law which would require the arrest of an offending citizen or a need to resolve and pacify the heated emotions of two or more angry citizens and to provide them with a strategy for living that should minimize the recurrence of the conflict. Conflict-management training is designed to improve a police officer's ability to judiciously distinguish between these two situations and to efficiently take either course of action. In a sense, it attempts to broaden the repertoire of trained responses which that officer is capable of making. Prior to 1966 no police departments in North America provided special training in conflict-management techniques (Liebman & Schwartz, 1972); by 1969 almost every large department in North America (and many smaller ones) provided such training.

It is a rare police officer who has not experienced many conflict-management situations, even in the narrow "domestic dispute" sense. In a city the size of Vancouver, British Columbia, with a population of approximately 400,000, an average of 283 domestic dispute calls per week were recorded in 1975 (Levens & Dutton, 1977, p. 29). Obviously, the public expects police intervention in such disputes (for reasons we will explore below), yet special training to enable police to provide such service has been a late arrival in police colleges. In part, this discrepancy can be traced to extreme reluctance by police with a traditional law enforcement orientation to get involved in domestic disputes. Only 53.8% of the domestic dispute calls in Vancouver received police service, and the majority of these dispatches were on a priority II basis (Levens & Dutton, 1972).

The successful implementation of a crisis-management training program requires a thorough understanding of the sources of such resistance to becoming involved in "family fights." As a prerequisite for effective attitude change among recruits, experienced officers, and management personnel, all such resistances must be met squarely and openly in the training program and at the organizational level. Failure to do so results in a "public relations" response to crisis intervention: The department halfheartedly supports it at the training level, and policy directives on crisis intervention get sabotaged at the mid-management level, blocking effective change in the implementation of new policies. In the following section the sources of such resistances are examined.

A variety of conflict-management training models exist for police. These have been reviewed elsewhere (Levens, 1978a) and will not be described in detail here. Some cities, such as London, Ontario and Regina, Saskatchewan, have emergency specialists who handle domestic crisis calls. Vancouver has a "Car 86" which performs a similar service. Such special "flying squads" usually operate on a 24-hour basis and provide a special coordinated police-social service resource for their respective communities. However, smaller communities can rarely afford such a special service, and in larger communities, such as Vancouver, family dispute calls are so frequent and come from so many areas of the city that one special flying squad can rarely cover them all. The "generalist" model of police training whereby each and every police officer is trained to a minimum standard in conflict-management skills is generally considered to be the most workable. Levens (1978a) reports that of 21 police departments in the U.S. and Canada who reported on their conflict-management training systems, 17 had opted for the generalist approach. For these reasons we will emphasize in this prescriptive package the generalist training model, with only passing comment on the specialist models used elsewhere.

"RESISTANCE" TO FAMILY CRISIS INTERVENTION PROGRAMS

Police resistance to a full-service commitment in domestic disputes comes from three main sources: a) job-related beliefs, values, and attitudes of police officers; b) bureaucratic-managerial resistances within the force; c) general societal beliefs, values, and attitudes. In establishing a new training program for police officers in domestic conflict management, special attention must be paid to changing (a) and (b) and at least making officers aware of (c).

General Job-related Resistances

Probably the most difficult officer to "reach" within a conflict-management program is the traditional, authoritarian officer who has done his job a certain way for a number of years and whose personal experience has forged a focus on "how to do police work" that is fixed as if it were set in concrete. To this officer, family dispute calls are viewed extremely negatively, as a type of "no-win" situation where any response short of arrest or cooling down the situation and giving a warning is a waste of time and not police work. This officer defines his job through what he is doing rather than through the goal or objective of his work. Hence, sitting in a private home interviewing, mediating, or making a referral to a social agency is considered "social work," not police work, which is seen as being in the cruiser, on patrol, waiting to respond to a crime call. This is the "on the surface" response of the traditional police officer. Just below the surface are a variety of reasons why such an officer resists changes in his approach to handling family dispute calls:

1) The calls do not fall under the general area of street policing—the officer is literally on "someone else's turf" where he feels a little uneasy. Rights of entry can present potential legal problems; even when this is not an issue, being in someone else's home subtly shifts the power balance from the officer to the homeowner, an uncomfortable shift for the traditional officer who is used to dealing from a position of power.
2) Such calls often involve emotionally upset people, which many officers find discomfiting and somewhat embarrassing, especially when personal emotional material is used as a weapon in a verbal dispute between intimates.
3) In many cases, the dispute strikes the officer, either consciously or not, as being similar to a personal dispute he may have had or be having with his own spouse. To the extent that the similarity is not conscious, it can create problems for the officer both in his inability to maintain neutrality in the present dispute and in the aggravation of his own domestic problem.

4) Untrained officers have no feelings of control in family disputes. Their only perceived control in the situation is the use of authority and toughness, but this often backfires, leading to violence that is touched off by the officer's own behavior (Bard, 1971). In other words, the rules that work for the officer in the street often backfire in a family dispute, and, if untrained, the officer has not yet learned a new set of workable rules or alternative sources of control in a situation.

5) Untrained officers have no feelings of accomplishment in family disputes. Improperly handled disputes lead to high recidivism rates. When police are called back to the same address time after time, a feeling of futility sets in. While some of these families may be locked into a chronic fight pattern, many others can be dealt with more successfully by trained police. In addition, many departments try to change policy on family dispute handling through training alone, without an accompanying change in the departmental reward system, so that correct application by the officer of the proper intervention procedures goes unrecognized and unrewarded. Police department reward criteria continue to support the traditional police role. The end result may be that training effects are lost.

6) Effective family dispute intervention requires some interpersonal sensitivity and verbal skills, both of which traditional police avoid. Yet no one could argue that a police officer's general performance on the job would not improve through the acquisition of either skill.

7) Police feel that laying of charges in a family assault is futile because the injured party (usually the woman) will not carry through on the charges after the crisis has passed. Yet alternative means of clearing the call are, by some twist of logic, similarly resisted. Police "gripes" about the lack of achievement they feel handling domestic disputes have some basis in departmental policies, rewards, etc.; yet these gripes are often not heard about similarly unrewarding parts of the more traditional police role, leading one to infer that they are in part a resistance to role change per se.

8) Probably no other aspect of police work straddles the tightrope between police law enforcement responses (if an assault is occurring police are expected to act with dispatch, power and authority) and order maintenance (in a delicate emotional crisis police are expected to be wise, good at communicating, and capable of effecting a resolution). To an extent, these two responses are somewhat antagonistic and incompatible. Consequently, a police officer answering a family dispute call is put in a sort of "double-bind" situation: He can make

a mistake by going too far in either direction (if too tough, he can trigger violence; if too soft, he can fail to contain it). Often police officers enter a family dispute situation without knowing which response will be required of them. This tightrope situation contributes greatly to the tension the officer feels in such situations. The training procedures described below attempt to remedy this dilemma by teaching police how to maximize their information about a dispute in progress prior to entry (Dutton, 1977).

The net effect of the points above is to create in the untrained officer a feeling of anxiety, lack of control, unease, and futility in handling family dispute calls. Each and every training session must deal openly with all of these resistances, as well as with any others that officers volunteer in an "open forum" type of atmosphere. Failure to do so simply leads to officers' keeping their negative feelings to themselves but passively resisting the skills, insights, and perspectives offered in the training workshop.

Managerial-bureaucratic Resistances

Even if general job-related resistances are dealt with in the training workshop, an effective family dispute program can be adversely affected by managerial-bureaucratic resistances to full implementation of such a program, as our own research seems to suggest.

An attitude survey of trained and untrained officers provides considerable evidence for the success of the training program in changing police perceptions, attitudes, and behaviors in family dispute situations (Dutton & Levens, 1977). Trained recruits were more likely to negotiate settlements of conflicts or to make referrals to outside agencies, were more satisfied both with their training for family disputes and their accomplishments in handling disputes, reported less violence toward them, less use of force after training, and greater citizen receptivity and satisfaction with their performance (as compared to pretraining experience). These results held for trained recruits up to seven months after graduating from training. (Longer time periods were not tested.) Hence, the results of the training per se appear quite positive. However, a follow-up study on departmental procedures for handling family disputes revealed little change from pretraining indices (Levens, 1978b; Levens & Dutton, 1977). While trained teams used referral to social agencies more than untrained teams and no police officer was injured handling a family dispute during the three-year period since the inception of the training, there was, until the end of the project, no change in the unsatisfactory screening of requests for service at the police switchboard, no change in departmental recognition of exemplary service by officers in handling disputes, and no change in the somewhat inconsistent application of priority codes assigned to domestic disputes.

What this pattern of data suggests is that the Vancouver training project succeeded, but that necessary bureaucratic changes in the Vancouver Police Department did not take place. This pinpoints a crucial problem in that personnel in charge of training rarely are in a position to bring about change in departmental policy; yet if these changes do not occur, much of what has been gained through innovative training techniques is eventually lost as new recruits are "resocialized" into the old traditional procedures. It is not that there was total "above-the-line-officer" resistance in the Vancouver project; indeed, it had full support from the Deputy Chief of the Vancouver Police Department and many of the Chief Inspectors. Rather, the failure was more related to middle-management resistance to the program, as has been fully documented elsewhere (Bard, 1975; Driscoll, Meyer, & Schanie, 1973; Katz, 1973).

Innovative programs such as family crisis intervention, if set up outside the formal chain of command, function to exclude members of the middle-management force from the planning stages (Bard, 1973). When the program reaches the implementation stage, that initial exclusion comes back to haunt those attempting to carry out the program, as the middle management, feeling deprived of control, takes little interest in the support or reinforcement of the program.

Bennett-Sandler (1975) has analyzed a variety of bureaucratic resistances to innovative programs in police departments. Her conclusion is that such efforts "cannot be appended to police organizations; rather, they must be assimilated into these organizations. That is, they must be examined for their philosophical and behavioral implications and then reinforced at every point in the organizational structure" (Bennett-Sandler, 1975).

Bennett-Sandler maintains that the management of innovation in police departments requires a number of steps:

1) analysis of the philosophical and behavioral goals and implications of the program;
2) analysis of the existing organization and its consistency with the program;
3) analysis of key points of resistance and blockages within the organization;

4) introduction of necessary organizational supports for the program.

For example, crisis intervention implies a police model whereby an officer's authority derives more from his interpersonal skills than from his possession of the legitimate use of force. This human-relations/community-relations model of a police officer represents a radical philosophical shift from a procedure-oriented, authoritarian/military model. To the extent that these basic philosophical differences are not resolved, Bennett-Sandler suggests, innovative programs will fail.

She further argues that existing paramilitary police organizations, while serving certain functions, are dysfunctional in that they lead to cynicism (due to what is perceived as arbitrary decisions by superiors) and demoralization (due to lack of participation in major decisions by those further down the hierarchy, plus a one-way direction of communication which makes the airing of grievances unlikely). The end result in such organizations can be the sabotaging of change efforts as a means of "getting even" and restoring one's personal sense of power within the organization.

In addition, paramilitary police organizations tend to emphasize procedures and productivity, which maintains a focus on the law-enforcement aspect of police work, the quantitative approach to performance evaluation with its heavy emphasis on arrest and summons, and the use of crime statistics as a measure of police effectiveness. Such structural factors preclude a reward system that is unrelated to arrest and interfere with the requirements of crisis-intervention programs.

Furthermore, specific mid-management resistances exist. Mid-managers are evaluated almost exclusively on the productivity of their commands. When productivity is traditionally defined, they are not likely to feel comfortable with programs such as crisis intervention which, at first glance, appear to reduce productivity. At the same time, middle managers have been socialized into a value system which may make them skeptical of the feasibility and appropriateness of crisis-management activities.

In addition, patrol supervisors who receive policy from middle managers, along with a mixed message as to its feasibility, may represent a second line of resistance due to similar pressures. Because patrol supervisors control officers' performance evaluations and recommendations for promotion, their lack of support is a major obstacle to implementation. Officers take their cues from patrol supervisors and act accordingly. Lacking organizational support, officers are unlikely to give crisis intervention a top priority. This leads to situations in which aspects of the job requiring crisis-management skills are relegated to a low status and fobbed off on "special units" or women officers, or split off in some other way from the "main function" of policing (i.e., law enforcement). Studies in New York and San Francisco (Levens, 1978a) support Bennett-Sandler's contention: In both cities police members of special squads were harassed by other police because they were not doing police work. Failure to align the philosophy of the department and the new program completely undercut the innovation. This is another reason why the present training program takes a generalist approach.

Societal Resistances to Family Crisis Intervention

Apart from the job-related resistances of officers and bureaucratic resistances within police organizations to family crisis intervention programs, there are some more basic or fundamental societal attitudes that are important to note. Police deal with the public in executing their duties, they are drawn from the public, and they carry with them into service these same societal attitudes. The three broad categories of attitudinal resistance to be examined here are: 1) attitudes toward violence; 2) male attitudes toward women; and 3) attitudes toward interference with violence between spouses.

Public attitudes toward violence. The work of both clinicians (Bach & Goldberg, 1975) and researchers (Steinmetz & Straus, 1974; Straus, 1977) points to the extremely high rate of violence between intimates. Although between 33-50% of homicides occur between intimates, there has been great reluctance on the part of the public to recognize this problem. In part this stems from the public's desire to think of violence as being committed by criminals—"bad people" who are viewed as being different from the public themselves. While there is no doubt that violence-prone individuals do exist, most homicides, especially domestic homicides, are committed by people who have no other criminal records for violent crime ("Domestic violence and the police," 1977). Thus, the citizen's belief that violent crime is only committed by people who are "different" from himself allows him to ignore his own potential for violence. Acknowledging domestic violence as a problem breaks down the distinction between criminal and upstanding middle-class citizen and forces us to look at the violence potential of intimate relationships —something we find very uncomfortable. Yet, a majority of North American men endorse violence as a means to an end (Bugenthal et al., 1972) and over one-third of "happily married" couples reported physical fights in a one-year period prior to a survey (Straus, 1977).

Male attitudes toward women. Although our society is currently undergoing a change in the status of women and male attitudes toward women, old attitudes linger. In England in March 1891 (Crown vs. Jackson), it was ruled that a husband no longer had the right to beat his wife, and a contemporary journal anguished that "marriage as an institution has ceased to exist in England." To the extent that women are regarded as possessions or objects, males will feel more justified in physically attacking them as a means of control. In 1975 a judge in Scotland told a husband who had punched his wife in the face: "It is a well-known fact that you can strike your wife's bottom if you wish, but you must not strike her on the face. I believe that reasonable chastisement should be the duty of every husband if his wife misbehaves" (Nicholls, 1978).

In British Columbia in November 1977, in a domestic case involving threats with a knife, property damage, and the forcible seizure of a 23-year-old woman, a provincial court judge was reported as saying regarding the women victims and witnesses: "They got scared because he was proving himself a macho man, was going to have one of them out and talk to her even if she got scared and ran back into the bedroom. So we've got a bunch of clucking females running around and they're all so scared that they have to call the police." And on another occasion in the same trial: "You know, women don't get much brains before they're 30 anyway" ("Reporting the comments," 1977).

The male attitude that violence toward women is justified as a means of control underlies the widespread incidence of domestic violence. Additionally, recent studies show increases in middle-class violence as males feel they are losing power to females and resort to violence in a desperate attempt to gain control (Whitehurst, 1974). These attitudes also sometimes result in violence in immigrant families where the male adheres to the older, traditional, male-dominant values and the females (spouses and daughters) opt for the more egalitarian values of the "new land."

Attitudes toward interference with violence directed at spouses. There is general public reluctance to interfere in domestic conflicts, and the police may reflect this attitude. A recent study (Shotland & Straw, 1976), in which staged man-woman fights were used to study the likelihood that witnesses would intervene, found that 69% did so when they believed the fight was between strangers, but only 19% intervened when an identical fight was believed to be between spouses. Witnesses were interviewed later and reported that if they perceived the man attacking the woman to be her husband, they believed her to be in less danger, less likely to want help, and less likely to help them fight off the man; the man was seen as more likely to put up a fight. Hence, the same assault was seen as less severe when occurring between spouses.

These traditional attitudes have, for a long time, stood in the way of effective family dispute intervention. However, evidence of change comes from the pressures and political stance of many women's groups in North America. A class action brought against the New York Police Department by the Litigation Coalition for Battered Women resulted in an agreement by the Department to arrest a man for felonious assault against his wife if there were reasonable cause to believe it had occurred ("New spouse abuse," 1978). In other words, the thrust of this movement is to treat an assault as an assault regardless of the relationship between the parties. It is important for police who have to deal with the public on a daily basis to be aware of these public attitudes.

REASONS FOR FAMILY CRISIS INTERVENTION PROGRAMS

Public Demand

Given all the sources of resistance outlined above, what are the reasons for police crisis intervention? First and foremost is public demand. In family disputes, especially where the use of force is a possibility, there is only one agency available on a 24-hour basis with an excellent response time and the legal authority to remove an offending party if need be. Most calls for police intervention come at a time when other agencies are closed (Levens & Dutton, 1977), and even if a "special flying squad" exists, it is rarely able to cover all requests for service of a domestic dispute nature. The police are highly visible and, given that the incidence of violence or potential violence is so high in these situations, they are the only professionals with the requisite legal authority and expertise to handle these crises.

In addition, many domestic calls originate from working-class households with families who are most likely to avoid other helping professions and any form of intervention that carries "mental health" connotations (Bard, 1969). Hence, many people feel more comfortable talking to a police officer who accepts their conflict at "face value" than to a psychologist or social worker who attempts to analyze it and discover its "deeper meaning."

Moreover, the reason for the call does not usually become clear until after the intervention has occurred, in which case, given that the police will still have to intervene, they had best be properly trained to do so.

Preventive Policing

Support for the second major reason for police domestic dispute intervention comes from a study done in Kansas City, Missouri, in 1970-71 ("Domestic violence and the police," 1977). Researchers found that 37% of the aggravated assaults were domestic assaults, and that for 90% of these police had answered at least one previous domestic crisis call from the household where the assault eventually occurred. In 48% of the cases police had intervened four or five times. Rarely did the person committing the assault have a criminal record outside the relationship. The picture that began to emerge from this study was one of a troubled relationship with frequent conflict, gradually escalating to a stage where the police are called. At that time the Kansas City Police took the standard short-term tactic of defusing the situation, issuing a warning, and leaving. We call this a "short-term" tactic because the root issue causing the conflict was not dealt with, so that the conflict reemerged later, and the police were called again to the same address, sometimes having to deal with an even more serious dispute.

This suggests that police handling domestic disputes are coming into contact with a group of people who have an extremely high likelihood of committing a violent and serious assault at a later date. The basis of conflict-management training is to teach police officers some techniques for reducing the likelihood of this future violence. Such techniques (mediation and referral to proper agencies) do not involve the criminal justice system, and, in fact, are designed to divert potentially violent people outside this system by dealing with their conflicts *before* they reach the stage of illegal physical violence.

The model of policing that is being presented here is a *preventive* one. Preventive policing suggests that, rather than simply responding to violent crime after it has been committed, the police officer takes a more active role in predicting situations where violence is likely to occur and then makes use of the totality of community resources available to reduce the likelihood of violence in the future. By contrast, the *reactive* model of policing (acting after the crime) is tantamount to shutting the barn door after the horse has escaped. The *preventive* model suggests that police can do more than this: They can, using new social science techniques for crime prediction and data analysis, assess the probability of crime occurring in various situations and reduce the violence potential by using techniques to aid the citizen in resolving the underlying conflict.

The concept of preventive policing may give rise to fears of a "police state" for many people, but the techniques of preventive policing do not involve legal system solutions, incarceration, or the use of force. They rely instead on persuasion, problem analysis, support, and understanding. To many traditional police, such techniques are the tools of social workers, not police officers. We suggest that police should define their jobs not so much through what they *do* (e.g., make arrests, patrol areas), but by the *outcomes* or *goals* of their activities (e.g., reducing the amount of violent crime in their jurisdiction). With our suggested orientation, the *means* by which they achieve this *end* can be more diverse and not as limited as a reactive model of policing would suggest. They can achieve the goal by talking to people in conflict rather than by simply making after-the-fact arrests. This kind of job definition frees the police officer from a narrowly defined, procedure-oriented role and allows entry into a more broadly based role as a professional with a wide variety of skills to offer the community.

Reduction of Violent Crime

While individual police officers differ widely in their aspirations and objectives, they tend to agree unanimously that reducing violent crime is important. Proper intervention in family disputes can serve this objective, since over half of all homicides and assaults occur in domestic situations. (In 1975 the FBI Uniform Crime Reports indicated that two-thirds of 20,510 murders studied were committed by relatives, friends, or acquaintances of the family, and over half of these involved a spouse killing a spouse.) Statistics Canada (Homicide Statistics 1977, 1978) reports that in 1977, for Canada as a whole, 32% of homicides were domestic (meaning immediate family) and another 33% of homicides resulted from lovers' quarrels, love triangles, fights between close or casual acquaintances or between people in business relationships—in other words, precisely the kind of situation the police are called upon to attend. By dealing effectively and efficiently with domestic disputes at an *early* stage of conflict, police can take some important steps toward realizing their objective.

A few further statistics help to underscore the enormity of this social problem: There are more domestic homicides in New York City in one year than there have been people killed in the violence in Northern Ireland in the last decade. The chances of being assaulted in the home by one's spouse are higher than those of a police officer being assaulted on the job (Straus, 1977; Kelley, 1975). Based on a representative sample of 2,143 couples in the U.S., Straus concluded that, even with underreporting, 28% had committed assault—one partner against the other. Extrapolated to the national population, this would mean 13 million couples committing at least one act of physical aggression. In North American and Western European cities, the percentage of all homicides that involve family members killing each other is about 40%.

These data often seem startling and surprising in a society that systematically downplays the seriousness of domestic violence as a social problem. As I have suggested elsewhere (Dutton, 1979), the fact that domestic violence is both literally and figuratively close to home prevents the average citizen from easily claiming that it was performed by a sinister "criminal element," as is the case with street crime. The "we-they" distinctions break down when a domestic assault is committed by an average upstanding citizen with no other record of violence outside the home. Yet the central characteristic of domestic violence is that it is mundane, occurring through all age groups, educational levels, socioeconomic classes, and geographic areas (Levens & Dutton, 1977; Straus, 1973, 1977; Whitehurst, 1974). Indeed, systematic examination of the many factors contributing to domestic violence reveals not only personality traits and family structural factors which may be particular to some families, but values, beliefs, and attitudes common to most North American men, such as acceptance of violence as a means of control (Bugenthal, Kahn, Andrews, & Head, 1972; Straus, 1973) and societal variables which affect us all (Straus, 1973, 1976, 1977).

Less Police Time in Repeat Calls

The Kansas City study and others (Fagin, 1976) suggest another more pragmatic, less far-reaching payoff for effective family dispute intervention. If mere short-term solutions are used in early interventions by police, much police time can be spent on repeat calls. Even police administrators who adhere to a more traditional concept of policing must realize that in the long run effective intervention training can result in more permanent solutions to family conflicts and less drain on police time spent on such repeat calls.

Safety

Proper training also reduces the likelihood of violence, perceived violence, and injuries to police officers sustained during the dispute intervention. Several studies cite the danger of family disputes for officers (Bard, 1971; Barocas, 1973; Coffey, 1974). Twenty percent of patrolmen who are killed on duty in the U. S. are killed handling a family dispute, and more injuries are sustained in family disputes than in any other category of police activity. "Not only is the interpersonal conflict situation a difficult one to handle from the standpoint of the intensity, intimacy and complexity of the social relationship; frequently the difficulty is compounded by the police themselves, who through the use of traditional methods of intervention become the catalytic element which escalates a verbal battle into a physically abusive fracas, and too often redirects the intra-marital violence towards the intervening officer" (Levens, 1978a, p. 216). The decreased likelihood of police injury and violence being directed towards police officers as a result of proper dispute intervention training (Bard, 1971; Dutton & Levens, 1977; "Domestic violence and the police," 1977) is a sufficient reason for instituting that training for all officers.

To sum up, police involvement in domestic disputes is as much a part of their existence as order maintenance and law enforcement efforts. It is, in fact, inappropriate to enlist surrogate agents to handle these situations when the potential for violence and law violation is so great. As unattractive as this aspect of their role may be to many officers, it is a legitimate police activity. What domestic crisis intervention training can do is reduce the time consumed by such calls, provide the officer with a more professional, efficient, and effective selection of techniques with which to handle the problems safely, and give the promise, through the employment of good diversionary and preventive tactics, of lessening the level of violence in the community.

HOW TO ESTABLISH A FAMILY CRISIS INTERVENTION TRAINING WORKSHOP

Types of Programs

The first step in establishing family crisis intervention training for police is to determine what kind of training is desired. Do we want to train a small group of police officers with good verbal skills as a special squad for handling family calls or do we want to train everybody? Do we want procedural training that gives police a set of procedures to use or do we want attitudinal training that is oriented toward personal growth? Fortunately, all these varieties have been tried by other researchers, so use can be made of their experiences.

Bard (1973) trained the New York Police Department using a specialist-attitudinal model based on the notion of changing officers' personal attitudes through insights obtained in the workshop sessions. Liebman and Schwartz (1972), however, point out that such training took 160 hours to accomplish, could not be assimilated into the recruit training program, resulted in a small group of trained specialists (18 men) who could handle only a small percentage of family calls, increased the amount of time spent on one call, created a "dependency" relationship with families whereby police would be called back in a social work capacity whenever future conflicts arose, and resulted in more referrals (three-fourths of all domestic calls) than social agencies could handle.

Liebman and Schwartz are also not enthusiastic about the use of non-police professionals—psychologists or social workers who accompany police on family dispute calls (as happens in London, Ontario, and Surrey, B.C.). They point out that such special squads cannot answer a large proportion of calls in big cities, they are expensive (since they require both psychologists and police on all calls—the police are still necessary in case a legal problem arises), and often police acceptance of other professionals is low because of differing philosophies and because the mental health professionals lack knowledge about the criminal justice system. If the mental health professional is good, much better service is provided than the average officer is capable of providing in such situations.

The generalist-procedural approach which Liebman and Schwartz used in Richmond, California, has been used in a variety of other departments (for a review, see Levens, 1978a). The advantages of such a generalist-procedural training program are varied: It is geared to train entire departments, so that any police officer handling any domestic problem has the requisite skills to do a good job. The procedural emphasis establishes a training system that fits quite well into other police training—providing a set of concrete skills and/or procedures for domestic disputes to which trainees are usually receptive. Police trainees are usually extremely practical and want concrete specific steps to take when confronted with situations they are being trained to handle. Procedural training is less likely than attitudinal training to meet resistance for being too "social work" oriented. Procedural training requires fewer hours in class and is thus better suited to in-service training, which is extremely important. (Experienced officers must not be led to feel resentful or jealous of new training techniques that only new recruits are getting, as this training can be important in reducing discrepant perspectives between recruits and experienced officers and can remove one source of resistance to innovative programs.) Generalist training minimizes the use of outside consultants. Psychologists are necessary only to help establish the training program, although they may be used to actually do some training or to train police trainers (see below).

Providing concrete procedures for police training can be a "thin edge of the wedge" for subsequent attitude change. Officers who learn how to effectively handle a domestic dispute will feel greater control and less apprehension about this type of work (Dutton & Levens, 1977). This can be used as a basis for subsequent further expansion of the police role and repertoire of skills, as long as it is supported by appropriate departmental policy (see next section). Generalist training is the only type of training that does not attempt to set family dispute intervention apart from regular police work, but confronts the reality that every police officer will at various times in his/her career be called upon to handle such calls. Hence, it is the only type of training that does not simply try to append a family crisis intervention program to existing police practice but challenges every officer who takes the program to define his/her proper role as a police officer. Thus, for police departments interested in moving towards police professionalism, the generalist training can serve as a vehicle for forcing trainees to think about their personal attitudes toward their jobs in a traditional-professional dimension.

The Training Package

In British Columbia we did our recruit training for family dispute intervention in a six-day package that not only touched on a variety of issues related to dispute intervention but also provided a concrete six-step procedure for handling disputes. The entire syllabus is outlined below. We kept lecturing to a minimum and used trainee participation, role-playing, videotapes, and simulations as much as possible to maximize learning in such a short time (36 hours). The training was procedure-oriented in that the behavioral objectives required demonstrated mastery of the intervention techniques (outside safety, interior safety, defusing, interviewing, mediation, and referral). Each step was presented via course notes and videotapes, which presented incorrect procedures followed by correct procedures. In addition, practice sessions were held which allowed for consolidation of one particular procedural step before moving on to the next step. As each new step was learned, old ones were reviewed, so that recruits gradually built a sequenced repertoire of skills. Also, maximum opportunity for practice occurred.

These procedures were the "core" of the dispute intervention workshop. All the theoretical material used related to them in obvious ways. This material included subjects for discussion and answers to many types of questions, such as:

1) Overview of domestic crisis intervention: Who calls the police and why? What do the police do? What are the resistances police have to family crisis calls? Why should such calls be police business?
2) Theory of domestic violence: What is the incidence and seriousness of domestic violence? Why does violence occur between intimates?
3) How can your personal attitudes or your own relationship with your spouse affect your handling of domestic calls?
4) What are the sources of stress for police on domestic calls? How can you reduce them? What are realistic expectations for a successful intervention?
5) What constitutes child abuse? What should you look for if you suspect child abuse? What should you do?
6) What special crisis intervention problems occur with minority communities (local ethnic, racial, and sexual minorities)? How do your attitudes affect your handling such calls?
7) What community resources exist to help you with crisis intervention? How can you find out more about such resources? How can you establish working relationships with other professionals? What do you expect from them? What do they expect from you? How do your differing philosophies affect your relationship?
8) What do you expect of your job as a police officer? What are your goals? What makes you feel like you have done a good job? How does crisis intervention relate to your goals as a police officer?
9) What can you reasonably expect from this course? What can it do or not do for you?

As can be seen from the above, although the core course is procedural, the entire workshop goes far beyond role or skill training. We found that the skill training was wanted by trainees, made the whole training package palatable, and integrated the program with the rest of their police training. It also could be used as the foot in the door to get recruits to explore many of the important attitudinal issues presented in the questions above.

The Course

The first morning is of extreme importance in dealing with trainee resistances and setting the rationale for the remainder of the workshop. After the introduction of the entire teaching team (preferably by the police college director or another police college person who has good credibility with the trainees) and a few statements about family crisis calls, we begin by drawing out the trainees' feelings, perceptions, etc., when they have handled family crisis calls during their field training. By demonstrating acceptance and understanding of any negative feelings which arise, an open forum atmosphere is established and receptiveness to the content of the workshop is increased. We usually facilitate this by expressing, as we understand it, police reluctance to handle family calls. We present this in the strongest way possible, often to the point of astonishing some trainees with our frankness and willingness to put out a strong position that appears to run counter to the goals of our workshop. Attitude change studies done at Yale University after World War II (Hovland, Janis, & Kelley, 1953) demonstrated that speakers facing audiences unsympathetic to their position can elicit more attitude change by making opening statements which agree with the audience's position than by ignoring or opposing that position.

It is also important on the first morning to probe for resistances among the recruits. Who is not saying anything? Why? Who is smirking and making asides? Who subtly shakes his/her head in disbelief at something said? It is important both not to leave these signs of resistance unprobed and not to appear to be bullying or "centering out" a trainee. Three qualities essential for the first morning are honesty, sensitivity, and a sense of humor (in addition to a clear presentation of the argument for police intervention).

The first morning works through three major sets of questions: 1) The Course Rationale—this is developed by answering the four questions listed as "rationale for workshop" in the syllabus; 2) Theory of Domestic Violence—addressed by the findings on incidence, reasons for, and causes of violence; and 3) Course Goals—an outline of the objectives of the program. To a certain extent we have answered these questions in Sections 2 and 3 of this prescriptive package. By combining those sections with the original materials (e.g., the Police Foundation Study, available on request), an instructor can develop his/her own materials for this part of the workshop. The second set of questions around a theory of domestic violence probably requires the aid of a psychologist-consultant, preferably one who is skilled and experienced in couple counseling, crisis intervention, and development of teaching programs. Contacting the educational psychology faculty at your local university can be a first step toward locating such a person.

We wind up our first morning session by clearly stating and explaining the goals and objectives of the course.* In this way recruits know exactly what we expect of them and we ask them what they expect of us—what they want to get from the course. Grading systems are discussed (we use written short-answer tests daily, a written exam on knowledge of procedures, and a behavioral check list to grade their performance during simulated crisis calls).

The procedural steps are all tough, and throughout the training we use essentially the same technique. First, we review the course notes with recruits. Then they observe a videotape we have made to demonstrate correct or incorrect procedures for that particular step of the intervention. We show the incorrect procedures once (straight through without stopping, asking trainees to point out the mistakes they see being made); then we go over it again with the built-in stop action on the tape. This stops the tape at a crucial feature and allows us to point out the subtle differences in technique that can have profound effects on the outcome of the intervention. This is particularly useful for interior safety and defusing where we teach recruits about proxemics, personal spacing, and nonverbal communication. The tapes allow us to demonstrate the origin and development of iatrogenic violence (caused by the specific behavior of the police officers).

Correct and incorrect procedure tapes often start with similar or identical situations so that trainees can see how the outcome diverges through police handling. The videotapes, in other words, are a crucial aspect of the total learning experience and can be properly constructed so as to aid learning at several different levels.

Day II of the course begins with training in communication skills and interview techniques. This section of the course is more difficult for the average trainee to grasp, especially if he/she is young and lacking in self-confidence and general verbal ability. However, if properly handled, even such a trainee will gradually establish some basic skills in this area. We use demonstration of overbearing communications (where one party totally controls the situation and does not give the other a chance to speak) and indirect communication (where the parties do not clearly communicate what they want and do not take responsibility for their

---

*It is important to distinguish between dispute calls where no assault has occurred, for which the present techniques are applicable, and those where an assault has occurred, where arrest and evidence-collection procedures are applicable.

own statements). These are presented in a general assertiveness training format.

The interviewing and communication skills section of the intervention procedures is one area where, in addition to teaching skills, we probe trainees' attitudes. One way to get trainees to do this is to make it clear to them that to the extent they are unaware of their own attitudes they will be susceptible to manipulation by citizens who play out a variety of "games" with them. We stress that we are not going to criticize them for their attitudes but simply show them how a particular attitude could interfere with their performance. Open-ended requests to "explore feelings" do not get very far in a police college atmosphere. Starting with a *procedure*, showing the *games* that people play to throw officers off the track, and then showing how their own *attitudes* can unconsciously put them into the hands of a manipulative citizen provides a rationale and basis for some attitudinal exploration that trainees would not otherwise risk. These "games" are described in more detail in our course notes, so trainees have handy access to their description.

Each procedural step is presented as a type of "tightrope" where an officer can err by going too far in either direction (e.g., being overbearing can make an upset citizen feel invaded, but being unassertive can cost an officer control of a situation). We also cover: adaptation to the dark, "sitting duck" moves, proper positioning inside a house, personal spacing, ordering confrontation techniques from light to heavy, appropriate force, legal rights, psychology of the citizens in these situations, establishing rapport in interviewing techniques for maintaining control, general theory of conflict management, listening responses, paraphrasing, perception checks, open-ended questions, mediation techniques, neutrality, argument or fight styles, fair-fight techniques, "edge of the wedge" questions for referrals, specific procedural techniques, and examples for each of the six procedural steps.

In the afternoon of Day II we continue with mediation techniques. Here the police officer serves as a conflict reducer by remaining neutral and attempting to bring parties in conflict closer together. Usually, in family conflicts people attempt to convince friends and relatives that they are the "wronged" party in a dispute. To the extent that each party wins support from well-meaning friends, he/she will become more convinced than ever that he/she is right and therefore will become more polarized from the other conflicting party. The long-term result is that the parties are less likely than ever to resolve their conflict. By remaining neutral and not feeding into either party's personal version of reality, intervening officers can alter this process.

At the same time, by modeling communication techniques for citizens, the officer serves a teaching function as well. Our approach to mediation is that officers never offer solutions to citizens (solutions "imposed" from without rarely are followed); rather they help citizens to arrive at their own solution to the conflict. This returns the responsibility for conflict resolution to the citizen.

Some disputes (especially between spouses) require long-term solutions and are not amenable to mediation. On the morning of the third day recruits are taught how to refer citizens to social agencies in such a way that the likelihood of the citizen following through on the long-term counseling significantly increases. Procedures involve foot-in-the-door questions to elicit agreement from citizens that they do have a problem, don't want it to continue, and would be agreeable to some free help with the problem.

Both mediation and referral techniques pay special attention to the "politics of intervention," the importance of neutrality from both a psychological point of view and the point of view of what will maximize the outcome of the intervention for police and citizens. Referral techniques are followed in the workshop by a session on social agencies that teaches trainees how to find out what resources their own community has to support them on crisis calls. These resources can vary from a complete agency directory (as in Vancouver) to a parish priest (in a small town). We also teach trainees how to establish working relationships with people in agencies and what realistically to expect in the way of support and follow-up.

Day IV is devoted entirely to an understanding of the origin and dynamics of prejudice and discrimination, and to the particular nature of police prejudice and prejudice toward (or against) the police. Two experimental exercises are used as additions to the lecture. One of these is a technique for exploring prejudice with people; the other subdivides the entire group into two groups (colored t-shirts can be used to facilitate this process) and provides each group with a task to perform. Game rules can be altered so that the groups come into conflict or a power imbalance occurs, and the resulting experiences can serve as a basis for discussion.

In addition, we brief police on their own prejudices (established partially through an exercise of handling domestic calls and partially via an independent assessment) and show them how their job often precludes contact with minority groups except under circumstances where the group looks "bad." With a lack of self-correcting contact, prejudice can be established. We have, from time to time, invited representatives of various minority communities to visit a trainee class. The results of this endeavor have been mixed. On some occasions exceptional "break-throughs" in terms of insight into reciprocal stereotypes have occurred; at other times the results have been counterproductive, especially with representatives of the gay community who received considerable hostility from trainees and became increasingly defensive. This section of the course pays special attention to police intervention in family disputes in minority communities, stressing family power structure, background information on the group, and special cultural rules that the police should know.

Day V continues with two further "special" topics. Child abuse can be discovered by police in the course of handling a family dispute call. We teach police to look for specific injuries to children and what to do if they suspect child abuse. Usually a representative of the child abuse team from the Child Welfare Department provides material for this section.

Finally, we conclude with a discussion of legal issues, in which we establish for police their legal rights in entering a premises if they suspect an assault, what they must do to enter, according to the law, and how they should give evidence in court. We include some test cross-examinations in this section to simulate court procedures.

We conclude the course with a review and overview, including an analysis of what the course is likely to do for the trainees in handling real disputes. These data are based on an evaluation of the course's impact on police in real disputes. This is done in order to give trainees as realistic a set of expectations as possible about what the course impact will be on them and what their goals should be in dispute intervention. Unrealistic or unattainable goals can be a source of stress. We attempt to alleviate this situation by presenting a more realistic set of goals.

Simulations on the final day provide both an evaluation and a practice opportunity. These two functions, it should be pointed out, are somewhat contradictory from a pedagogic point of view, and trainers may want to place more emphasis on one than the other.

Teams of trainees take part in a variety of dispute scenarios, written so as to elicit many of the issues brought out in the course. Actors are coached in the forms of obfuscation that citizens sometimes use. In general, we train actors to follow their instincts in reacting to the officers' behavior (e.g., Do they feel crowded, angry, calm?). Actors can usually be obtained by contacting a local acting school. It pays to develop a small pool of actors who are familiar with the workshop objectives and can react accordingly.

At the end of each simulation we review a videotape with the trainees in which the trainees intervened into a simulated dispute. By comparing their performance with the standards developed during the course, we can point out their strengths and weaknesses. Often nonverbal habits are the most difficult to alter. The video feedback is a useful first step in this regard. If the trainees feel they were weak in some respect in their interviewing, conflict resolution, etc., we ask them how they would perform if they had it to do over again. If a team's performance is clearly inadequate, they will be asked to perform again using a different scenario.

In conclusion, we should add that on occasion trainees do commit serious errors in simulations. We have recorded examples of trainees who have generated violence in a script that was intended to be peaceful—an example both of Bard's concept of iatrogenic violence and of how role-plays can take on a reality all their own.

DEPARTMENTAL SUPPORT FOR FAMILY CRISIS INTERVENTION PROGRAMS

What changes can police departments make so that the skills acquired by recruits in training programs will not be lost upon return to street policing?

Recruitment and Selection

In recruitment, police departments should advertise policing as a "person" profession. The avoidance of active recruiting on the grounds that "we already get more applications than we have jobs for" overlooks the quality, background, and orientation of the applicants and results in a stagnant department. Applicants should perhaps be required to pass more stringent criteria for demonstration of interpersonal skills in line with a professional police orientation.

Recruitment advertising should be directed at countering media stereotypes about police work. The total police role should be stressed in advertisements, not just the "cops and robbers" mystique. It should be kept in mind that trying to change an organization through personnel change alone is arduous and time-consuming; the organization is at least as likely to change the personnel. Hence, changing recruitment and selection policies is necessary but not sufficient to ensure departmental innovation.

Training of Communication Operators

We have stressed recruit training in the preceding section, but training of "com-ops" is also important. The personnel who field calls from citizens and the dispatchers who alert patrol cars need to be taught what information is necessary for police handling domestic disputes (Levens, 1978b). For example:

1) Who made the call and how many persons are present?
2) Where is the call being made from and is the offender on the scene?
3) Is the assault in progress or threatened (i.e., the violence potential of the situation)?
4) Is a weapon involved, available, mentioned, or suspected?
5) What is the emotional state of the disputants or caller—agitated, upset, etc.?

This involves spending at least one day training "com-ops" and ensuring that new personnel receive comparable training. Efficient intervention begins with proper intake and dispatch of information.

Performance Evaluation

Training must be reinforced by a performance evaluation system which expands traditional criteria and deemphasizes arrest and summons. A crisis intervention program which emphasizes defusing, mediation, and referral as techniques to divert violence-prone families outside the criminal justice system cannot rely on rewards for officers based on the intake of people into that very system. Rather, officers should be evaluated on the quality of referrals, follow-ups, call-backs, changes in assault statistics (both on officers and between disputing parties), and the nature of complaints and commendations—all of which are indicative of the broader criteria of communication skills, work quality, judgment, knowledge of the community, flexibility, crime prevention, and decision-making (Bennett-Sandler, 1975). Appropriate observation of these skills by patrol supervisors suggests that supervisors respond not only to crime calls but to calls for service as well.

Reward System

Clearly, promotion and reward must follow from the performance evaluation used, otherwise role conflict, confusion, dissatisfaction, and lowered morale will result. Thus, for purposes of crisis-management programs, police need to be rewarded not only for bravery, but for exceptional sensitivity, community service, and ability to defuse potential violence. While these things are often difficult to measure, they are worthy of attention and need to be upgraded and recognized if police are to be comfortable with their total role. Interpersonal skills are necessary in all aspects of police work, even in investigations by detectives, yet they are not considered criteria for promotion.

Management

The most important of all organizational processes is management. Management sets the tone of the organization and controls the resources which mold it. Techniques which require flexibility and professional judgment (as do dispute intervention techniques) are incompatible with rigid management structures. Hence, paramilitary organizational structures tend not to be conducive to the operation of domestic dispute intervention programs. Decentralized management (including team policing, peer review, and peer panels) is more promising in terms of structuring police organizations for crisis intervention.

Finally, any efforts to implement crisis intervention programs must be "sold" to management in order to enlist its support and cooperation. Such selling requires, as much as possible, that management personnel be briefed and consulted for their feedback on proposed changes. They must feel that they have some control over the implementation of new programs. In addition, management must be apprised that organizational change, with an emphasis on decentralized management and a full service model, is necessary if crisis intervention efforts are to have their full effect.

PROGRAM EVALUATION

Description of Study and Method

In order to evaluate the impact of such training on recruits' attitudes toward the handling of family crisis calls and their general perception about this type of police work, a survey was undertaken in the spring of 1976 of 70 police officers, comprising 20 experienced officers who had not received the family crisis training package and three groups of recent British Columbia Police College graduates who had received the training. All respondents were randomly chosen from Vancouver Police Department staff lists. Length of service for each group is shown in Table 1.

One group (Class III) had just graduated two weeks prior to the survey. Class II had graduated three to four months previously, and Class I had graduated six to seven months previously. Thus, by comparison of responses from the three recruit classes, the study also allowed for assessment of the longevity of any effects due to family crisis training. Prior research on police training has discussed a much publicized discrepancy between "street training" and "academic training," whereby recruits are "resocialized" from innovative practices acquired during street experience with veteran officers who have not had the training and have not accepted the new techniques.

Since little in-service training had been done with the Vancouver Police Department to establish a more general acceptance of some of the more innovative procedures of family crisis intervention, it was believed that the effects of such training on recruits might be lost to resocialization and would disappear as more time was spent on the streets. By comparing the attitudes of B.C. Police College Classes I, II, and III, some evidence bearing on this contention was obtained.

All interviewing was conducted by telephoning police officers and scheduling interviews either at officers' homes or at the police station prior to the time the officers were to go on shift. Five male interviewers

TABLE 1
Composition of Survey Sample

	Vancouver Police Population	Sample	Length of Active Service at Time of Interview
Experienced Officers	480*	20	Average 9 years Range: 3-20 yrs
Class I Recruits	95	15	6-7 months
Class II Recruits	87	15	3-4 months
Class III Recruits	62	20	Two weeks

*This figure refers to the Patrol Division, Uniform Branch, and is the actual number of such officers at the time of this study.

identified themselves as working for the United Way on this project and divided the 70 interviews among them.

The interviews were structured around a 31-item questionnaire with probes inserted on specific items or at other appropriate times (to be determined by the interviewer).

After a few "icebreaker" items, interviewers began to sound out the police officers on their attitudes and perceptions toward domestic crisis intervention. Basically, six categories of attitude were measured, each being related to an objective of the family crisis workshop. These were: police procedure for family crisis calls; attitudes toward the role of the social scientist in police training; attitudes toward handling family crisis calls; attitudes toward people involved in domestic conflict; attitudes toward social agencies; and perceptions of danger, alcohol use, and ability to control domestic crisis situations.

Results

The results of this survey, reported in detail elsewhere (Dutton & Levens, 1977), can be summarized as follows. Trained recruits are:

1) more likely to negotiate settlement of problem or to make referral to outside agency;
2) more likely to use long-term conflict reduction strategies as opposed to short-term strategies;
3) more satisfied with their family crisis intervention training as compared with experienced officers who received "traditional" training;
4) more likely to report greater feelings of accomplishment on family crisis calls and greater willingness to get involved in such calls;
5) less likely to conclude that couples in crisis should resolve their problem by living apart;
6) less likely to hold negative attitudes about social agencies than untrained officers;
7) less likely to perceive a high incidence of alcohol usage and to feel alcohol use by citizens impaired police handling of family crisis calls;
8) likely to report decreases in violence and the use of force after training (compared to pretraining experience);
9) likely to report increases in citizen receptivity and satisfaction with their own performance after training (compared to pretraining experience).

None of the above findings disappeared with time: Trained recruits seven months after training did not differ from trained recruits who had just completed training (both groups differed from untrained officers).

All of the above results are significant at the .05 level or better (Levens & Dutton, 1977). The results generally indicated that the training sessions had succeeded in instilling greater fellings of control, safety, and accomplishment in crisis interventions and greater use of long-term strategies (mediation, referral). However, at this time, recruits still have to function in a police system which may be at odds with the goals and philosophy of crisis intervention work.

REFERENCES

BACH, G., & GOLDBERG, H. *Creative aggression.* New York: Avon Books, 1975.

BARD, M. Family intervention police teams as a community mental health resource. *Journal of Criminal Law, Criminology and Police Science,* 1969, *60*(2), 247-250.

BARD, M. *Family crisis intervention: From concept to implementation.* U. S. Department of Justice, Washington, D. C.: U. S. Government Printing Office, 1973.

BARD, M. *The function of the police in crisis intervention and conflict management: A training guide.* U. S. Department of Justice, L.E.A.A. Washington, D. C.: U. S. Government Printing Office, 1975.

BARD, M. Iatrogenic violence. *The Police Chief,* Jan., 1971.

BAROCAS, H. Urban policemen: Crisis mediators or crisis creators? *American Journal of Orthopsychiatry,* 1973, *43*(4), 72-81.

BENNETT-SANDLER, G.: *Structuring police organizations to promote crisis management programmes.* Presented at Symposium on Crisis Management in Law Enforcement, National Conference of Christians and Jews and California Association of Police Trainers, Berkeley, CA, 1975.

BUGENTHAL, R. L., KAHN, F. M., ANDREWS, F. M. & HEAD, K. B.: *Justifying violence: Attitudes of American men.* Institute for Social Research, Ann Arbor, MI, 1972.

COFFEY, A. R. *Police intervention into family crisis.* Santa Cruz, CA: Davis Publishing Co., 1974.

Domestic violence and the police: Studies in Detroit and Kansas City. *Police Foundation,* 1977.

DRISCOLL, J. M., MEYER, R. G., & SCHANIE, C. F. Training police in family crisis intervention. *Journal of Applied Behavioral Science,* 1973, *9*(1) 172-192.

DUTTON, D. *Domestic dispute intervention for police.* West Coast Social and Behavioral Research Enterprises, 1977.

DUTTON, D. *Domestic violence and the female as victim/offender.* Simon Fraser Conference on the Female Offender, Jan., 1979.

DUTTON, D., & LEVENS, B. Attitude survey of trained and untrained police officers. *Canadian Police College Journal,* 1977, *1*(2), 75-92.

FAGIN, J. *Delivery of paraprofessional mental health services to victims of crime and in crisis intervention and conflict management.* American Society of Criminology Meetings, Tucson, Arizona, 1976.

Homicide Statistics, 1977, Statistics Canada, Justice Statistics Division, Cat. No. 85-209, Ottawa, October, 1978.

HOVLAND, C., JANIS, I. L., & KELLEY, H. H. *Communication and persuasion.* New Haven: Yale University Press, 1953.

KATZ, M. Family crisis training: Upgrading the police while building a bridge to the minority community. *Journal of Police Science and Administration,* 1973, *1*(1) 16-27.

KELLEY, C. M. *Crime in the United States,* 1973. Uniform Crime Reports, Washington, D. C.: U. S. Government Printing Office, 1975.

LEVENS, B. R. A literature review of domestic dispute intervention training programs. *Canadian Police College Journal*, 1978(a), *2*(2 & 3).

LEVENS, B. R. Domestic disputes, police response and social agency referral. *Canadian Police College Journal*, 1978(b), *2*(4), 356-381.

LEVENS, B. R., & DUTTON, D. Domestic crisis intervention: Citizens' requests for service and the Vancouver Police Department response. *Canadian Police College Journal*, 1977, *1*(1), 29.

LIEBMAN, D. A., & SCHWARTZ, J. A. Police programs in domestic crisis intervention: In J. R. Snibbe & H. M. Snibbe, (Eds.), *The urban policeman in transition*. Springfield: Charles C. Thomas, 1972.

New spouse abuse policy for New York Police. Centre for Women Policy Studies, Washington, D. C. *Response*, 2(1), Oct., 1978.

NICHOLLS, M. *Vancouver Province*, Nov., 1978.

REITH, C. *The police idea: Its history and evolution in England in the 18th century and after.* London: Oxford University Press, 1938.

Reporting the comments of His Honour Judge Bewley in the trial of Anthony Tourangeau. *The Vancouver Sun & The Province*, November 2, 1977.

SHOTLAND, L., & STRAW, M. Bystander response to an assault: When a man attacks a woman. *Journal of Personality and Social Psychology*, 1976, *34*(5), 990-999.

STEINMETZ, S., & STRAUS, M. A. *Violence in the family*. New York: Harper and Row, 1974.

STRAUS, M. A general systems theory approach to a theory of violence between family members. *Social Science Information*, 1973, *12*, 105-125.

STRAUS, M. Sexual inequality, cultural norms and wife beating. *Victimology*, 1976, *1*, 54-76.

STRAUS, M. Societal morphogenesis and intrafamily violence in cross cultural perspective. *Annals of the New York Academy of Sciences*, 1977, *285*, 718-730.

STRAUS, M. A. Violence in the family: How widespread, why it occurs and some thoughts on prevention. *Proceedings from United Way Symposium on Family Violence*. Vancouver, March, 1977.

WHITEHURST, R. N. Violence in husband-wife interaction. In S. Steinmetz, & M. A. Straus (Eds.), *Violence in the family*. New York: Harper and Row, 1974.

WILSON, J. Q. What makes a better policeman? *Atlantic Monthly*, March, 1969.

9
Preventing Violence in Residential Treatment Programs for Adolescents

DEAN L. FIXSEN, ELERY L. PHILLIPS, THOMAS P. DOWD, and LOUIS J. PALMA

The summaries of some institutional practices provided below may sound like a description of institutional life at the turn of the century, before the advent of modern-day concern for mental health, child development, and children's rights. Unfortunately, the descriptions were extracted from a court case that began in 1973 regarding some of our "modern-day" child-care institutions. To be sure, the degree of violence and neglect cited below is not common in most institutions. However, some degree of violence and neglect does occur in many institutions and represents a serious problem in our society.

We want to express our gratitude to Fr. Robert Hupp, Executive Director of Boys Town, and to the Board of Directors of Father Flanagan's Boys' Home. Their support, encouragement, and flexibility have been invaluable to our efforts. We also want to thank Joan Fixsen for her assistance in preparing the manuscript and Richard Baron for his contributions of ideas, logic, and good sense.

Partial support for preparation of this manuscript was provided by Grant #1-T01-MH15699 from the National Institute of Mental Health (Center for Studies of Crime and Delinquency) to Father Flanagan's Boys' Home (Department of Youth Care).

INSTITUTIONAL PRACTICES

Some Definitions*

"Peel": A peel is administered by forcing a youth to bend over, then striking him hard on the back with a fist or opened hand.

"Tight": A tight is applied by forcing a youth to bend down, holding his ankles or toes, then striking him on the buttocks with the handle or straw-end of a broom.

"Brogue": A youth is subjected to broguing when he is kicked in the shins.

"Make work": Make work refers to requiring a youth to pull grass without bending his knees on a large tract of ground not intended for cultivation or any purpose; forcing him to move dirt with a shovel from one place on the ground to another and then back again many times; making him buff a small area of the floor for an excessive period of time.

"Confinement": Placement in a 6' x 12' locked room, with a solid door that has a small window which is painted over and a narrow slit for food trays.

"Picking": When picking, youths are lined up foot-to-foot, heads down, and are required to strike the ground with heavy picks swung overhead as the line moves forward. Nothing is ever planted in the picked ground.

Some Applications

While on "make work duty" a youth became tired after three hours of pulling grass and bent his knees. For this, he was kicked in the back and punched in the mouth by a staff person and told to go back to pulling. When he again became tired and started to stand up, another staff person kicked him in the head with his booted foot. (The staff person's height was 6 feet 3 inches; he weighed about 200 pounds. The youth was 5 feet 6 inches, and weighed approximately 110 pounds.) When the youth complained that his side hurt, the staff person told him to keep pulling, and later kicked him twice more in the head. Apparently

---

*The "Definitions," "Applications," and "Examples of Life in the Institution" are summaries of testimony and arguments prepared in the *Morales v. Turman* case in the Eastern District Court of Texas. We extend our appreciation to the U.S. Department of Justice who invited us to participate in this case and to Patricia Wald and Peter Sandman who, as lawyers, have done a lot for children.

desperate, the youth escaped from the work detail and ran to the superintendent's office. There he met yet another staff person who pulled him into his office by the neck, slapped him, and told him to get up against the wall and put his hands in his pockets. This staff person struck the youth many times in the jaw and stomach with fist and open hand, kicking the youth when he fell down. The staff person then ordered another boy to bring the youth clean clothes (to replace his bloody ones), and made the youth sign a false incident report written by the staff person. Subsequently, the staff person directed the youth to run back to grass-pulling duty. The staff person followed closely in a pick-up truck, all the while racing its engine. Late that evening, the youth was placed in confinement for running away from work duty.

Some Examples of Life in the Institution

As revealed in the court case, the most striking characteristic of daily life is overwhelming monotony and regimentation. In the institution for girls, rooms are like cells; each is furnished with a bed, a dresser, and a small cubicle for clothes. The doors have locks, as well as safety chains on the outside that permit them to be opened about four inches when latched. The light switches are outside in the corridor. Girls may not use the restroom at night, but must relieve themselves in chamber pots. During the time they are locked in, they must call out if they are sick or in need of assistance. Whether a girl is latched into her room often depends solely on the convenience of her housemother.

The justification given by a staff psychologist for latching girls' doors was the impossibility of making individual decisions about who should or should not be latched in. He conceded that not all girls require such close confinement, estimating that 20% to 50% of the girls need to be latched in. The superintendent stated that latching would be altogether unnecessary if he had a larger staff.

The girls arise at 6 a.m., weekends included. Doors to their rooms are unchained for showers (two students at a time), unchained again for breakfast and smoking at 7 a.m., and again for brushing teeth, using the bathroom, and emptying chamber pots. Girls then wait in their rooms until 8:45 a.m. when they go to school, then to lunch and a smoke break, then back to school. A "line lady" checks to see that all girls are present when they return to their cottages at 4 p.m., when they are chained in their rooms (except for bathroom call) until supper and smoking time at 5:30 p.m. To line up for each meal, the houseparents "call sides," unlatching first one tier of doors and then the other. Girls are ushered into the dining room to the calls of "east side," "west side," "let 'em out," "put 'em up." The dishes are plastic. Meals are eaten quickly, and it is obligatory that conversations be quiet. Even the cook can order silence. At the end of the meal the staff members demand that the girls sit with their hands in their laps while the silver is collected and counted.

After dinner girls are chained in their rooms again, except for chores such as brushing teeth and washing faces, using the bathroom, and emptying chamber pots and trash baskets. At 7 p.m. girls are let out of their rooms, one side at a time, for recreation, during which time they sit in the commons area, play cards, and talk quietly. After using the bathroom at 8:45 p.m., the girls are chained and locked in their rooms at 9 p.m., and their lights must be out between 9:30 and 10 p.m. At 11 p.m. the night watchman shines a light in each girl's window. On weekends the routine is basically the same. The girls move through the institution as a group with no autonomy, but rather subject to a routine which is based upon institutional convenience.

In the institution for boys the dormitories house approximately 30 boys each. The beds are lined up "military camp head-to-toe fashion." The boys are awakened between 6 and 6:30 a.m. every day by their dormitory officer. Dressed in the day's underwear, in which they had slept the night before, the students are ushered into the bathroom. They then walk from the sleeping area to the dayroom area where they retrieve their clothes, which were carefully folded and placed upon chairs the night before.

Everyone in a dormitory is scheduled to eat at the same time, around 7 a.m. Boys who get dressed early either go back to sleep or merely sit around; however, they are not permitted to return to the sleeping area once in the dayroom. The youths walk in a file to breakfast in another building, return to the dayroom area for a short period, and then form another line to go to school.

After school the students return to the dormitories where they usually sit around, fall asleep, or line up in chairs watching television programs. On one occasion a witness observed nearly an entire dormitory of boys sitting before a broken television set. They spend up to two hours in the dormitory before going to dinner. (Students are not permitted to take school books back to their living units, but even if they were, the lighting is such that reading is difficult at best.) In most units the only time youths go outside during this two-hour period is at the specific directions of their staff. Occasionally the staff persons on duty will participate in some of the indoor or outdoor activities, but generally they do not.

The boys also go to dinner in a group. Seating arrangements depend upon which school is being fed. Generally the arrangement is one of the following: a) Boys are seated as they come in, four to a table; b) no more than two blacks may sit at a four-person table; or c) no more than two blacks, two whites, or two Mexican-Americans may sit at a four-person table, and the two persons of the same racial or ethnic classifications must sit across the table from each other.

After returning from dinner to their living unit, the boys may be allowed to play outside for a short period. They then polish their shoes or perhaps buff the dormitory floors. The youngsters are then required to shower and shave; this process begins around 7 p.m. The boys put on clean underwear and walk around in this manner until time for bed. Unless a student is on medication, in which case he may retire around 8 p.m., he is required to go to bed between 9 p.m. and 10 p.m.

The students' weekend schedules are not unlike those of the week days, with chores replacing the time spent in school. Occasionally, movies or interdormitory competitions are planned, but the major portion of the boys' weekends is spent doing nothing.

SOLUTIONS

As a society, we are very concerned with children, and considerable effort and expense are devoted to their rearing and education. When the family unit fails to rear a child properly, social mechanisms have been developed to provide extra support for the child and his family or even to remove the child from the family unit and place him/her in an environment that offers the child a better chance to develop normally. Thus, when our child-care institutions are exposed as being violent or neglectful, the public becomes very concerned and begins looking for solutions.

Legal Solutions

When the violence is extensive and of long duration, the most common attempt at a solution is the "legal solution," especially when the legal rights of youths have been seriously compromised within an institutional setting. Perhaps some of the more dramatic court cases in recent years have centered on the abuse and neglect some children have suffered in institutions, all in the name of "treatment." The *Wyatt v. Stickney* case regarding retarded children, *Morales v. Turman* concerning delinquent and predelinquent youths, as well as others, have pointed out the violent, abusive, and neglectful nature of some programs. These court cases have served very useful purposes. They have brought national attention to many child-care problems and raised the level of social awareness regarding the need for better, more humane treatment. They have also forced some changes in the worst programs by writing into law some basic standards for child care.

While the legal solutions have produced beneficial effects, they suffer from two basic problems. One problem is the enormous cost of developing and prosecuting a case against a treatment program. It requires many years of dedicated effort on the part of dozens of lawyers, mental health experts, parents, and youths to develop the testimony and investigate the facts of a case. The total cost of one case may be more than five million dollars spent over a five-year period. Another problem is that legal solutions are often unimaginative and do not really solve the problem. For example, most of the solutions recommended in "right to treatment" suits are concerned with standards for living space, number of staff, staff qualifications, types of activities, grievance procedures, recordkeeping, and prohibitions against excessive use of force. These recommendations are usually unimaginative because of the adversarial nature of a court case and the need to have reasonable documentation and professional support for each requirement written into law. Innovations or simply "good ideas" usually do not fare well under these conditions.

Professional Solutions

Another kind of solution is commonly suggested by professional groups (e.g., psychologists, psychiatrists, social workers, correctional officers) who point out that violence, abuse, and neglect in programs would be alleviated if only more of their kind were employed by those programs. Because of the influence of professional groups, some of this thinking is written into law and can be seen in most of the court cases which attempt to specify the standard credentials of those who should be allowed to work with youths. Like the legal solution, the professional solution has had a national impact on many programs. There has been a general concern for increasing the number of staff, upgrading staff qualifications, and assuring professional and humane treatment of youths. Also like the legal solution, the professional solution is costly and may actually slow the process of making needed fundamental changes because people may think that "we have solved our problem by hiring these added professional staff and meeting these legal standards for child care."

Programmatic Solutions

Another possible set of solutions has been germinating for the past 15 to 20 years. Researchers have been developing new treatment methods, evaluation techniques, program-monitoring procedures, and feedback systems to provide positive learning experiences for children, to organize and administer programs to prevent abuse and neglect, and to be accountable for the outcomes. Since these programs are innovative, many would require making fundamental changes in the institutions that adopt them and the qualifications of the people who operate them. Thus, these research-based, programmatic solutions will have to overcome considerable institutional inertia and survive the attempts at replication and dissemination before they can be thought of as a real solution to the problem. Nevertheless, our attempts at developing a treatment program we call the Teaching-Family Model and our experiences over the past four years at Boys Town have taught us a great deal about programmatic solutions to many problems in child care.

PREVENTING VIOLENCE

The most basic element in preventing violence in institutions is the treatment program which prescribes how staff members are to interact with the youths. Without explicit guidelines for staff behavior and clear methods for monitoring staff/youth interaction, staff members are left to their own devices for dealing with a wide range of problem behaviors each day. Consider for a moment the situation in which we place many good, well-intentioned staff. First, we build institutions that are more or less isolated from normal social monitoring or control, either because of physical isolation in rural areas or social isolation via imposing structures, fences, or lack of "outside" people coming through. Next, we collect a large number of youths who, for one reason or another, have been banned from their homes because of their misbehavior or their inadequate home life. Then we add staff who are often recruited from the area near the institution and, with little preparation, ask them to "help the children." Next we hire professionals to make treatment policy, supervise staff, monitor progress of youths, establish budgets, write reports, and carry on the other myriad tasks required to operate an institution. And we ask the professionals to do this "in their own way" based on their experience and expertise.

The final ingredient is time. Each institution develops a history of dealing with problems that becomes the standard for all new staff persons being hired. New people may be repulsed at first and some quit after a few weeks or months. Others adapt quickly to the historical standard and soon become adherents to the standard. Because of this, Moos (1974) could collect longitudinal data on the social climate of institutions and find little change in the data, even though there had been nearly 100% turnover of staff and youths over a two-year period.

Given the informal manner in which many institutional treatment programs are established and the emphasis on institutional stability, violence in institutions would appear to be a logical outcome.

Boys Town

Since we arrived at Boys Town in 1975, we have changed the institution from a self-contained town to something more like a suburban neighborhood. Instead of cottages and larger buildings that each housed 15 to 60 youths cared for by shift-work staff, we now have 41 homes with 8 to 10 youths and a full-time, live-in married couple (teaching-parents) in each home. Instead of a bulk-ordering system, each home shops at local grocery stores. Instead of an on-campus medical clinic, teaching-parents select their own doctors and dentists in the community; instead of a centralized transportation system, each family has its own van, and so on. These changes have had the effect of opening up a closed institution, but they also require that we invest a great deal of responsibility and authority in the teaching-parents who live and work with the youths every day. Being a teaching-parent is stressful, much like being a parent to any 10 teenagers would be—only more so. To prevent .neglect or abuse in the homes, we carefully select and train teaching-parents and supervise the operation of each home.

Selection of Teaching-Parents

We advertise and make recruiting trips nationally to locate good couples and encourage them to apply. The applications are screened and those who do not meet some basic criteria are rejected: They must be married, have no more than two children of their own, and be available to move to Boys Town. Couples meeting these criteria are then interviewed on the telephone, where we explain the duties and responsibilities, trials and tribulations, and reinforcers associated with being a teaching-parent. Those couples who sound good on the telephone are invited to come to Boys Town (at their own expense) for a personal interview. These couples are interviewed by the Community Directors who are responsible for the overall operation of the five "communities" of homes at Boys Town. During this interview the teaching-parent position is explained in detail and the couple is asked to role play a few situations to see how well they interact with people and take feedback. Considerable attention is also paid to how good a model the couple would be for the youths: Are they friendly and warm? Are they at ease? Do they share with one another? Do they have good social skills? Are their values sound? In brief, do they have the skills we want our youths to learn? Based on this final interview and a review of references, couples are hired as teaching-parents.

During 1978, 201 couples applied to be teaching-parents at Boys Town, 138 couples were interviewed on the telephone, 73 couples were interviewed by the Community Directors, and 20 couples were eventually hired.

Teaching-Parent Training

After they are hired, the couples begin a one-year training program leading to certification as professional teaching-parents (see Figure 1). We emphasize teaching skills more than a theoretical framework for rearing children. The couples first go through a seven-day, intensive *preservice workshop* to teach them the rudimentary skills they will need to work effectively with youths and to operate a home. The workshop covers all aspects of the Teaching-Family Treatment Model (Phillips, Phillips, Fixsen, & Wolf, 1974) including learning theory, developing positive relationships, teaching new behaviors, motivating youths, self-government, counseling, appropriate tolerance levels, and working with parents, teachers, social agencies, and the public. The workshop also includes training on developing and maintaining professional relationships, developing and using treatment plans for each youth, organizing the activities and business operations of a home, and legal issues related to the care and treatment of youths.

Following the preservice workshop, a couple moves into a home and begins working with the youths. At this point, *support* is provided by a consultant and by the community administration. The consultant is a certified teaching-parent who has gone through special training to be a consultant. The consultant spends time in the home helping the new couple implement the teaching-family program, organize their home, and become familiar with the Boys Town organization and the Omaha community. The community administration consists of a community director, two assistants to the community director, and a secretary. The community administration consults with the couple regarding the operation of the home, business practices, movement of youths in or out of the home, and reviews requests for special treatment or referral of youths. The consultant and community administration are on call 24 hours a day to help with any situation that arises.

Teaching-Parent Evaluation

Another hallmark of a Teaching-Family home is frequent evaluation. The first evaluation shown in Figure 1, the minor evaluation, occurs 30 to 60 days after a couple completes the preservice workshop. For the minor evaluation, two evaluators visit a home for 30-45 minutes and use standard criteria to look at the cleanliness and attractiveness of the home, the social skills of the youths, and the teaching skills of the teaching-parents. Also, the youths are interviewed privately and asked to rate the pleasantness, concern, and helpfulness of the teaching-parents. The feedback from the evaluation is given to the couple, the consultant, and the community administration, so they can see the strengths and weaknesses of the home and devise a plan to provide additional support and training as needed.

After about four months in the home, the couple goes through a major evaluation. As one part of the major evaluation, two evaluators visit the home for about four hours for a professional in-home visit. During the visit the evaluators use standard criteria to assess the implementation of the treatment components such as teaching new skills, self-government, motivating youths, relationship development, and so on. They also look at the physical condition of the home, the organization of the record-keeping system, and the youths' knowledge of their program and their individual goals. The evaluators again interview the youths privately to obtain their opinions about the program and the teaching-parents.

Another aspect of the major evaluation is the home consumer evaluation. This consists of questionnaires that are sent to the parents and teachers of the youths, to the agency (e.g., social welfare, juvenile court) workers who are responsible for youths in the home, to the community administrators who oversee the home, and to the employers, neighbors, or others who have some contact with the youths. The results of the major evaluation are summarized and given to the teaching-parents, consultant, and community administrators as feedback on the progress of the home. Further, the teaching-parents' continued employment is contingent on the outcome of these evaluations. If the major evaluation results are poor, the teaching-parents might be asked to leave (after a

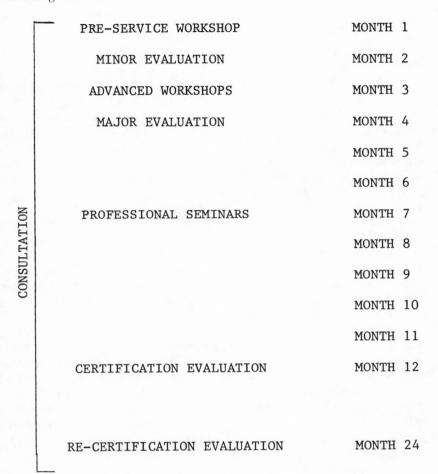

FIGURE 1. This figure shows the sequence of training, evaluation, and consultation services provided to each couple during their first year as teaching-parent trainees.

period of attempted correction of the problem). If they do well and meet all the criteria, they receive a substantial pay raise.

About 12 months after the preservice workshop, the major evaluation is repeated. This time, if the teaching-parents meet all criteria, they receive another pay raise and, most importantly, they are certified as professional teaching-parents. Each year thereafter the teaching-parents need to go through another major evaluation and meet all criteria to maintain their certification and to receive an annual pay increase.

TEACHING-FAMILY MODEL

The selection, training, consultation, and evaluation procedures only make sense when they are focused on a set of procedures for dealing with youth behavior. We call this set of procedures the Teaching-Family Model. The specific treatment procedures have been evolving since 1967 when we first began working with youths in Achievement Place, a group home in Lawrence, Kansas. From the beginning our goals have been to develop a treatment model that is humane, effective, and satisfactory to the participants (e.g., youths, parents, teachers). To be humane, treatment staff must have understanding and compassion for the youths and their problems and be willing to advocate the best interests of the youths. To be effective, treatment staff must be able to teach a wide range of prosocial skills that can serve as appropriate alternatives to the youths' antisocial behaviors. To satisfy the participants, treatment staff must be pleasant, maintain open communication with all participants, be responsive to the feedback and concerns of others, and educate participants about the purposes and procedures of the program to invite their help. These goals are often difficult to achieve simultaneously, but each is critical to the success of a program.

Two other goals are to develop treatment procedures that have a reasonable cost and that can be described in sufficient detail to allow their use on a broad scale. These are goals because we want to develop a replicable treatment model that can be used to benefit youths in group homes in communities and institutions across the nation. In 1978 there were over 150 teaching-family group homes in the United States.

Before we describe the basic treatment components of the teaching-family model, we need to explain some of the philosophy that governs our approach. As applied researchers, we understand "shaping" or the use of successive approximations to teach a goal behavior. For example, if we wanted a mute child to say a complete sentence, we might first reinforce any sound the child makes, then reinforce only those sounds that make up a word, then reinforce only those words that make up a complete sentence. Serious antisocial behavior, such as violence, follows a similar path. First, one youth bumps into another, then words are exchanged, then the words get louder, then one youth pushes another, then the punches begin to fly. To "stop a fight" the staff might wait until the punches begin to fly, then two staff members intervene, pull the youths apart, restrain them, and lock them up to let things cool down. Youths and staff members often get hurt in the process. Another way to "stop a fight" is to intervene very early in the sequence. When one youth bumps another or words are exchanged, staff can intervene and "stop the fight" with a few words. The staff could go further and teach the youths how to handle situations like this in the future (e.g., apologize when you bump into someone) and how to maintain control over their anger (e.g., when you are upset by something, think about the situation and a solution before you act). And the staff could reinforce "good relations" between the youths in the future. Thus, our philosophy is to intervene early, teach youths to avoid problem situations, and teach appropriate alternative behaviors.

Teaching

The primary technique that the teaching-parents use is the "teaching interaction," which is one of the key components of the teaching-family model. In essence, the teaching interaction is simply a way of teaching youths new, appropriate behaviors which, at the same time, discourages inappropriate behavior. It is critical, in using the teaching approach to change behavior, that the steps be broken down into small, learnable components so that a youth can receive reinforcement for each successive approximation that he attempts. By breaking the learning task into small steps, the youth finds that the learning process is easier and more fun than when vague, global requests to change are made.

For example, when teaching a youth how to "follow instructions," that vague concept becomes a fairly routine task when broken down into four steps: a) look at the person giving instructions; b) acknowledge the person ("OK, I understand"); c) complete the task; and d) check back after the task is done. The teaching process that takes place in the teaching-family model is one of describing the inappropriate behavior in enough detail that the youth recognizes what he was doing wrong, describing the appropriate behavior you are asking of the youth in sufficient detail so that he understands what you are asking him to do, and then asking the youth to describe it to you so you are sure he understands it. Then he is expected to practice it in front of you so you can provide feedback and reinforcement, depending on the quality of his performance. At later points in the day, the youth has the opportunity to practice that behavior and receive more feedback in more natural settings; also, of course, when he uses that behavior without prompting in a more natural environment, he receives large, positive consequences.

Systematic Consequences

Since the teaching program is the primary change procedure used in the teaching-family model, it is critical that a systematic program of reinforcement be used to develop the new behaviors that you expect a youth to learn. This is done through a systematic motivation system where the youth starts out on a structured system of reinforcement and is later faded to a less structured program of consequences more like those that occur in the natural environment. The specific motivation system that we use in the teaching-family model is one where a youth lives in the program for two weeks while being on an assessment or diagnostic program where the day-to-day behaviors are recorded and the youth's sensitivity to natural consequences is determined. If during this assessment period it is determined that the youth can operate on the normal consequences that most children and adults use to change behaviors, then the motivation system selected for him will likely be the negotiation system. In this system the teaching-parents and youths set individual goals for behavioral change each day and assess that change at the end of the next day during a counseling session where the youth is given feedback on how he has done. On the other hand, if during the assessment period it is determined that the youth cannot operate with normal consequences, he will go on to a token economy system, the point system, where a more structured consequence system exists. On the point system he will receive points for appropriate behavior and will lose points for inappropriate behavior throughout the day. Of course the teaching-parents are still very concerned about setting specific goals each day, but the point system allows the teaching-parents to have more control over the type and frequency of consequences the youth receives. Once a youth has been on the point system for a period of time, he can graduate to the negotiation system to see if he is ready for a natural consequence system. Finally, the youths graduate to a responsibility system which is designed to allow a youth who has learned all the new behaviors asked of him to operate on the same system that exists in the real world, hoping that the new behaviors he has learned will continue when exposed to extended periods of time without more structured reinforcement. This system will continue for the remainder of the time that the youth is in the program, although on occasion he may need a "refresher course" on either the negotiation system or the point system. The final goal of the systematic consequence system is to have the youth on the responsibility system.

Another aspect of the motivation system is that reinforcement occurs even under relatively negative conditions. One of the main concerns that we had in teaching the youths new behaviors is that our "problem youths" had a tendency to get into trouble more often than "normal youths." Thus, it is possible for punishment to become a frequent occurrence. In order to avoid the problem of the environment becoming too negative when a youth must be punished for a behavior he has engaged in, we try to make sure there are enough reinforcing events, even during punishment, to maintain his motivation and insure that the youth will "keep trying" to improve. For example, if a youth must lose a large number of points because he has engaged in an agressive act with one of the other youths, then it is very likely that each day he will need to earn three or four times the normal amount of points to maintain some of his privileges. But we make sure those points are available more often than they would be normally and that he receives more occasions for positive feedback. For instance, the youth may begin to earn points immediately following his point fine by appropriately accepting the consequence (e.g., good eye contact, acknowledgment of the fine, absence of inappropriate behavior such as frowning, cursing, etc.). It is very critical that there not be a period of time without some opportunity to make points. If we do not use this system, then many youths simply stop trying because there is no reinforcement in the system and they cannot see any way out.

Family Conference

Another aspect of the treatment program is the family conference. The family conference allows every youth to have a voice in the treatment program. No matter how minor the incident, he may bring it up at this group meeting, which is designed to solve the day-to-day problems of the youths living together. This is not a counseling session but a problem-solving group session. At the daily family conference a youth may bring up a particular issue with another youth. The youths and the teaching-parents discuss the issue and attempt to arrive at a solution that is satisfactory to all the youths involved. The kinds of problems that are dealt with at the family conference range all the way from how many times do you have to knock before you enter someone's room, to more important issues such as the problem of one youth bullying another. The family conference process is a semi-democratic process designed to insure that every youth feels he has some say and control over the program.

Individual Counseling

Individual counseling for each youth is the opportunity for that youth to sit down with just the teaching-parents and express concern over a particular problem he is having. In many of these counseling sessions there are no solutions immediately available to the problem except talking to someone about the difficulty. These problems range from sex to religion to parents to fear of a particular teacher. The major purpose of the individual talk is to insure each youth the opportunity to talk to adults and let someone else in the world know that he has fears and needs love and respect.

Preventive Teaching

Preventive teaching is most important in the control of violence and abuse of children. Most of the youths have been reinforced for their emotional and violent behavior prior to coming to the program. We simply assume this when a youth arrives and we begin immediately (before we even see the tendency toward lack of emotional control) to teach him how to control his emotional behavior. We know it is frustrating sometimes to lose something you have, or not to receive what you think you should. If not taught how to control his emotions and to accept occasional disappointment, a youth will fly into a rage even when he loses points on the motivation system. What we attempt to teach, even before we take off points, is how to lose points. He earns points for learning how to accept feedback. He earns points for taking off points without getting emotional, and we gradually try to teach the youth that it is more reinforcing over the long run not to throw temper tantrums and show aggression.

Intensive Teaching

Intensive teaching is our method of handling a youth when he is bordering on out-of-control behavior or has actually thrown a temper tantrum and has become aggressive. Intensive teaching is a method by which the teaching-parents stop all other interactions, clear the room of other youths who might taunt him or encourage his aggressive behavior, and engage in a systematic set of steps to concentrate on the negative behaviors he is engaging in, no matter how far he tries to lead the teaching-parents astray. For example, an aggressive interaction might start off by a youth becoming angry and yelling at the teaching-parents that "It is unfair! I never get to go anywhere when I want to and I should be able to go out tonight!" The teaching-parents immediately clear the room of other youths; one of the teaching-parents stays with the angry youth, and the other teaching-parent takes care of the household and continues the normal routine so that the house is not disrupted. (It is important that the youth throwing the temper tantrum not receive re-inforcement for disrupting the house.) The teaching-parent staying with the youth who is angry begins to ask the youth to concentrate on the real problem. "Now, the problem at first was that you wanted to go out and did not want to do dishes even though it was your turn, but now the problem is that you have become angry, you are looking defiant, and you've got your fists tightened up. You insisted that you are going to have it your way, and you stood up and knocked the chair over." The youth says, "Well, I don't give a damn! It's my life and I'll lead it the way I want to!" The teaching-parent again focuses on the problem and starts to suggest alternative behaviors. "Now, the problem is that you are starting to curse. You need to calm down, you need to sit down. You need to say 'Lonnie, I want to talk to you about a problem that I have tonight.'" The youth at that point may say something like, "Dammit, I never get to go anywhere!" The teaching-parent again does not leave the immediate subject and at that point says, "You need to sit down and stop cursing; you're losing points but you can earn some of those points back if you sit down." By doing this, the teaching-parent is handling the situation by *dealing with the ongoing behavior* and not with the content of the youth's argument about the fairness of staying home or going out. The teaching-parents have something effective and practical to do when a youth is out of control. The problem is *not* that the youth wants to go out tonight; the problem is that the youth is showing aggressive behavior and the teaching-parents must deal with that problem first. It is easy to be trapped into talking about what the youth wants to talk about when he is angry. It is critical that teaching-parents do not reinforce that behavior by talking about his topic. That can always be rectified after he has calmed down. Of course, the youth must never get his way with one of these temper tantrums and the final line must be that he would have been better off *not* becoming aggressive.

DEALING WITH VIOLENT BEHAVIOR OF YOUTHS

When a youth does become violent, it is important that the teaching-parent have a prescribed format to follow to deal with the youths, that an official "backup" system be available, and that a routine review of each incident take place.

Assaultive Behavior Checklist. The teaching-parents are taught to use the Assaultive Behavior Checklist whenever a youth becomes uncontrollable. As shown in Table 1, the Checklist prescribes the actions to be taken to

TABLE 1

The Checklist Used to Teach and Remind Teaching-Parents About the
Procedures to Deal with the Behavior of a Violent or Assaultive Youth

PHYSICALLY ASSAULTIVE YOUTH PROCEDURE

Introduction
Occasionally the teaching-parents will have a youth in their home who will
become assaultive with a teaching-parent, the children of the teaching-parents,
other youths living in the home, or pets, or will become violently destructive.
The behavior of the youth may be shoving, pushing, kicking, biting, hitting,
throwing objects, or threatening with weapons or dangerous objects.
Purpose
The purpose of this procedure is to familiarize teaching-parents with a course
of action should such an event occur. The final goal, of course, is for the teaching-
parents to be able to maintain enough control to allow for the resolution of the
conflict within the home or community.
Prevention
The following suggestions are made to assist the teaching-parents in preventing assaultive behaviors or escalation of intense situations in their home.
— 1. Educate the youths during the orientation process as to the benefits of
living at Boys Town, the home's operation, rules, etc. It is also helpful to
occasionally review this checklist with the youths so they know the procedure used to deal with serious disturbances.
— 2. Behavioral Rehearsal. Develop and practice with each youth appropriate
responses to criticisms and intense emotional situations that might be
encountered in day-to-day living. Goals should be to teach:
—a. Responding to "no."
—b. Objecting constructively.
—c. Following instructions.
—d. Accepting criticism.
—e. Engaging in rational conversation.
—f. Expected response to a cue word such as "stop."
— 3. Record approximations to assaultive behavior and threats in the Home
File on each youth.
— 4. Keep consultants, the community director, parents, and social agency
workers informed of approximations to assaultive behavior and threatening behavior.
— 5. Monitor youths engaging in aggressive or threatening behaviors or "out-
of-control" behaviors very closely.
— 6. Review and practice the Intensive Teaching Process.
Procedure
In the event that a youth should become assaultive, uncontrollably threatening,
or destructive, utilize the following procedure:
— 1. Ask the other youths to leave the room and have one teaching-parent
maintain the normal routine of the home.
— 2. If the youth is continuing threatening or destructive behavior, contact
neighbors for assistance. (If a youth has assaulted a blood relative, it is

imperative that some nonfamily member be called to assist, since the temptation for overreaction is present.)

— 3. Contact the Boys Town Police Department for assistance.
— 4. Contact the community director.
— 5. Upon the arrival of the Boys Town Police Department:
    —a. Isolate the youth in the home.
    —b. Use the minimum restraint necessary to stop *aggressive physical behavior*. (Note: This does not include preventing the youth from running away.)
    —c. In the event that the youth is still engaging in aggressive, physical behavior, the police may need to remove the youth from the home. The teaching-parent must accompany the youth.
— 6. Await the return call or arrival of the community director.
— 7. If, after a discussion with the community director, it is decided that the youth will be going to a closed setting, perform the following:
    —a. Describe to the youth where he is going, why he is going, how long he might be there, what he needs to do, and the measures you will take if he does not.
    —b. Do not leave the youth alone.
    —c. Prepare the youth with toilet articles and clothing for 24 hours.
    —d. Contact a neighbor to help with transportation, since the Boys Town Police Officer will not be able to wait with you at the closed setting.
    —e. Have an adult check the outside of the home to make sure no "spectators" are around and to disperse them if present (the youth should not be humiliated or embarrassed).
    —f. The youth should be placed in the back of a Boys Town Police vehicle with an adult on each side of the youth. (Note: The youth will be under a great deal of stress; the temptation to leave the vehicle or interfere with the driver of the vehicle is very real.)
    —g. In some cases, the youth may be handcuffed by the Police for transporting. (Note: As suggested under "f" above, the purpose is to prevent the youth from harming himself or others which would further intensify the difficulty the youth is in.)
    —h. Transport the youth to the designated closed facility.
    —i. After arriving at the closed facility, check in at the admissions desk before going to the closed section.
— 8. Recontact the community director and complete appropriate reports. (Note: If charges are to be filed regarding the incident, be sure it is first discussed with the community director.)
— 9. Notify the director of youth care.
—10. Notify within 24 hours:
    —a. Youth's parent(s) or guardian.
    —b. Other concerned agencies.

Follow-Up
— 1. Discuss with the youths at the next family conference:
    —a. The precipitating incident.
    —b. Other youths' actions during the incident.
    —c. Any inappropriate action.

— d. Rationales.
— e. Consequences.
— f. Expected response of the family members when the youth returns.
— 2. Check back with the youth in eight hours to see how he or she is. Visit (in person) the youth sometime the following day and each day the youth is in the closed facility.
— 3. Begin to prepare the youth for release from the closed facility. (Note: Make sure the release is coordinated with the community director and the person responsible for releasing the youth from the closed facility.)
  — a. If the youth is returning to Boys Town, discuss *where, why,* and *when* the youth is going and what the expectations are.
  — b. If the youth is returning to the community that referred him or her, discuss where, why, when and *to whom* the youth is going and what the expectations are.
— 4. Transport the youth to Boys Town.
— 5. Schedule a community council meeting to review the entire episode.

summon help, the preparations to make if the youth needs to be removed from the home for a period of time, and the people who should be notified of the incident. The main purpose of the Checklist is to protect the youth. If the teaching-parents understand that it is all right to call in other people, then they are less likely to resort to other means that might harm a youth. In other words, having a prescribed procedure limits the "approved" actions that might be taken under these difficult circumstances. Also, the Checklist helps the teaching-parents to accurately report each incident and provides an easy way for the Community Director to follow up and review each incident.

Official backup system. It is critical in any treatment program to have the backup systems well designed ahead of time so the teaching-parents can routinely go through their use when the time comes. Of course, the primary system is the teaching-parents and the techniques they use with the youth. The first backup system is the Community Director who is available 24 hours a day, seven days a week, and who has a "pageboy" in order to be reached any time, night or day, so he can help with a problem. The second backup system is our on-campus Police Department that responds immediately to any calls on campus and can restrain a youth or hold a youth until a decision is made as to what should happen to him. The third backup is a local juvenile treatment center for out-of-control youths. We may place a youth in this setting for up to 48 hours until a decision is made as to his long-term disposition. While there, the youth is evaluated, and that information is given to the Community Director to be used in determining whether the youth should stay in the treatment program or be removed.

Routine review of incidents. All actions of a teaching-parent are routinely reviewed by the Community Director, who acts as a consultant to each home and who is notified of each incident in a home. An additional level of review by a community council is also required when consideration must be given to unusual punishment or restriction procedures used by teaching-parents, to incidents involving youths who are violent or abusive, or to recommendations for dismissal of a youth from Boys Town. The community council is composed of a Community Director, two teaching-parents, two school teachers, and two youths. At council meetings, the teaching-parents and/or youth whose behavior is subject to review are present to describe the incident and answer questions. After all questions are answered, the council meets privately to vote on a course of action.

The primary concern of the council is to protect the youths from practices that may cause them injury or harm. Teaching-parents operate their programs with the knowledge that the council has the right to review their decisions and behavior. This enhances the teaching-parents' accountability for following the procedures outlined in their training program and in the Assaultive Behavior Checklist. Also, the membership of the council is broad enough so that many points of view are represented. This results in a mutual education process where reasonable tolerance levels are established for both youth and teaching-parent behavior.

From a legal point of view, the community council serves as a mechanism for considering "least restrictive treatment" and "due process" requirements. The least restrictive treatment principle requires that more severe or confining treatment should not be used unless less severe treatments have already been tried and have failed. Due process requirements mean that a youth has the right to represent his point of view and that a systematic process is used to make decisions.

DEALING WITH ABUSE

Despite any institution's best efforts, violence, abuse, and neglect will occur on some occasions. The problem here centers around detecting it, investigating the facts, rectifying the situation, and seeking ways to prevent it in the future.

Detecting Violence and Abuse

Frequent interaction with the youths and staff is probably the best method to detect violence and abuse. Consultants, program directors, evaluators, and visitors are frequent guests in a home at Boys Town, and they are constantly alert to the conditions that might be associated with violence and abuse: Are the youths unhappy and do they avoid the teaching-parents? Do any youths have bruises or cuts or scratches? Do the youths or parents or teachers complain about conditions in the home? Do the teaching-parents complain about the youths or avoid them? Considerable judgment is required to interpret the behavior and conditions in a home and conclude that violence or abuse is occurring there. However, it is best to be very sensitive and to investigate even the slightest hint of abuse.

Investigating the Facts

It is rarely the case that a clear-cut incident occurs. There are always varying interpretations and conclusions, even among eye witnesses. At Boys Town we have a small group of people who are called together to investigate each alleged incident. It is their task to interview the youths, teaching-parents, teachers, and others who may be involved and to arrive at a judgment based on the available information. This judgment is presented to the director of youth care, who then takes appropriate action.

Rectifying the Situation

If the evidence clearly indicates that an adult physically abused a youth, that adult is fired, the youth is cared for, and all concerned parties are notified of the incident. If the evidence clearly indicates that no abuse occurred, the situation is more difficult because reputations are often affected during the investigation process. In these cases, it is important to explain to each person who had been interviewed what the total facts of the case were and to caution them against spreading rumors or discussing the situation with anyone else. Often, however, the evidence is not clear, but a judgment still has to be made. The consequence for the staff person may range anywhere from termination or an official reprimand to increased monitoring for a period of time.

Preventing Future Incidents

After each incident of abuse or alleged abuse, the program managers meet to discuss how the situation could have been prevented. Did we select and hire the wrong person? Do we need to change our training and evaluation program? Were the consultant and Community Director doing enough monitoring? Do we need to change the treatment model? Or were the circumstances so unique that they are unlikely to be repeated? This meeting is very important not only for making needed program changes but also for keeping everyone alert to the potential problem.

Voluntary Placement

Another important consideration is that all youths who come to Boys Town do so voluntarily. This is emphasized throughout the admissions process, where detailed information about the Boys Town teaching-family program is provided to youths, parents, and referral agents, and the youths and parents are asked to consent to placement in the program. In these materials, the process for voluntarily leaving the program is specified and the procedures are detailed in writing. The youths can leave any time they are dissatisfied with what we do and how we do it. Thus, the youths maintain some (at least implicit) consequences for staff behavior that makes them unhappy. This fact, coupled with the youth consumer evaluation that is done as part of our minor, major, and certification evaluations, serves to make all of us accountable not only for helping the youths learn new skills but also for doing this in a way that is satisfactory to the youths.

CONCLUSION

Violence, abuse, and neglect are a way of life in some institutions and are more or less frequent occurrences in all institutions. We feel the most basic element in preventing violence in institutions is the treatment program that prescribes how the staff are to interact with the youths. But this has to be coupled with procedures to recruit and select the best staff, train the staff to use the treatment procedures humanely and effectively, evaluate the use of the procedures and the youths' progress, and support and help the staff in their efforts to work with the youths.

With the emphasis society places on children and their development, it is unconscionable for society to remove children from their homes and place them in institutions where they are abused and neglected. It is our clear responsibility as institutional managers to treat the youths humanely and effectively and in a way that encourages normal development. At Boys Town, we continue to strive for this ideal.

REFERENCES

Moos, R. H. *Evaluating treatment environments*. New York: John Wiley and Sons, 1974.

Phillips, E. L., Phillips, E. A., Fixsen, D. L., & Wolf, M. M. *The teaching-family handbook*. Lawrence, Kansas: University Printing Service, 1974.

10

Drug and Environmental Interventions for Aggressive Psychiatric Patients

ROBERT PAUL LIBERMAN,
BARRINGER D. MARSHALL, JR.,
and
KAREN L. BURKE

Central to concerns with aggressive mental patients is the question: "Are psychiatric patients more dangerous or violent than the population at large?" The prevailing layperson's view of this, stimulated by sensational journalism, is that individuals with psychiatric illnesses are more dangerous than nonpatients (Rapkin, 1972). Many of the commitment

This chapter was written with the support of NIMH Research Grant No. MH 30911. The opinions are those of the authors and do not reflect official policy of the California Departments of Mental Health or Developmental Disabilities or the Regents of the University of California. The authors acknowledge the crucial contributions of the CRU nursing staff whose assessment and treatment skills were responsible for the successful outcomes reported in this chapter. In particular, the leadership provided by Val Baker, R.N., Tim Oliver, R.N., and Lily Horton, R.N. and the professional training and program development given by Jim Teigen, M.S.W., Larry Licker, M.S.W., Lorelle Banzett, M.S.W., Dennis O'Bosky, M.S.W., Charles Wallace, Ph.D., and Roger Patterson, Ph.D have been instrumental to the productivity and creativity of the CRU. The administrative support given by Clinton Rust, M.P.A. (Executive Director), Samuel Rapport, M.D. (Medical Director), and Doug Van Meter, B.A. (Clinical Director) at Camarillo State Hospital has been vital to the operation of the CRU as a special evaluation and treatment unit.

laws and codes regulating psychiatric hospitalization, derived from popular opinions and social stereotypes, are tantamount to equating mental illness with dangerousness and violence. On the other hand, the professional view, based upon data from surveys and follow-up studies, is that psychiatric patients are less aggressive, violent, or dangerous than the population at large. However, methodological critiques of the research which led to this view and new research findings may lead us to revise our current conceptualizations of the issue.

Studies carried out between 1922 and 1962 provided data which led the National Commission on the Causes and Prevention of Violence to conclude that "Most studies indicate that the discharged mentally ill, as a whole, are significantly less prone than the general population to involvement in violent behavior . . . the mentally ill are no more likely than the general population to be involved in crimes such as assault, rape, or homicide" (Mulvihill & Tumin, 1969, p. 444). The studies supporting this conclusion were carried out by following up large cohorts of mental patients one to 10 years after their discharge from state hospitals. Arrest rates for these patients varied from four to 12 per 1,000, as compared to 27-99 per 1,000 for the general population. Four more recent studies, however, offer contradictory findings, with discharged psychiatric patients showing higher arrest rates, especially for assault, robbery and homicide, than the general population (Giovannoni & Gurel, 1967; Rappeport & Lassen, 1965, 1966; Zitrin et al., 1976).

Methodological limitations of the earlier studies suggest that it may be necessary to increase our concern about the dangerousness or aggressiveness of psychiatric patients. The earlier studies did not take into account that the more dangerous or violent patients are kept in the hospital longer and are the ones who are discharged last, and hence would be underrepresented in any follow-up period. These studies also did not take into account the "revolving-door phenomenon" which results in many discharged mental patients returning to the hospital for one or more readmissions. Thus, patients' "days at risk" in the community for committing an arrestable offense are much lower than the general population's. A final methodological problem comes from inadequacy of arrest rates and police records for determining the occurrence of violent crimes. Many ex-mental patients are dealt with administratively by police officers. These patients rarely get to the point of a formal arrest or adjudication for a violent offense. Instead they are channeled into the mental health system or referred to human service agencies for social control. Much of their threatened and actual aggression takes place within the family which brings the ex-patient to a mental health center or hospital. In sum, the earlier studies probably under-estimated the problem of dangerousness in psychiatric patients (Jacoby, 1978).

Aside from aggressive acts and criminal offenses committed by former patients in the community, how much of a problem is aggression within mental hospitals? A prevalence study was done at Camarillo State Hospital, which contains 1,400 patients, one-third of whom are retarded or developmentally disabled and two-thirds are psychotic, severely depressed, alcoholic, or acting-out personality disorders. Each month at Camarillo approximately 400 violent incidents are reported administratively. Incident reports are filed when either a staff member, a visitor, or a patient is injured. To arrive at a more accurate estimation of the frequency of aggression in the hospital, this number can be multiplied by a factor of five because the majority of aggressive incidents in psychiatric hospitals are not recorded (Lion et al., in press). When there is no obvious tissue damage to the staff or patient victim, and if a physician does not have to provide medical treatment, an incident may go unreported. Using the fivefold correction factor, there may be as many as 2,000 aggressive acts each month which comes to about two acts per patient per month in this hospital.

At a regional psychiatric hospital in Illinois where Gordon Paul (Paul & Lentz, 1977) developed two intensive treatment units based on milieu therapy and social learning principles, careful records were kept over a five-year period on aggressive behavior. On the two experimental wards, which had fine positive programming with high staff/patient ratios, there was one aggressive act occurring per half-hour of waking time. This rate might be expected to be even higher on other units which are not so richly staffed or so positively programmed. In summary, aggression by psychiatric patients poses a problem both inside psychiatric facilities and in the community. From a social learning perspective, since there is a high frequency of aggression within psychiatric hospitals—with manifold opportunities for overlearning, intermittent reinforcement, and modeling—we might expect generalization of aggressive behavior from the hospital into the community.

A SOCIAL LEARNING ANALYSIS OF AGGRESSION IN PSYCHIATRIC SETTINGS

Now that the significance and scope of the problem of aggression among psychiatric patients have been outlined, how might we conceptualize the determinants of this problem? Aggressive behavior is rooted in both biological and environmental factors. Our genetic endowment and neural substrates determine the qualities and boundaries of our psychosocial functioning, including our capacity for violent and aggressive behavior. The search for neurophysiological causes and correlates of violence and aggression has been sensationalized by the popular press, but has yielded little data. There are only sporadic, well-documented clinical cases where lesions in the temporal or frontal lobes—particularly involving the limbic system in the area of the amygdala and hippocampus—have been implicated in violent outbursts. Temporal lobe epilepsy is occasionally associated with periodic episodes of aggressive behavior, but even in cases where cerebral dysrhythmias and seizure phenomena have been recorded, psychological and environmental factors play an important part in determining where and when the violence occurs (Mark & Ervin, 1970). In such patients, drinking even a small amount of alcohol can precipitate aggressive attacks. Thus, a multiplicity of variables—past history and childhood development, drugs and alcohol, socioenvironmental stressors, existing behavioral repertoires, and organic neuropathology—all interact together to determine aggressive activity (Daniels, Gilula, & Ochberg, 1970). In this section, the environmental and personality or person-linked variables will be covered.

A behavioral or functional analysis of aggressive behavior starts with topographical descriptions of the problems so that observers and clinicians can reliably record and count their occurrence. Such descriptions are graphic and clear; one does not have to split hairs or use refined and sophisticated behavioral codes to encapsulate aggressive acts among hospitalized psychiatric patients. We are dealing with grossly apparent behaviors such as hitting, kicking, scratching, hair pulling, biting, and throwing objects. If untrained observers walk onto a psychiatric unit, there would be little difficulty in obtaining high levels of interobserver agreement in determining the occurrence of an aggressive act. Here are some examples of aggression:

> Sally, a 20-year-old, frail-looking, moderately retarded young woman slammed doors, tore pictures off the wall, and pushed staff members and other patients.

> Ronald, a 53-year-old man, continuously hospitalized for almost 30 years, punched patients without provocation and walked around the unit with a clenched fist intimidating people.

> Valerie was a 28-year-old schizophrenic who surprised staff and

patients alike with sudden attacks from the rear, often pulling her victim's hair out by the roots. Her attacks resulted in several staff members having to be hospitalized for injuries.

Joe, a burly 22-year-old ex-athlete with an organic brain disorder, broke windows and TV sets, and used his cane to thrash other patients.

Thus, one way to conceptualize aggression is by describing the behavioral excesses which they reflect. What, then, are the antecedents and consequences in the environment which sustain aggressive behavior?

In terms of antecedents, the context of institutional settings influences aggression. Most mental hospitals are confining, with locked, crowded wards. There is little privacy, few staff, and a lot of inactivity, boredom, and deprivation of both biological and social needs. Thus, the contextual cues on psychiatric units tend to elicit frustration-induced aggression.

The consequences of aggressive behavior include getting staff attention, a scarce commodity in understaffed institutions. Aggression reliably and consistently generates a concerned response from staff, and given the levels of social deprivation on many psychiatric wards, even negative attention can be reinforcing. Instrumental needs are also met via aggression. Grabbing other people's food and stealing cigarettes and other things have their own rewards. In prisons we are familiar with the verbal and physical intimidation that promotes sexual favors and other personal comforts and conveniences. Because aggression is maintained by its antecedents and consequences, perhaps we should spend more of our time planning modifications of the institutional environments, rather than focusing on individual cases and their behavioral problems.

As an example of the functions subserved by aggression in an institution, let's picture a scenario with Valerie, the young schizophrenic woman whose violent behavior caused injuries sufficient to warrant hospitalizing a few staff members:

The staff are sitting in the nurses' station drinking coffee or doing interminable paper work. They might be complaining about the psychologist and psychiatrist who never come down to the unit, but instead spend all their time reading journals in their offices. Valerie is looking through the window of the nurses' station checking out the nurses. She is lurking around the bend of a corridor, waiting for another patient to approach. When the patient comes by, she pushes the patient, knocks her down to the floor, and jumps on top of her, beating her and screaming. The nursing staff then come running out of the nursing station, pry the patients apart, and administer a *prn* intramuscular dose of chlorpromazine. After the injection is given, Valerie is allowed access to her room and bed which previously were locked and not available to her. She is encouraged to calm down, and a staff member, speaking soothingly, periodically checks to see how she is feeling. For the time being, the aggressive act is dealt with and chronicled in a hospital incident report; however, Valerie's behavior has been powerfully reinforced. In addition, her aggression serves as a model for other patients on the unit to emulate.

Thus, in most psychiatric facilities aggressive patients do get the "goodies." That is, they get scarce staff attention and other things as well. From the functional point of view, it matters little whether the topographical description of the aggression is hitting, biting, or kicking; they are all prompted by the same antecedent conditions and are all reinforced by the same consequences. Functionally, these qualitatively different aggressive acts are equivalent.

PERSONAL VARIABLES IN AGGRESSION

While the situational antecedents and consequences undoubtedly affect aggression in mental hospitals, variables linked to the person are also implicated. Certain individuals appear to create "tornados of aggression" in a variety of situations and against a range of targets. Aggressive behavior is learned and incorporated into a person's repertoire and endures over time and across places and targets. Not only is the aggressor influenced by features of the environment he or she encounters, but the aggressor also selects the situations in which the aggression occurs. The aggressive patient's acting-out affects the character of the environment, producing, through modeling, more aggression and, through expectations of others, a self-fulfilling prophecy of more aggression.

This interactional view of aggression, in which the aggressive individual helps to mold the nature of the responsive environment, is highlighted by the work of Toch (1969) who studied 128 men who had exhibited repeated violent encounters. The research reconstructed the chain of interactions between aggressor and victim and elaborated the sequential developments in encounters resulting in aggression. The methods used included detailed interviews with aggressors and their victims and analysis of relevant reports of the violent incidents. Ten categories of "violence-prone" persons were determined, including those for whom aggression served to maintain their reputation, their social status, or their self-image. Violence-prone individuals appear to have consistent interpersonal orientations in which they perceive, process, and then respond to social situations in a way that produces a high likelihood of violent interactions. These persons respond aggressively to certain cues that others do not respond to in an aggressive way.

For example, Joe tended to respond with aggression to minor frustrations. If a nurse said, "I'm sorry, I can't get you a cup of coffee now. You'll have to wait until later," he might respond by breaking a window or pushing someone. He tended to view frustrations as provocations. He did not have cognitive or verbal alternatives to respond differently to frustrating situations. Unsocialized, aggressive children have been studied by Patterson and his colleagues, who find them to be veritable storm centers of violence. Wherever they go and whomever they interact with, they seem to generate aggression in both themselves and others (Patterson, 1979, this volume, Chapter 5).

Aggressive behavioral trends that endure over time and across situations and interpersonal targets may be the result of inadequate problem-solving skills and inept social relationship skills. Toch (1969) points out, for instance, that a majority of the violence-prone individuals he studied were deficient in verbal and interpersonal skills. He was able to retrospectively determine that many of his subjects appeared to slip into violence because of social clumsiness. For example, a subject convicted of repeated rapes had never learned to engage in seduction and courtship rituals. A man charged with armed robbery used his gun when his verbal bluffs were unconvincing. Much domestic violence stems from the protagonists' inability to work through a problem using verbal interaction.

All of us have social and emotional needs for attachment, interdependency, concern, affection, and recognition. When these needs are deprived or frustrated, violence can ensue unless the individual has requisite social and problem-solving skills for restoring and satisfying his/her needs. If deficits in social and problem-solving skills do indeed predispose an individual to aggressive behavior in the pursuit of basic needs, then methods for remediating these deficits should have a high priority in the armamentarium of helping professionals.

DRUG TREATMENT FOR AGGRESSIVE BEHAVIOR

Psychotropic drugs are the standard treatment in most psychiatric facilities for dealing with violent psychiatric patients. In one textbook, detailed instructions are given on how to administer medication to aggressive patients: "The medication should be prepared, if possible, before the patient is restrained, so that it can be given as soon as possible, usually before placing the patient in 4-point restraint. By giving the medication intravenously and slowly, the level of sedation can be titrated, side effects minimized, and control gained quickly" (Tupin, 1975, pp. 132-133). For aggressive behavior, drugs are used most commonly, followed by mechanical restraints, and then seclusion.

There is an empirical rationale for using drugs, but only in cases where a well-defined psychiatric disorder or illness produces symptoms that indirectly or secondarily lead to violent behavior. Table 1 gives the indications for using one or another of the psychotropic drugs when aggression stems from one of the major psychiatric disorders. For example, in schizophrenics, aggression is usually bizarre and stems from delusions of persecution, grandiosity, or religiosity which produce poor perception and processing of interpersonal situations that may lead to aggression.

A person who suffers from schizophrenia can be given a major tranquilizer or neuroleptic, like chlorpromazine, which reduces the paranoid delusional misperceptions of the world that may lead a person to belligerence and aggressive acts. Individuals who are manic and suffering from manic-depressive psychosis can become excited with delusions of grandeur which then, secondarily, lead to aggressive behavior. For example, a manic patient of the senior author recently felt that he was chosen by God to bring a message to the city and to destroy a local synagogue. When his wife and parents refused to accompany him on his "mission" down the main street of the town, he lashed out and became violent with them. Later, he smashed windows in the synagogue. The patient's elation and delusional manic state "unlocked" his usual high

TABLE 1
Psychotropic Drug Treatment for Aggression Associated with Specific Psychiatric Disorders

Disorder	Type of Drug	Example
Schizophrenia	Major tranquilizer or Neuroleptic	Chlorpromazine (Thorazine)
Manic-depressive psychosis	Mood stabilizer	Lithium (Eskalith)
Severe depression	Antidepressant	Imipramine (Tofranil)
Psychomotor epilepsy	Anticonvulsant	Primidone (Mysoline)

level of social inhibition and moral self-restraint. An aggressive person suffering from a well-defined manic illness responds well to lithium. When lithium and perhaps a supplementary neuroleptic are administered, effects are seen in a few days. The patient's mood is stabilized, the symptoms subside, and when the symptoms subside, the aggression goes away.

People who are severely depressed may also act out violently as a result of their hopelessness, feelings of worthlessness, agitation, and delusions of being evil. Depressed persons sometimes feel the need to kill loved ones, so that their loved ones will not be as miserable as they feel themselves. Contrary to psychoanalytic lore, depressed persons actually exhibit more outward-directed hostility than do nondepressed individuals. Homicide and suicide situations occur quite frequently in depressed individuals. For potentially aggressive depressed persons, antidepressant drugs such as imipramine or amitriptylene can be effective, with suppression of symptoms and elimination of the secondary aggression.

Likewise, appropriate drug therapy can eliminate aggression elicited by psychomotor epilepsy or temporal lobe epilepsy. If aggression linked to temporal lobe epilepsy is diagnosed early, anticonvulsants successfully stop the secondary episodes of rage, Hyperactivity in children is sometimes associated with provocativeness, agitation, poking, pushing, and other forms of aggressive behavior with peers. In some cases, stimulant drugs like methylphenidate (Ritalin) or amphetamines can be helpful in reducing these symptoms and the aggression.

Antiandrogen and progestational agents are recently-tried, controversial treatments for aggression which have not yet been tested in double-blind controlled clinical trials. While testosterone levels have been correlated with aggression in laboratory animals, no similar evidence has been collected for humans. These drugs, which lower serum testosterone levels, have been employed for hypersexual aggression (Blumer & Migeon, 1975). Anecdotal reports suggest that these agents are effective, especially with sex offenders such as rapists. Progestational agents have been used successfully for crisis intervention with very dangerous sexual offenders (Gene Abel, personal communication). The drug quickly enables doctor, patient, and family to raise their hopes and gain some control. While this hormonal treatment has spread more by word of mouth than by scientific publications, a number of experts in the field are suggesting that this may be an effective therapeutic approach to aggression, particularly where the aggression is linked to hypersexuality (Lion, 1975). Much evaluative research still has to be done before hormonal agents become an accepted mode of treatment.

Most of what we know about drugs tells us that they do not have a direct calming effect on violence unless used in a psychiatric setting as a "chemical straightjacket," sedating the person to the point of drowsiness, so movement of any kind is impaired. But aside from "snowing" an aggressive out-of-control patient for his/her and others' safety, the only appropriate use is for well-defined, well-diagnosed psychiatric illnesses from which the aggressive behavior appears as a secondary problem.

The minor tranquilizers, or antianxiety agents, are more prescribed than any other type of drug in the world. Valium, Librium, and other similar drugs in the benzodiazepine category have definite taming effects on aggressive animals, but they have not been shown to have beneficial effects on aggression in humans. Despite their lack of demonstrable antiaggressive effects, the benzodiazepines are frequently used for dealing directly with aggression.

Because drugs are so easily administered and appeal to the belief of many psychiatric personnel that aggression is biologically driven, misuses of medication frequently occur. Some years ago there were anecdotal reports in the psychiatric literature on lithium's purported effectiveness in reducing violence in prisoners and other deviant populations. Because aggression is common among residents at state schools and hospitals for the developmentally disabled or retarded, physicians began using lithium. When, in some states, rules were promulgated that lithium could only be used for patients diagnosed as manic-depressive (the only proven indication for its use), some physicians changed or added to the diagnosis of these retarded people the label of manic-depression so they could continue using the lithium.

In large institutions housing patients with serious and omnipresent aggression, there is tremendous pressure from the nursing staff on the physician or psychiatrist to misprescribe and to misuse psychotropic medications. Prescribing and administering drugs serve important social control and personal functions among all levels of staff. Because something tangible is being done "therapeutically," much staff anxiety is relieved. And it should be pointed out that the extent and dangerousness of violence in psychiatric settings do promote realistic fear among staff.

Illustrating the magnitude of staff beliefs in medication, a study we carried out a number of years ago at Camarillo State Hospital was aimed at evaluating a change in the schedule of administration of major tranquilizers on one of the chronic care units, from the typical four times a day to once a day at bedtime, with the total daily dosage remaining constant. Nursing staff were very upset and very resistant to having this experiment carried out. They felt that the 45 patients on the ward would become out of control, that aggression would increase, and that people would be hurt. The ward psychiatrist and research team reassured them that the evaluation was just for a brief period of time. The nursing staff were further told that the results of the change in schedule of drug administration would be reevaluated frequently. If, in fact, patients became out of control, four-times-a-day administration of the medication would be resumed immediately.

Direct observations by reliable and "blind" raters were taken 18 times a day, measuring a variety of behaviors, including aggressive acts. The 45 patients on the ward were observed during four-times-a-day administration and once-a-day administration, using a within-subject, repeated measures design. The only difference in behavior found was that, when the medication was given once a day at bedtime, patients tended to have their *eyes open* more often during the day. There weren't any other significant changes whatsoever. The nursing staff, however, were convinced that aggression increased during the once-daily drug period. Even when the staff were shown the data, they still averred that the patients had gotten out of hand. This failure of empirical evaluation to sway staff opinions highlights the tremendous problems posed by staff attitudes, concerns, and anxiety in the rational use of psychopharmacological agents (Callahan et al., 1975).

PARADOXICAL EFFECTS OF PSYCHOACTIVE DRUGS ON AGGRESSION

Almost every psychoactive drug has been reported to elicit aggressive and hostile responses in man. Alcohol is the drug most often associated with violence. Sedative-hypnotic drugs, such as barbiturates, Quaalude, Doriden, and chloral hydrate, rank second to alcohol in their implication in criminal assaults. There is mounting evidence that the omnipresent minor tranquilizers such as Valium and Librium may also elicit hostility and aggressive acts (Salzman, Kochansky, & Shader, 1974). Stimulant drugs, epitomized by the amphetamines, are well-known as elicitors of aggression. In chronic use, amphetamines can produce a paranoid psychosis, with the individual often acting out delusions in a violent manner. More recently, the increased use of phencyclidine, also called PCP and "angel dust," has been associated with violence and self-injury.

Case Example of Paradoxical Aggression Produced by a Neuroleptic

While neuroleptics or major tranquilizers are considered to have therapeutic effects in diminishing aggression linked to psychotic symptoms, the following case illustrates the paradoxical effects which can occur with this class of drugs.

Ronald was 53 years old and had been continuously hospitalized for 30 years with a diagnosis of schizophrenia. He was kept hospitalized not because of his paranoid delusions, but because he was repeatedly violent and aggressive. Because of violent behavior, three lobotomies were performed on Ronald over this 30-year period, the most recent one being in 1968. That highlights the desperation of staff who had to manage his violence, because by 1968 very few lobotomies were still being done. Over the years Ronald had over 100 electroconvulsive treatments and had been tried on all types and combinations of drugs.

He would hit, without warning, fellow patients and staff members, generally from behind and by surprise. These aggressive episodes resulted in serious injuries. In fact, the first week that he was on our Clinical Research Unit, he knocked out two teeth from two patients, broke another patient's nose, and lacerated the forehead of one of our staff members.

By the time we evaluated him, Ronald wasn't very verbal or articulate, and thus historical information was lacking. As often happens in long-term hospitalized cases, Ronald's medical records were lacking details and little was known about his prehospital life. However, he may have been a boxer, because he often would stand with a boxer's stance in the middle of the ward, jabbing at people who walked by. He had cauliflower ears, which may have come from his boxing days or from his violent encounters in the hospital.

Prior to lashing out and hurting people physically, he made frequent and well-defined threats, characterized by making a fist or pointing his right index finger at someone, scowling, and furrowing his brow. Thus, he showed clear behavioral premonitory signs before mounting an aggressive outburst. These threats occurred about four times a day, while actual assaults averaged about two a day.

When Ronald was admitted to the Clinical Research Unit (CRU), he was receiving haloperidol (Haldol), a neuroleptic, and phenytoin (Dilantin), an anticonvulsant. The anticonvulsant was given not because Ronald had a seizure disorder, but because years before it had been reported, anecdotally, to reduce violent behavior among psychiatric patients. The frequency of aggressive acts is shown in Figure 1 under the baseline condition, with Ronald receiving both drugs. While receiving haloperidol and phenytoin, Ronald averaged two aggressive incidents per day. During this time, he was placed in a time-out room for 15 minutes contingent upon each aggressive act, since time-out from reinforcement is a standard CRU policy for aggressive and destructive behavior. Despite the systematic application of time-out, Ronald continued his frequent violent acts while he was receiving the two drugs. When he was taken off his medication, with the time-out contingency remaining constant, he showed a rapid decline in aggression to almost zero, with maintenance of that low rate for the final two months of his stay on the CRU.

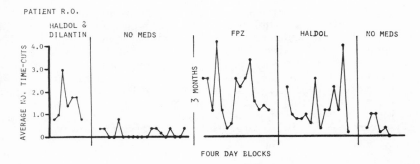

FIGURE 1. Number of time-outs for Ronald's aggressive behavior averaged over four-day blocks. Doses of medication were Haldol = 30 mg/day; Phenytoin (Dilantin) = 300 mg/day; Fluphenazine (FPZ or Prolixin) = 20 mg/day. A 3-month period separated his two hospitalizations on the CRU.

He was discharged from the CRU and returned to his referring hospital. Inexplicably, the staff at the other hospital resumed the administration of neuroleptic medication, in this case fluphenazine (Prolixin). It is almost axiomatic, unfortunately, that when a patient is admitted to a psychiatric hospital, psychotropic medication is ordered. As can be seen in Figure 1, the aggressive behavior returned and continued when Ronald was switched to his original neuroleptic haloperidol. Aggression was eliminated quickly when he was taken off all medication. During his second period of treatment on the CRU, he was again exposed to the same time-out contingency for aggression; however, the environmental program did not control the aggression until medication was withdrawn.

There are several possible reasons why Ronald may have had a paradoxical aggressive reaction to psychoactive medications. For one, the neuroleptics produce uncomfortable and subtle neurological side effects such as akathisia, or severe restlessness and muscle tension. Many patients speak of akathisia as an "inner turmoil" that can "drive them up the wall." It has been shown that patients' symptoms can increase, even their psychotic symptoms, as a result of agitation and attempts to escape from the restlessness. Another possible explanation for the drug-related aggression lies in the disinhibitory phenomenon seen most typically with alcohol. It is possible that the neuroleptic blurred Ronald's ability to appreciate the social deviance of his behavior. In a similar vein, the drug may have interfered with Ronald's learning from his environment—only with the withdrawal of drugs did he appear to respond to the time-out program on the Unit. Finally, the drug may have directly affected the patient's limbic system, increasing excitation and belligerence.

For Ronald's threatening behavior, a program was developed based upon *differential reinforcement of other behavior* (DRO). For

every 15 minutes that he did not engage in any threatening behavior—defined as holding his fist up or pointing his finger—he
earned tokens which could then be exchanged every half-hour for
cigarettes and coffee. Gradually this 15-minute interval was increased to 45 minutes. If he did threaten during any of these
intervals, he was fined tokens. This resulted in his threatening
behavior going down to almost zero. The DRO program affected
the behaviors that preceded the actual violent outbursts. If premonitory signs of aggression can be identified and reliably observed, it is helpful to target those for intervention.

ENVIRONMENTAL CONTROL OF AGGRESSIVE BEHAVIOR

Since its inception in 1970, the CRU at Camarillo State Hospital has
treated many mentally and developmentally disabled patients with
aggression and/or property destruction as their referral problem. The
CRU's therapeutic environment gradually evolved to effectively respond
to severe problems such as aggression. Even now, the environment is
evolving, as evidenced by the continual revisions in the CRU's official
policy manual. A description of the CRU and its programs is important
since the control of aggression requires a systematic, consistent treatment
environment aimed at strengthening prosocial behaviors as well as reducing violent ones.

Patients are referred to the CRU from other hospital units, from
community agencies, from private therapists, and from psychiatric facilities in other parts of the state and country. Each referred patient is
evaluated by the entire staff in an interdisciplinary team process. Many
times a nursing staff member will accompany the social worker or psychologist to evaluate a referred individual. Active involvement of the
nursing staff at every phase of treatment, starting from the point of
referral, is important, since the nursing staff are instrumental in carrying
out the 24-hour-per-day observation and treatment of the patients. Referrals are discussed at team meetings where an inventory is made of
the patient's assets, problems, and kinds of reinforcers that might be
effective in developing a treatment program.

If the patient is accepted to the Unit, a more intensive behavioral
assessment is undertaken. Observations are made by nursing staff
around the clock. Narrative notes are made, in a continuous fashion, of
antecedents and consequences of the patient's problem behaviors. Systematic entries are made which rate the patient's self-care or daily living
skills such as eating, room-cleaning, bed-making, and completion of

housekeeping chores. The number of prompts required for the patient to achieve acceptable grooming and dress criteria is recorded.

Evaluations are made four times a day by nursing staff of the patients' social interaction and conversational skills. Each patient, in turn, is observed and rated as interacting or isolated. If the patient is interacting, a judgment is made regarding the positive or prosocial vs. negative or antisocial nature of the interaction. If the patient is isolated, a judgment is made regarding the activity or engagement of the patient with reading, games, or TV. After making momentary cross-sectional observations of each patient, the nursing staff then approach each patient in turn and engage in a five-minute conversation, using a topic from a glossary of themes. After the conversation, the patient is rated on verbal and nonverbal components of expression and any bizarre or symptomatic behaviors are noted. These social and conversational data serve as points of departure for developing individualized social-skills training programs.

The frequency of aggressive and destructive incidents is noted, as well as violations of Unit rules and policies. Each patient is given a multi-axial DSM III diagnosis. When appropriate, an MMPI, a Psychiatric Assessment Scale, and a Present State Examination are administered to assess the patient's psychiatric phenomenology and psychopathology. More elaborate assessments are provided when applicable.

Within one to two weeks of admission, the assessment data are summarized and pooled, and one of the professional-level staff members takes responsibility for writing a treatment program. Two types of treatment programs are developed: One, a credit system, is semi-standardized for the CRU and focuses on personal hygiene and daily living skills. The second program is highly individualized to meet the unique needs of each patient.

The individualized program is written in problem-oriented medical record (POMR) format (Marshall, Wallace, Burke, & Liberman, 1979) as a treatment memo that is given to all members of the CRU staff. The treatment memo and its associated data sheet are placed on a clipboard which is hung on a pegboard in the nurses' station. The memo and data sheet serve as a 24-hour-per-day guide or prompt to the nursing staff to carry out consistent observations and interventions with the patients. The data that are recorded by the nursing staff during the day are then summarized and graphed by the night shift who come on duty at 11:30 p.m. In this function, the night staff is brought into the treatment program in an active way. The behavioral graphs are used at twice-a-week team meetings to make decisions about changing the individualized treatment programs or to continue them. Figure 2 outlines the assessment and treatment programs of the CRU.

Credit System

The Unit-wide credit system is primarily for maintenance behaviors like self-care skills, grooming, bed-making, and cleaning-up activities. The aim of the credit system is to reinforce self-care and interactional

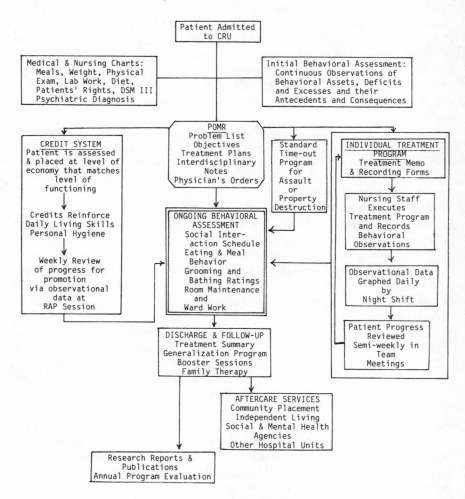

FIGURE 2. Outline of assessment and treatment programs on the CRU.

skills which occur many times during the day. Fines are also used to discourage infractions and antisocial acts. While credits possess symbolic and social reinforcing value (Liberman et al., 1977), they are backed up by tangible, primary reinforcers in a canteen that has a variety of candy, cigarettes, ice cream, coffee, tea and notions. Credits are exchangeable for these items three times daily.

The credit system has five levels in a hierarchy based upon immediacy of reinforcement, degree of self-evaluation, and range of privileges. The lowest level is a *continuous reinforcement program* where actual tokens are given out immediately to low-functioning patients who need shaping of self-care skills like grooming, simple conversational behaviors, or cleaning up after themselves. Most of the patients enter the program at the second level, a *tri-daily level*, where three times a day they have an opportunity to exchange at a canteen tokens that they have received. At these times pateints can buy cigarettes, coffee, candy, soda, and ice cream; they can also purchase privileges such as extra room time or permission to leave the Unit and go out on the hospital grounds. At the tri-daily level and higher, patients are rated on a five-point scale for their adequacy and initiative in carrying out maintenance tasks. Each time a task (e.g., teeth-brushing, mopping a floor) is completed *satisfactorily without prompts*, five points are awarded. If one prompt has been given to produce satisfactory performance, four points are awarded. A patient receives 30 credits for a five-point performance and 15 credits for a four-point performance.

If a patient averages at the scale level of four on all tasks performed during a week, has less than 60 credits debt because of fines, and has fewer than two destructive or aggressive incidents during the week, he or she is eligible for promotion to the *daily level*. Promotion from one level to another is subject to ratification by a two-third's vote of patients and staff present at one of two weekly "RAP" sessions, during which the patients are encouraged to discuss issues and concerns related to their programs and living on the CRU, and to suggest changes in the CRU's procedures, activities, and credit system.

At the daily or third level, credits are exchanged once a day during the evening canteen, when a patient can purchase a "daily ticket" for cigarettes, coffee, and grounds passes at a better bargain than at the tri-daily level. Using the "daily ticket" requires planning and budgeting one's credit earnings. In addition, during the time that a person is at the daily level, he or she has the responsibility for initiating and carrying out self-care tasks and Unit chores and reporting to the nursing staff monitor how well the job was done. The patient in the daily level is expected to request credit reinforcement upon completing each task, with the request including mention of the correct number of credits to be awarded for the task. The nursing staff member then double checks the job performance and gives credit if the performance is at a satisfactory level. Thus, at this step there are more opportunities to self-monitor and self-evaluate. The patient at the daily level can also accumulate up to 200 credits of debt each week without demotion.

If a patient continues to do well at the daily level for a week and has fewer than one aggressive outburst requiring time-out, does not acquire a credit debt more than 60 credits in a week, and continues to function at a high level in evaluations of the task and self-care performances, he or she is then eligible for promotion to the *weekly level*. At this level, patients can purchase a "weekly ticket" for privileges and access to the items available at the canteen. At the weekly level patients may also borrow up to 400 credits to be repaid over a two-week period. Patients at this level self-monitor and self-evaluate their performances on self-care and ward-wide tasks, with staff members making spot checks on a 20% random basis.

As criteria for promotion to the highest or *credit level*, the patient must go seven consecutive days without an aggressive incident, must maintain task performance at four or better, and not have fines in excess of 40 credits. Promotion must also be ratified by the patient-staff RAP session. At the time of promotion, the patient and a responsible nursing staff member negotiate a contingency contract focusing on some individual problems that are seen as needing change. The focal goals in the contingency contract might be increasing social interaction with the nursing staff, getting up earlier in the morning, or developing a skill in industrial or occupational therapy. At the credit level, patients monitor and evaluate their own behavior. Determination of continuing at the credit level is made at a weekly RAP session, with global ratings by the staff and patients on the individual's ability to maintain autonomy and responsibility and to adhere to terms of the contract.

Time-out Contingency

Time-out from reinforcement by placement in a quiet room is used as a general procedure for any assaultive act directed toward patients or staff on the CRU and for any act of property destruction, including slamming a door. The period of time-out in the quiet room does not exceed 15 minutes, with the following exceptions:

1) A patient must be quiet for two consecutive minutes before he/she is let out.
2) If a patient has to be physically prompted by staff to go to the quiet room, the time-out increases from the usual 15 minutes to one hour. Physical prompts include having to be pulled away from any patient or staff member.
3) If a patient does not enter the quiet room within one minute of being told to do so, time-out is increased to 60 minutes.
4) A specific patient's treatment program may be written to include longer periods of time-out, particularly for life-threatening assaultiveness.

Any aggressive or destructive incident also results in loss of grounds privileges for 24 hours, unless stated otherwise in individual programs. Time-out is also implemented for stealing items from nonpatient areas of the CRU. The specific behavioral components used by staff in implementing time-out are to:

1) remain calm;
2) state the rule broken and the time-out consequence;
3) ignore extraneous verbalizations and excuses by the patient;
4) follow through quickly.

Following removal of the patient from time-out, as soon as the patient shows cooperative or adaptive behavior, the staff member immediately praises the patient by:

1) looking at the patient;
2) smiling;
3) coming close to the patient;
4) making a positive verbal statement;
5) praising the behavior, not the patient;
6) using a friendly gesture or touch.

Time-out from reinforcement, operationalized by brief social isolation in a "quiet room," is the mainstay of treatment for aggressive behavior on the CRU. We have not had favorable results using overcorrection for aggressive behavior of adult psychiatric patients. In using time-out we have introduced some precautions against abuses. Our time-out program and its implementation are clearly and specifically described so that there is no room for "interpretation" and bias. Each new staff member is instructed in the use of time-out and "certified" as competent before using it. The time-out program is ratified by the hospital's Human Rights Committee. A large alarm clock sits in the nursing station and is set for the 15-minute time-out period to prompt the nursing staff to check whether the patient is able to come out of the time-out room. If the patient is not aggressive or destructive, he or she can then come out. As another quality assurance, there is close monitoring of the utilization of time-out, with notations on a clipboard.

CASE EXAMPLES OF BEHAVIOR THERAPY WITH AGGRESSIVE PSYCHIATRIC PATIENTS

With the therapeutic environment of the CRU outlined as the exceedingly important context for conducing behavioral treatment of aggressive patients, some case examples will be presented. The patients are referred for treatment on the CRU as a last resort, when all other forms of treatment have failed. They are individuals with many episodes of aggression in the community and in their previous hospital experiences. The results with these patients are based on evaluative data, not controlled studies; therefore, conclusions about the role of the treatment procedures or treatment components in the clinical outcomes cannot be made with confidence. However, the patients' long preexisting baseline periods of unrelenting aggression and destructiveness suggest that when reductions in violent behavior occurred on the CRU, the environmental interventions were influential in the behavioral changes. The cases presented are a biased sample of those in which successful outcomes were achieved.

The Case of Fred

Fred was 31 years old when he came to the Clinical Research Unit. He was transferred from another State hospital in California. He was broad-shouldered, over six feet tall, and weighed 190 pounds. He spoke fast, he walked fast, and he swung his fists fast. He'd spent most of the previous six years in a succession of hospitals. In fact, he had been in 12 different hospitals all over the State of California—fancy, luxurious private hospitals, as well as state hospitals. He systematically wore out his welcome in each hospital because of his aggressive behavior.

Fred was abusive verbally, obnoxious in his lack of social amenities, and he hit and spit on people. When he arrived on the CRU, we counted his rate of spitting: Many days it was over 1,000 spits per day. Staff members described his spitting as being like a "machine gun." Some of them were tempted to wear rain gear to work. The floor and furniture were covered with his spittle. He carried a towel around his neck which was soaked with sputum.

Fred also pinched, pushed, and hit other patients whom he tended to prefer as targets over staff. A typical example of his aggressive behavior occurred at night when he would stand over his sleeping roommate and jab the latter in his ribcage with his finger or fist until he awakened. Obviously his agitating other patients led to his being victimized in turn, serving himself as a target of aggression, so he was not only an assailant, but also a victim of aggression. His body showed the residue of absorbed beatings: He had many of his teeth knocked out, had black eyes frequently, and had episodes of broken bones over the years.

Besides spitting, hitting, and provoking patients, he had other problems. Fred, and other patients like him, do not simply show a unidimensional aggressive pattern; they usually come to us with many other difficulties, deficits, and excesses. Fred, for example, was destructive of property, banging doors and walls and slamming doors. One of his behaviors was particularly disturbing to the nursing staff. When he would leave the nursing station, he would subtly click the lock on the door so that he could get in and avail himself of cigarettes, notepaper, pocketbooks, and other personal effects which were kept there. He also stole items from other patients and set fires in ashtrays. One of his most annoying behavioral excesses was stuffing toilets, which made the odors on the CRU very unpleasant, since the state hospital plumbing crew doesn't always respond to the first call for repairs.

His provocativeness extended to his social speech as well. He spoke in a rapid-fire and lewd way, propositioning and cursing nursing staff by saying such things as, "Hey Joan, let's go to bed. Let's go to bed and screw, Joan. Joan, let's go to bed." or "Fuck you, John. Fuck you, John, fuck you John." Thus, the content and form of his speech were a problem for him and for others who were living with him. He was incontinent of urine during almost every day and night. In sum, Fred was a very disturbed and disturbing young man.

Seven years before, at the age of 24, Fred had been a business administration major in a college in California. He worked nights and weekends as a bartender for a catering firm. Driving home late one night from his job, he drove off the road, having fallen asleep at the wheel. He crashed his car into a tree, was unconscious for two days, and suffered a skull fracture and an epidural hematoma. Twice he underwent neurosurgery which revealed a gaping gash in the left fronto-parietal section of his brain. His accident had resulted, in effect, in a massive prefrontal lobotomy. He left the neurosurgery with an acrylic plate in his skull and returned home to live with his parents. Soon thereafter he began to exhibit the kinds of behaviors described above.

Before the accident he lived a fairly normal life. He was described by his parents and siblings as being somewhat immature for his age and not having a lot of social graces, but he was a happy-go-lucky, friendly person who had a job, friends, schooling, and was getting on with life. After the accident he continued his happy and friendly social manners despite the aggressive behavior. If you came onto the CRU between one of his spits or hits, he would smile, greet you, and even invite you to play a game of cards with him.

His parents were politically prominent and well-connected in the state, and when it appeared that none of the hospitals were helping him, they arranged through the Governor's office to have him transferred to the CRU. Receiving a "political referral," incidentally, can be helpful if you are running a special unit and need special resources. Taking in very difficult cases on a political basis can amplify your support from the power structure. In Fred's case, we did a favor for the administrators of the mental health system in the state capitol who were relieved to find a satisfactory placement for the patient, since it reduced the hassling and pressure they were getting from Fred's parents.

We have worked with Fred on the CRU for almost three years. This time duration is not unreasonably long when treating aggressive patients who have had a long history of intermittently reinforced aggression. It is often necessary to take the variable of time or the duration of treatment into consideration when planning a program for patients with longstanding aggressive behavior. Rapid changes rarely occur, and it may be necessary to maintain programs for a long period of time without changing them too often.

The first program used with Fred was our standard Unit policy for aggression, which was 15 minutes in the locked time-out room for any incident of aggression, agitating others, property destruction, stealing, setting fires, or spitting on people. During the next phase of treatment we added a period of social and material deprivation and extinction to the locked time-out for each instance of aggression or destructiveness. After being in the time-out room for 15 minutes, Fred endured a 24-hour period of deprivation when he was unable to exchange his credits for coffee or items at the canteen, and staff ignored him except for necessary interactions. Since he was a very sociable man and liked interacting with staff, we thought we were controlling a critical reinforcer by having staff turn their backs on him for 24 hours. During this time of deprivation, he received his meals and sleeping accommodations; however, none of the other small luxuries available to others on the Unit were available to him during that 24-hour period. To reenter the regular CRU program, he had to go 24 hours without assault, property destruction, or spitting on people. As can be seen in Figure 3, the second intervention phase seemed to have an effect in reducing Fred's aggressive and destructive behavior. The 24-hour period of time-out was gradually faded to a four-hour period. He was given state-supplied clothing

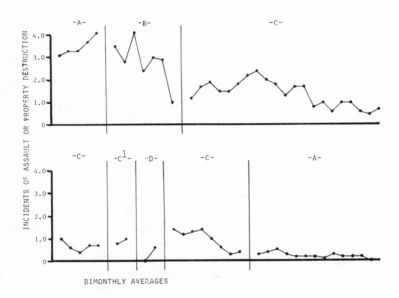

FIGURE 3. Behavioral interventions employed in the case of Fred over a 30-month period. Each data point represents a 2-week average of the number of assaultive and destructive acts. The intervention phases were:

    A = Locked time-out for 15 minutes contingent upon each aggressive or destructive act

    B = Same as A plus 24-hour period of time-out from all CRU reinforcers and total staff ignoring. This was reduced gradually to 4 hours of time-out by the end of the phase

    C = Same as B plus deprivation of personal clothing for same 4-hour time-out period

    C^1 = Same as C except that time-out period lasted 6 hours

    D = Required relaxation (10 minutes) contingent upon each episode of aggression or property destruction

to wear during the four-hour period. Even though his behavior was much improved, he was still averaging over one aggressive or destructive incident a day. The nursing staff wanted to bring his violent behavior under more thorough control. Since Fred liked wearing his own clothes, as all of us do, it was felt by the treatment team that this additional brief deprivation might further diminish his aggression. Indeed, as seen in Figure 3, this new program, lasting over a year, resulted in another decrease in the frequency of Fred's problem behaviors. At this point, Fred's aggressive and destructive behaviors occurred approximately once every two days.

The next phase, lasting one month, increased the period of time-out and deprivation to six hours. However, no further reduction in problem behaviors was noted. Feeling frustrated with their failure to eliminate Fred's aggressive and destructive behaviors, the staff members decided to implement a required relaxation intervention (Webster & Azrin, 1973). In this program, any time Fred engaged in any spitting, aggression, or property destruction, he had to lie down on the floor for 10 minutes motionless without talking. If he spoke or moved he would have to start all over again for 10 minutes. The almost total suppression of aggressive behavior for the two weeks following the start of the required relaxation, as shown in Figure 4, was a result of Fred's having to spend most of his time lying on the floor and not engaging in much behavior at all. The aggressive and destructive behavior returned, however, after this brief "honeymoon" effect.

Next, we reinstituted the previous four-hour time-out program that seemed to have been beneficial. Fred spent 15 minutes in the locked time-out room for each incident, plus lost access to all CRU reinforcers and his clothes for four hours. After four months of this program, Fred was placed on the standard CRU program for aggression, which enabled him to live on the Unit as any other patient would. Engaging in an assaultive or destructive act led quickly to 15 minutes of time-out in a quiet room.

In addition to the time-out programs, positive interventions were instituted for Fred to strengthen his adaptive behavioral repertoire. It is important, ethically and clinically, that any behavior therapy unit avoid using deprivation in excess of positive programs. The CRU policy manual states that any negative reinforcement, punishment or extinction program be balanced in the patient's treatment plan with a positive reinforcement program on a 1:1 basis.

In accord with this CRU policy, positive programs were developed for Fred. Focusing on his lewd speech, staff provided differential attention—they responded avidly and with conversation when Fred spoke politely and respectfully, but totally ignored him and walked away when he cursed or spoke lasciviously. When approaching a staff member, instead of saying, "Hey, Joan, let's go to bed. Let's fuck," he was taught in sessions to say, "Excuse me, please, Joan. I would like to talk to you for a little while." Natural reinforcers, such as spontaneous conversation or playing cards or chess, were programmed as consequences for his appropriate speech content. We also taught him to speak more slowly, since he often spoke in a rapid-fire, unintelligible manner. He received training sessions in which he learned to pace his speech by using his fingers and talking in cadence.

Positive practice and cleanliness training programs (Azrin et al., 1974) were instituted for Fred's day and nightime incontinence. Each episode of incontinence was consequated with 20 positive practice trials of walking to the toilet and going through the motions of urinating. After each incident of incontinence, Fred was prompted to clean himself thoroughly, obtain fresh clothing or bed linen, and change clothing or remake his bed. These efforts effectively decreased his incontinence from three times a day to less than once a month. One problem of Fred's that has resisted treatment has been his strong tendency to shred massive amounts of paper, which then leads to toilet stuffing and plumbing stoppage. We have tried six different interventions for this problem, including a satiation exercise, all to no avail. This problem poses a hurdle to Fred's leaving the hospital and living in the community.

However, the improvements in Fred's behavioral repertoire over the past three years has led to functionally important changes in his quality of life. He no longer takes psychotropic medication—having been taken off all drugs shortly after his arrival on the CRU—and is free from the annoying and debilitating side effects which accompany these drugs. He is able to leave the hospital for brief trips to a local town and for extended visits and holidays with his parents, sometimes for as long as two weeks. He has even gone to Las Vegas with them for a vacation, which was a real treat for him as his favorite pastime is card-playing. His daily life on the CRU and in the hospital also has changed for the better. Staff and other patients no longer avoid him, but rather engage him in a high rate of social interaction. He has a hospital job assisting the custodian and takes pride in his work and the credits he has earned. He has moved up in the credit system to the weekly level. Overall, he is viewed as one of the most successful outcomes treated on the CRU. His parents are pleased, the state mental health administration is pleased, the Hospital Director is pleased, the staff of the CRU are pleased, and Fred is pleased.

The Case of Barney

Barney was a 40-year-old mentally retarded man when he was transferred to the CRU from another hospital unit because of aggressive behavior. He had lived in state hospitals for 23 years. At this point in his long hospital career, he was urinating on the floor and in trash cans, spitting in ash trays and on the floor, picking his nose, masturbating publicly, and tearing his clothing. But the reason for his referral was his putting his arms around people and giving them uninvited bear hugs, which were frightening and injurious and which were frequently sexually intrusive. Barney did not wash and shave himself, make his bed, write his name, or talk with another person.

At first the staff reacted to Barney's grabbing, touching and feeling behavior in an inconsistent manner, sometimes ignoring it, sometimes scolding him. This led to an increased frequency of the problem, with grabbing occurring approximately three times daily. The next step was a planned program of extinction which consisted of 1) withdrawing all attention for the inappropriate grabbing behavior for a period of 30 seconds, followed by 2) our approaching him and explaining that we would talk to him if he called a staff member by name without touching or grabbing. During this phase of treatment, Barney's behavior did not improve because it was impossible to ignore his grabbing, and the actual contact gained by touching someone was reinforcing in itself. A graphic example occurred two weeks after the start of extinction. When the supervising nurse stepped out of the nurses' station, Barney bear hugged her from behind with his hands firmly cupped on her breasts. He held on for dear life as she tried to "ignore" him, charging up the hallway toward the doctor and dragging Barney along with her.

Our next effort combined mild punishment with frequent positive reinforcement for socially acceptable behavior. The person he touched slapped his hand while withdrawing all other attention. On the other hand, any time a staff member approached Barney and he did not respond by touching or grabbing, he was lavished with praise and conversation. With this new procedure, Barney's inappropriate touching of others declined to less than once per day, as Figure 4 indicates. During this period Barney was also taught to shake the hands of people with whom he interacted. Although he used handshakes with people he knew from the CRU, we still observed him grabbing people he didn't know and who were not familiar with our treatment procedure. We then recognized the need to generalize his appropriate social behavior by systematically exposing him to people outside the CRU.

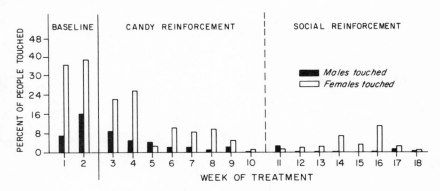

FIGURE 4. Average number of people inappropriately touched and grabbed by Barney per week during three treatment conditions.

Each day Barney was taken for a 30-minute walk to assorted areas of the hospital, especially near groups of people. At first we placed no contingencies on his touching behavior in order to obtain a baseline. As can be seen in Figure 5, Barney grabbed and hugged people frequently, especially females. After two weeks the training procedure found effective on the CRU was introduced. Each time Barney touched someone, his hand was slapped. If he passed within ten feet of any person and either did not grab him/her or shook his/her hands, he was given some candy and verbal praise such as "Right on, baby," "Far out," and "I can dig it!"

The results, as shown in Figure 5, were generalized to all staff members who alternated taking him for the daily walk. The interpersonal distance of people encountered on the walk was decreased from ten feet to five feet, and candy was gradually eliminated until only the social reinforcement was necessary to maintain his improved behavior.

While Barney's maladaptive grabbing behavior was all but eliminated, he needed to develop many self-care and social skills. Behavior therapy techniques were applied to building up these deficient skills. He was reinforced with credits and consumables for increasing the volume and articulateness of his speech. He learned to shave and shower himself and to keep himself well groomed throughout the day. His incontinence ended, as did his spitting, when the appropriate contingencies were applied. He worked independently with simple wooden puzzles, solved discrimination problems, colored on paper, sanded pieces of wood, and socialized with groups by playing volleyball and badminton. Now, seven years later, Barney lives in a less restrictive environment but still shakes

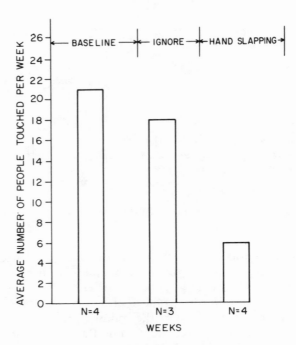

FIGURE 5. Percent of people inappropriately touched or grabbed by Barney during daily off-unit walks on the hospital grounds. The percentage was computed from the number of people who came within ten feet of Barney during his walks.

hands with people he approaches. When he's not shaking hands, you can see him walking down a path holding his hands behind his back.

The Case of Joe

Joe was a handsome, tall, well-built 22-year-old young man whose aggressive behavior began seven years before he came to the CRU. At that time he was hospitalized with a subarachnoid hemorrhage which resulted from a congenital arteriovenous malformation at the base of his brain. Until that time he had been a fine student, an outstanding athlete, and very popular with his friends. After the hemorrhage he was irritable, depressed, and subject to frequent outbursts of anger and violence. Joe's neurological problems produced incoordination requiring the use of a cane. At times his incoordination and ataxia were so severe that he had to use a wheelchair.

This incapacity made Joe dependent on other people—his family and medical personnel—for mobility, transportation, and meeting daily needs. As his dependency and frustration increased, his violent outbursts increased both in frequency and in seriousness. They occurred at about four per month when he came to the CRU. He threatened his sister with a gun, shot a rifle into her car, and knocked his mother down a flight of stairs. He smashed windows and innumerable objects in his home and on various psychiatric units. The incident precipitating his admission to the CRU was his assaulting his elderly roommate with whom he lived in a nursing home in the community. Angry and unable to express his feelings verbally, Joe used his cane to hit the old man on the head. Subsequently the man died of his injuries.

Treatment spanned 37 days and consisted of the simultaneous application of two techniques: contingency contracting and assertive training. Because of the demonstrated severity of Joe's aggressive behavior, it was felt essential to suppress such behavior during Joe's stay on the unit. Hence, a contingency contract, signed between Joe and the CRU staff on the third day of treatment, specified that home visits would be contingent upon Joe's not performing any assaultive behavior for the preceding seven days.

However, it was also felt essential not merely to suppress aggressive behavior, but to train Joe to respond to potentially frustrating situations with appropriately assertive behavior. A program of daily assertive training began on the fourteenth day and lasted for 22 days.

Since Joe needed continual medical care, situations for assertion were limited to primarily institutional ones. Hierarchies were constructed on the following four themes:

1) making a request of the nursing staff;
2) having problems with other patients;
3) complaining about treatment;
4) making small talk with other patients or staff.

Each hierarchy had from four to eight scenes in ascending potential frustration. Thus, the hierarchy of making requests of the nursing staff contained eight scenes which varied the quality of nursing staff response (yes or no) and the time between onset of request and answer by nursing staff (five seconds to no response at all). There were a total of 25 scenes for the four hierarchies.

Each assertive training session was conducted by members of the nursing staff under the supervision of the psychologist and social worker.

Joe was required to role play each scene appropriately twice in succession before he could go on to the next scene. Appropriate performance was defined as correct voice volume, eye contact, posture, gestures and content of conversation.

To determine if the rehearsals were effective in modifying behavior, a number of the situations role played during the sessions were deliberately enacted in the actual living situation without Joe's knowledge. If Joe's response to this was inappropriate, he was required to role play that specific scene again before he could advance in the hierarchy.

Of the 25 scenes, all but two were role played without the need for repetition. Eight scenes were tested in the living situation, and on each occasion Joe's behavior was appropriate. Only one aggressive incident occurred during treatment and this was on the first day of Joe's admission to the unit. A 12-month, posttreatment follow-up in the community disclosed only one aggressive incident, the relatively minor one of turning a bed over. No aggressive incidents toward other patients have occurred. According to those who were familiar with Joe's behavior, this was the longest time that he has gone with so little aggressive behavior.

The Case of Sally

Sally was 20 years old and diagnosed as moderately retarded. She was small, slender, with a frail, innocent appearance, and looked about 15 instead of 20; however, she was a destructive dynamo. She was referred to the CRU because she was literally tearing up her other unit at the state hospital. She slammed doors, tore pictures off the wall, ripped furniture, swore at staff, threatened to kill them, and pushed and shoved staff and other patients. She irritated and frightened people by approaching and standing very close to them and violating their personal space. Then, if they tried to walk away, she followed, stalked, and leered at them. This behavior, of course, provoked attacks on her as well.

To reduce the frequency of her hitting and shoving, Sally was placed in the quiet room for 15 minutes of time-out each time these aggressive incidents occurred. Female staff escorted her to the time-out room, since struggling with male staff appeared to be reinforcing her aggression. At the same time, positive programs were established to promote improvements in interpersonal behavior and in self-care skills.

Sally was given social-skills training both in special sessions and *in vivo* on the Unit. The training was aimed at remediating her inappropriate interpersonal behavior, such as standing too close to others, stalking them, slouching, slurring her speech, whining, and complaining. Sessions focused on role-plays of typical Unit interactions. The *in vivo*, spontaneous training yielded one minute of undivided staff attention contingent upon Sally's:

1) approaching a staff person with an appropriate verbal request or greeting;
2) showing upright posture and remaining at least three feet away from the person;
3) speaking clearly enough to be understood at that distance.

She was also involved in the credit system and received both credits and praise for completion of assigned chores and self-care skills.

The results of treatment were gratifying. Her tantrums and aggressive behavior declined by 93% over a six-month period, from once a day to once every 20 days. Her stalking behavior was reduced by 70%. Her satisfactory completion of daily living and personal hygiene skills—grooming, bathing, room-cleaning, chore completion—increased to 95% without prompting or correcting.

DISCUSSION AND SUMMARY

Aggressive behavior in psychiatric settings is a major problem which occurs at a high rate. The aggressive behavior of psychiatric patients can be understood and assessed from several vantage points:

1) as excesses in violent and destructive motor acts—a topographical description;
2) as resulting from deficits in social and instrumental skills;
3) as being prompted and reinforced by its environmental context;
4) as resulting from interactions between the predispositions of the person and the situational context.

Each of these perspectives sheds useful light on the problem and points toward treatment interventions.

Psychotropic drugs have their place in the treatment of aggression, but only where there is a clearly diagnosed psychiatric illness such as mania or schizophrenia and where aggression is secondary to the symptoms of the illness. Drugs are not a ready answer to aggression and are most often misused as "chemical straightjackets" for the mentally ill. While newer applications for drugs in reducing violence may emerge with future research, there is the risk that a wide variety of currently used drugs are actually producing aggressive and destructive behavior, paradoxically. Thus, psychotropic drugs should be used carefully, conservatively, and pointedly for aggressive behavior clearly linked to the symptoms of a major psychiatric illness.

More generally useful for dealing with aggressive behavior in psychiatric institutions are a variety of environmental interventions based upon social learning principles. The most effective way, and perhaps the only ethical way, to use behavior therapy for aggression is to combine interventions that suppress the aggressive and destructive acts with interventions that strengthen social and self-care skills. Building up prosocial and daily living skills in psychiatric patients provides the patients with alternatives to meet their needs for social attention and primary reinforcers instead of using aggressive, bullying, or provocative behaviors. When properly applied, behavior therapy can also reduce the amount of psychotropic medication dispensed on a psychiatric unit for dealing with aggressive patients and anxious staff members.

Social-skills training is a recently developed technology for reducing aggressive and acting-out behavior and for teaching patients how to solve interpersonal problems. Aggression can be conceptualized as resulting from a patient's deficit in problem-solving and interpersonal skills. Research underway at the Camarillo/UCLA Mental Health Clinical Research Center for the Study of Schizophrenia is predicated on the assumption that successful interpersonal problem-solving requires three steps that are interconnected: 1) accurate social *perception* of a situation; 2) clear cognitive *processing* of response alternatives in that situation, including the weighing of consequences of the alternatives and choosing an alternative that seems like a reasonable one to implement; 3) effective *sending* of social messages or responding to the other(s) in the situation with the use of verbal and nonverbal skills (Liberman et al., 1980).

As an example of deficient problem-solving, Fred was not able to weigh and anticipate the consequences of his obnoxious and aggressive behaviors. When asked how people felt about him because of his spitting, he wasn't able to articulately respond. It didn't occur to him that he was being ignored and ostracized for his destructive behavior. Social judgment was not in his repertoire. [Joe, the young man who bludgeoned his roommate to death, had a variety of problems in each of the problem-solving areas of perceiving, processing, and sending. He misperceived the entire world as threatening, frustrating, and depriving. He rarely generated alternatives to violence in getting his way or meeting his needs. Regarding sending skills, he didn't know how to put his feelings into words, or how to appropriately assert himself.]

Fred, Joe, Barney, and Sally were all exposed to social skills training as one component in their multifaceted treatment programs. Fred learned to speak more coherently and politely; Joe learned how to make reasonable requests of staff rather than "expect" them to meet his needs automatically; Barney practiced shaking hands as a nonverbal means of interacting and expressing his desire for personal contact with others, as well as increasing his speech volume; and Sally benefited from special sessions and *in vivo* unit practice in maintaining an appropriate interpersonal distance and posture and in making polite requests for conversation. From our experience working with aggressive patients, social-skills training axiomatically should be a component of treating such individuals.

Others have carried out social-skills training with aggressive patients. Most notable among workers in behavior therapy are the Achievement Place/Boys Town researchers who have effectively used a "teaching interaction" method of training within the context of a point economy (Willner et al., 1978; Fixsen et al., this volume, Chapter 9). Fredericksen, Jenkins, Foy, and Eisler (1976) reported reductions in verbal outbursts on the ward as a generalized effect of social-skills training with two aggressive psychiatric patients. Four chronically hospitalized, aggressive, female psychiatric patients who received one to two weeks of daily social-skills training showed marked reductions in arguing and fighting (Matson & Stephens, 1978). However, analysis of the data indicated that the favorable results were as much a function of the additional attention and expectations funneled by the special sessions than of the specific training procedures.

A caveat emerging from collective experiences using social-skills training with psychotic and organically impaired patients is that much attention needs to be given to developing maintenance programs to continue the progress generated in special training sessions. Simple acquisition of social skills by severely impaired patients does not sufficiently imprint the verbal and nonverbal responses to produce a durable repertoire. Skills need to be repeatedly practiced *in vivo* with natural reinforcers—for example, prompting and praise from nursing staff or relatives—to sustain appropriate social behavior.

While workers in the field of behavior therapy have made some progress in developing methods for reducing the frequency of aggressive behavior, much more needs to be done. For example, a well-run token economy on a 66-bed state hospital ward for chronic female patients reduced incidents of aggression from 44 per week to 24 per week through token fines contingently applied for violent behavior (Winkler, 1970). While this reduction obviously made a difference to staff and patients alike, the residual rate of aggression was still a major problem.

The limitations of current behavioral practice are similarly reflected in the work of Paul and his colleagues, who compared the effectiveness of intensive milieu therapy and social learning methods with two wards of long-stay, chronic psychotic patients (Paul & Lentz, 1977). They found that principles of the therapeutic community actually led to increases in violent behavior, with the rate of "intolerable behavior" being as high as 120 incidents per week. As can be seen in Table 2, time-out from reinforcement, used on the ward with social learning principles, was considerably more effective in reducing violent episodes. However, the rate of aggressive acts at the end of the project was actually higher than during the baseline period, suggesting the need for new methods beyond those currently available. Paul and his colleagues found that a combination of methods worked best in controlling aggression, including: 1) time-out for 72 hours; 2) heavy response costs through token fines; 3) overcorrection or restitution therapy; and, most importantly, 4) the presence of sufficient male staff members on the ward, especially at nights and on weekends. These methods controlled aggression in approximately 75% of the patients and enabled the staff to significantly reduce the use of psychotropic medication from 100 to 11% of the patients.

Environmental interventions, thus, do not provide a wholly satisfactory solution to the problem of aggression in psychiatric settings. The state of the art leaves much to be desired. Our own eight years of experience with 34 patients exhibiting assaultive behavior on the CRU has been only moderately successful. We evaluated our effectiveness with each of the problem behaviors presented by our patients, using a four-point scale of improvement. The rates of targeted problem behaviors during the

TABLE 2

Average Weekly Incidents of Aggressive Acts ("Intolerable Behavior") as Charted by Clinical Staff on Two Intensive Treatment Units for Chronic Mental Patients (Adapted from Paul & Lentz, 1977)

Duration of Expulsion from Unit (Milieu Therapy) or Time-Out (Social Learning)	Units	
	Milieu Therapy	Social Learning
Baseline (none)	21	32
Up to 72 hours	53	10
2 hours	120	53
72 hours	50	38

first three weeks of each patient's stay on the CRU were compared to the rates of the same behaviors during the last three weeks of the patient's stay. A percentage reduction of inappropriate or increase in appropriate behavior was then calculated, and the degree of improvement of each behavior was rated using a four-point rating scale:

1 = Marked improvement	= 75-100% improvement
2 = Moderate improvement	= 50- 74% improvement
3 = Slight improvement	= 26- 49% improvement
4 = No improvement	= less than 25% improvement

As can be seen in Table 3, we have been able to reduce the frequency of assaultive incidents through a variety of punishment plus reinforcement programs on the average of 50%. We have been somewhat more effective in reducing the rate of property destruction. In comparison to assaultiveness, we have been more effective in treating self-care skills, sexual deviance, work behavior, self-injury, pesty demandingness, and verbal abuse. While we have had some success with overcorrection procedures with the self-injurious behavior of autistic children, our staff have encountered poor results and implementation problems using them with aggressive adult retardates and psychotics. These patients almost always actively resist the manual guidance required to gain their compliance and appear to be reinforced through struggling with staff. While the credit system is helpful in motivating aggressive patients to respond to reinforcement of alternative behavior, a certain proportion of our patients lack interest in the usual backup reinforcers in the credit system and hence are nonresponders. With some, the biggest reinforcer in their life space is continued institutionalization, and they exhibit aggression because they know it is a problem which cannot be tolerated outside the hospital. Some of our patients have responded to time-out as a reinforcer, preferring periods of isolation and privacy to the hubbub of the ward.

Our future efforts need to consider ways of "treating the institution" and not just the patient. Inpatient units that are overcrowded and noisy, with too much unstructured time, will continue to breed aggression. Unless a unit has a majority of its patients who are nonaggressive, the aggressive patients will tend to influence the others to act out as well. Thus, careful mixing of patients, rather than sending all acutely ill and agitated patients to the same unit, may be helpful in reducing the violence level. We will need to infuse programs, funds, and attractive residential

TABLE 3

Average Levels of Improvement for Behavioral Problems Treated in
122 Patients on the Clinical Research Unit, 1970-77

Patients had an average of 2-9 problem behaviors targeted for intervention. Improvement
was evaluated on a 4-point scale which describes the percentage reduction in maladaptive
behavior or increase in adaptive behavior between the first 4 weeks and the final 4 weeks
on the CRU:
1 = 75% or more improvement
2 = 50-74% improvement
3 = 26-49% improvement
4 = 25% or less improvement

Behavioral Problem	No. Behaviors Treated	Average Improvement
Self-care	84	1.83
Social skills	42	1.76
Assaultiveness	34	2.00
Work	33	1.58
Bizarre movements or posture	29	1.90
Verbal abuse	28	1.43
Property destruction	24	1.50
Pesty demandingness	17	1.53
Delusional speech	15	1.93
Self-injury	14	1.50
Social isolation	12	1.83
Depression	12	2.00
Sexual deviance	7	1.57
Hallucinations	3	3.67
Total No. Behaviors	354	
Average Improvement Level		1.62

alternatives for the community life of chronic psychiatric patients so that
they will have adequate incentives to give up their aggressive hold on
the institution. And finally, we must extend our expectations for successful treatment to longer durations of active treatment within institutions and maintenance treatment for generalization in the community.
Most importantly, we need to develop and evaluate new methods of
intervention for aggression at the biological, individual, and environmental levels.

REFERENCES

AZRIN, N. H., SNEED, T. J., & FOXX, R. M. Dry bed: Rapid elimination of childhood
enuresis. *Behaviour Research and Therapy*, 1974, *12*, 147-156.
BLUMER, D., & MIGEON, C. Hormone and hormonal agents in the treatment of aggression.
Journal of Nervous and Mental Disease, 1975, *160*, 127-137.

CALLAHAN, E. J., ALEVIZOS, P. N., TEIGEN, J., NEUMAN, H., & CAMPBELL, M.D. Behavioral effects of reducing the frequency of phenothiazine administration. *Archives of General Psychiatry*, 1975, *32*, 1285-1290.

COHEN, S. Aggression: The role of drugs. *Drug Abuse and Alcoholism Newsletter*, 1979, *8*, 1-4.

DANIELS, D. N., GILULA, M. F., & OCHBERG, F. M. (Eds.) *Violence and the struggle for existence*. Boston: Little, Brown, 1970.

FREDERICKSEN, L. W., JENKINS, J. O., FOY, D. W., & EISLER, R. M. Social skills training to modify abusive verbal outbursts in adults. *Journal of Applied Behavior Analysis*, 1976, *9*, 117-125.

GIOVANNONI, J. M., & GUREL, L. Socially disruptive behavior of ex-mental patients. *Archives of General Psychiatry*, 1967, *17*, 146-153.

JACOBY, J. E. Dangerousness of the mentally ill—a methodological reconsideration. In D.J. Frederick (Ed.), *Dangerous behavior: A problem in law and mental health*. Washington, D.C.: DHEW Publication No. (ADM) 78-563, 1978, pp. 20-36.

LIBERMAN, R. P., FEARN, C., DeRISI, W. J., ROBERTS, J., & CARMONA, M. The credit-incentive system: Motivating the participation of patients in a day hospital. *British Journal of Social and Clinical Psychology*, 1977, *16*, 85-94.

LIBERMAN, R. P., WALLACE, C. J., VAUGHN, C. E., SNYDER, K. S., & RUST, C. Social and family factors in the course of schizophrenia: Towards an interpersonal problem-solving therapy for schizophrenics and their relatives. In J. Strauss (Ed.), *Psychotherapy for schizophrenia: Current status and future directions*. New York: Plenum, 1980, pp. 21-54.

LION, J. R. Conceptual issues in the use of drugs for the treatment of aggression in man. *Journal of Nervous and Mental Disease*, 1975, *160*, 76-82.

LION, J. R., SNYDER, W., & MERRILL, G. L. *Hospital and Community Psychiatry*, in press.

MARK, V. H., & ERVIN, F. R. *Violence and the brain*. New York: Harper and Row, 1970.

MARSHALL, B. D., WALLACE, C. J., BURKE, K., & LIBERMAN, R. P. Adaptation of the problem-oriented medical record to a behavior modification unit. *Scandanavian Journal of Behaviour Therapy*, 1979, *8*, 57-67.

MATSON, J. L., & STEPHENS, R. M. Increasing appropriate behavior of explosive chronic psychiatric patients with a social skills training package. *Behavior Modification*, 1978, *2*, 61-76.

MULVIHILL, D. J., & TUMIN, M. M. *Crimes of violence*, Vol. 12, Staff Report to the National Commission on the Causes and Prevention of Violence. Washington, D.C.: U.S. Government Printing Office, 1969.

PATTERSON, G. R. A social learning approach to aggressive children. Presented at Banff International Conference on Behavior Modification, March, 1979.

PAUL, G. L., & LENTZ, R. J. *Psychosocial treatment of chronic mental patients*. Cambridge, Massachusetts: Harvard University Press, 1977.

RAPKIN, J. K. Opinions about mental illness: A review of the literature. *Psychological Bulletin*, 1972, *78*, 153-171.

RAPPEPORT, J. R., & LASSEN, G. Dangerousness-arrest rate comparisons of discharged patients and the general population. *American Journal of Psychiatry*, 1965, *121*, 776-783.

RAPPEPORT, J. R., & LASSEN, G. The dangerousness of female patients: A comparison of the arrest rate of discharged psychiatric patients and the general population. *American Journal of Psychiatry*, 1966, *123*, 413-419.

SALZMAN, C., KOCHANSKY, G. E., & SHADER, R. I. Chlordiazepoxide-induced hostility in a small group setting. *Archives of General Psychiatry*, 1974, *31*, 401-405.

TOCH, H. H. *Violent men: An inquiry into the psychology of violence*. Chicago: Aldine, 1969.

TUPIN, J. E. Management of violent patients. In R.I. Shader (Ed.), *Manual of psychiatric therapeutics*. Boston: Little, Brown and Co., 1975, pp. 125-136.

WEBSTER, D. R., & AZRIN, N. H. Required relaxation: A method of inhibiting agitative-disruptive behavior of retardates. *Behaviour Research and Therapy*, 1973, *11*, 67-78.

WILLNER, A. G., BRAUKMANN, C. J., KIRIGIN, K. A., & WOLF, M. M. Achievement Place: A community treatment model for youths in trouble. In D. Marholin (Ed.), *Child behavior therapy*. New York: Gardner Press, 1978, pp. 239-273.

WINKLER, R. C. Management of chronic psychiatric patients by a token reinforcement system. *Journal of Applied Behavior Analysis*, 1970, *3*, 47-55.

ZITRIN, A., HARDESTY, A. S., BURDOCK, E. I., & DROSSMAN, A. K. Crime and violence among mental patients. *American Journal of Psychiatry*, 1976, *133*, 142-149.

11

Explosive Behavior:
A Skill Development
Approach to Treatment

LEE W. FREDERIKSEN
and NANCY RAINWATER

INTRODUCTION

Explosive behavior, high intensity outbursts of physical and/or verbal aggression, present a major challenge to society. On one hand, the intensity of the attack often represents a very real danger. On the other hand, explosive episodes may occur at relatively low frequency and be followed by remorse, denials of responsibility, and promises that "it won't happen again." To further complicate matters, there is no clear line of responsibility for who ought to help. Depending on which theory you subscribe to, the explosive individual may be: 1) a criminal to be apprehended and punished; 2) a victim of his physiology to be treated with drugs and surgery; or 3) a mentally ill patient to be controlled, counseled and rehabilitated.

The situation is not a simple one. There are undoubtedly individuals

The authors express their appreciation to their colleagues and students whose input has been so important in the development of the approach described in this paper.

who clearly fit into each of these categories: the professional criminal who uses violence to achieve his ends; the victim of temporal lobe epilepsy who strikes out blindly at those around him; or the psychotic individual carrying out a gruesome command hallucination. Yet there is a large group of people who do not fit neatly into any of these categories. These individuals have been labeled "explosive personality," "explosive behavior disorder," "episodic dyscontrol," or the like. We have focused our efforts on this group of people.

The purpose of this chapter is to summarize and review the development of an approach to treating explosive behavior. Drawn from a clinical population, individuals have been studied intensively, generally within single-case research designs. Over a four-year period, the approach has evolved into a working model which integrates the findings and suggests new directions for research and treatment. We will: 1) describe the population we are working with; 2) present our working model of explosive behavior; 3) describe a comprehensive assessment approach (including behavioral, physiological and cognitive measures); 4) outline our treatment paradigm; and 5) present results (including follow-up) from a small group of patients receiving treatment. Finally, we will discuss some limitations of current understanding and suggest directions for further work.

Selection Criteria

All individuals were assessed or treated while they were inpatients on a psychiatric ward at the Veteran's Administration Hospital in Jackson, Mississippi. Our selection criteria were as follows (cf. Fredericksen & Eisler, 1977):

1) We ruled out individuals with evidence of severe mental retardation, organic brain syndrome, or a history of psychotic behavior. (All individuals had complete medical and, in most instances, neurological workups.)
2) We included individuals with documented histories of episodic violence (either verbal or physical) which contrasted with their typical patterns of behavior (i.e., we ruled out the professional criminal who used violence solely for instrumental gain).
3) We required validated evidence that these episodes had significant negative impact on the individual's life functioning (e.g., job loss, legal difficulties, negative impact on family life, injury to self and/or victims, etc.).

4) The individual had to evidence signs of subjective distress following the episodes (e.g., anxiety, depression, remorse, or guilt, etc.).
5) Finally, the individual had to report subjective "loss of control" during the episodes.

The individuals meeting these criteria were exclusively male (which is to be expected since they were drawn from an almost exclusively male population). They ranged in age from their early twenties to late forties, with the majority being in the 25-30-year age range. They all had at least a two-year history of problems. The typical pattern involved an escalating pattern of episodes starting in adolescence. All individuals had documented histories of both verbal and physical attack. About two-thirds reported the use of weapons in these attacks (e.g., guns, knives, clubs), and about one-third reported inflicting fatal wounds on at least one victim. It seems safe to say that by almost any criteria these individuals displayed severe patterns of explosive behavior. While many had histories of repeated minor legal problems (e.g., arrests, assault charges, short jail sentences), none had been sent to prison as a consequence of his attacks. However, it is important to note that these individuals were typically seeking treatment because the explosive episodes had recently begun to produce increased aversive consequences, e.g., their wives had left them, they had lost their jobs, they were involved in legal problems, they suffered from depression, etc.

MODEL

In developing a working model of explosive behavior, several characteristics have been observed and are hypothesized to be important.

1) *These individuals show a deficit in social skills.* This deficit is particularly apparent in those situations which require assertive responding. The typical response is characterized by extreme passivity *or* aggressive outbursts. Put another way, there seems to be a deficit in "middle ground" assertive responding. For example, in eight of the cases discussed in this paper, there was an opportunity to systematically obtain overall ratings of social skill prior to therapy. In five cases these multiple ratings (5-point scale: 1 = very unskillful, 5 = very skillful) were obtained unobtrusively on the ward, and in three cases they were made during role-played, laboratory situations (see the Assessment and Results sections for more details). The mean rating for the explosives was 1.38. This is compared

to a mean rating of 1.64 for low assertive and 4.15 for high assertive, but nonexplosive, psychiatric patients participating in another study (Eisler, Frederiksen, & Peterson, 1978).

The importance of developing appropriate social functioning in aggressive individuals has been emphasized elsewhere. Bandura (1973) has stressed the importance of helping individuals develop prosocial responses that aid them in achieving their objectives. In making their case for employing assertiveness training with aggressive individuals, Rimm and Masters (1974) state that "many individuals resort to physical violence or threats of violence simply because they are deficient in the verbal skills that would accomplish their goals effectively and without the severe negative consequences often associated with acts of extreme belligerence" (p. 105). Further, social-skills training has been reported as an effective component in a number of other clinical studies (e.g., Matson & Stephens, 1978; Rimm, Hill, Brown, & Stuart, 1974; Wallace, Teigen, Liberman, & Baker, 1973).

2) *These individuals report atypical cognitive behavior.* These differences are prevalent both in their generalized expectations regarding social interactions and the labeling of social situations and in their selection of appropriate behavior. Recent theoretical work has put a greater emphasis on the importance of how an individual labels a situation and the kinds of expectations he/she has regarding the probable consequences of certain responses as determinants of social responding (e.g., Bandura, 1977; Mischel, 1973). Further, recent experimental evidence indicates that there are important cognitive as well as behavioral differences between high- and low-assertive individuals (Eisler et al., 1978; Fiedler & Beach, 1978) and that cognitively oriented interventions may be useful in effecting change in aggressive individuals (Meichenbaum, 1977; Novaco, 1976).

The explosive patients in our sample tend to expect a high frequency of negative interactions with others. To quantify these expectations we have administered the Generalized Expectations of Others Questionnaire (Eisler et al., 1978) to a small group of patients (N = 5) prior to treatment. This instrument asks the individual to estimate the proportion of social interactions on which a certain outcome will happen. (For detailed items refer to Assessment section.) The responses on this instrument can be contrasted with those given by groups of high- and low-assertive, nonexplosive psychiatric patients drawn from the same population (Eisler et al., 1978). These results are shown in Figure 1. While the extremely small number of patients requires caution, it seems that

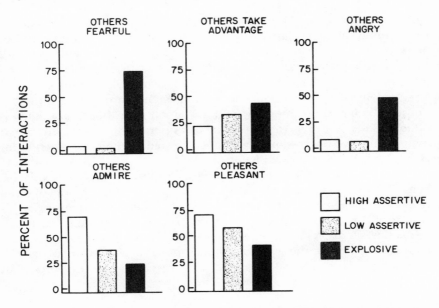

FIGURE 1. Mean expectation scores for high- and low-assertive psychiatric controls (from Eisler et al., 1978) and a sample (N = 5) of explosive individuals. Full item descriptions are in the Assessment section of this paper.

the explosive population may indeed have expectations regarding day-to-day social interactions that deviate in important ways from their non-explosive counterparts. It is not difficult to imagine how these expectations might tend to increase the probability of explosive behavior. For example, whereas nonexplosive controls expect to encounter aggression about 7% of the time, explosives report expecting aggression during *almost half of all social interactions.*

3) *The individual's physiological state seems important.* Virtually all of the explosives report heightened levels of subjective arousal associated with explosive episodes. The data in support of this are only preliminary; however, it seems that heightened arousal tends to be interpreted in such a way as to increase the probability of attack. Another consideration is the use of alcohol. About half of the patients in our sample display explosive episodes only when they have been drinking.

4) *The consequences of explosive episodes tend to reinforce their occurrence.* First, explosive behavior often serves the function of getting the indi-

vidual what he wants. Others give in or attempt to placate him in hopes of avoiding further episodes and/or physical harm. Negative consequences (if any) may be quite removed in time from the episode. Second, the individual may gradually develop "amnesia" for the episodes, patterns of remorse, "blackouts," etc., all of which tend to absolve him of any responsibility for his behavior. The evidence supporting these hypotheses is based on interview and anecdotal data, but is nonetheless quite striking. Further, the importance of operant reinforcement in the maintenance of aggression is well documented in the experimental literature (cf. Bandura, 1973; Knutson, 1973).

To integrate these observations and hypotheses regarding explosive behavior, we have found it helpful to develop a schematic model of social responding (Figure 2). The model starts with a stimulus situation, in this case social. Faced with a social situation (A), the individual must first assess that situation (B). This assessment will result in some sort of evaluation or "label" for the situation. Based upon that assessment or "label," the individual must select an appropriate response (C). It is important

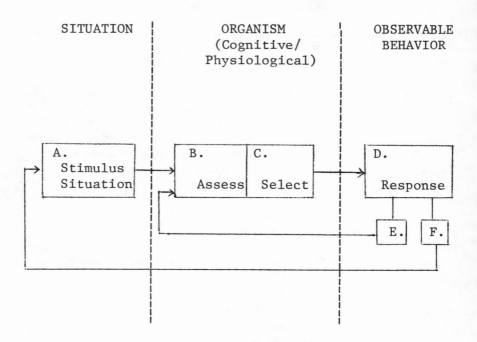

FIGURE 2. A working model of social responding.

to note that these assessment and labeling functions involve an inter-action of both cognitive and physiological response systems. Next, the individual emits the overt response (D). The emission of a response then serves to provide feedback to the individual (E), as well as to affect the stimulus situation (F). Such feedback may, of course, function as a rein-forcing or punishing stimulus.

Within this model there are several points at which problems can develop. First, an individual could inappropriately assess a situation (B). Where most people would label a situation as mildly annoying, an ex-plosive individual may see the same situation as a serious personal threat. Such atypical labeling could be related to cognitive activity (e.g., inap-propriate expectations), physiological activity (e.g., heightened arousal), or an interaction of the two. A second possible point where problems could develop would be in the selection of an appropriate response (C). The explosive individual could have a limited range of alternatives from which to select (e.g., passive or explosive responses but no assertive ones) or could tend to select responses that escalate the situation. Another possibility is that the individual may assess the situation accurately, select an appropriate response, but not be able to emit it (D) because the desired response is not within his repertoire (e.g., a social skill deficit) or is somehow inhibited (e.g., excessive physiological arousal). A final complicating factor is the natural consequences of explosive episodes (E and F). While the long-term consequences of such behavior are prob-ably quite negative, the short-term consequences can often be positive. The explosive individual often gets his way. The perceived threat is terminated, the feared consequence avoided. It seems reasonable to ex-pect that this short-term success would tend to reinforce the explosive pattern.

ASSESSMENT

Behavioral Interviews

Initial assessment focuses on detailed interviews of each patient, mem-bers of his family, and sometimes his employer to determine the history, topography, antecedents, and consequences of his outbursts. These in-terviews of a variety of significant others, as well as the patient, provided a large, useful, and reliable data base for assessment and treatment based on information from multiple data sources (Linehan, 1977). Based on this information, a number of explosive scenes in which the interactions have reliably precipitated physical attack in the past are developed to be used in social-skills training and physiological assessment. Each scene consists of a short description of a situation and an initial statement by the other person in the interaction. For example:

> You're at a party with a date that you want to impress. A person that you haven't seen in a while comes up to you and says, "Well, if it isn't old snaggletooth. I haven't seen teeth that crooked since the last time I saw yours."

In addition, neutral scenes are developed to be used in the physiological assessments. Neutral scenes also require interaction with another person, but have never precipitated an outburst in the past. For example:

> You go into a grocery store to pick up some bread. A clerk comes up to you and says, "Can I help you find something, sir?"

Social-skills Assessment

Role-playing sessions were conducted in a studio furnished with comfortable livingroom furniture and a microphone. Each session consisted of explosive scenes which were role-played with the therapist. A research assistant read the scene descriptions over an intercom from an adjacent control room and the respondent followed with a one-line prompt. All sessions were videotaped.

After each session a research assistant reviewed the videotape and scored the social-skills components in each scene to assess deficits and changes. Reliability of the social-skills components was assessed by having two research assistants independently rate 33% of the total number of sessions (including at least one session in each phase). For the measure of "looking" (see below), each assistant calculated the percentage of looking for each scene. Agreements were scored if the independently obtained percentages did not differ by more than ± 2%. Discrepancies of greater than 2% were scored as disagreements. Percent agreement for all frequency measures was calculated by dividing the total number of agreements by the total number of agreements plus disagreements x 100. The range and mean reliability of observations for each of the components of social-skills behavior, as well as the operational definitions, are shown below (cf. Frederiksen, Jenkins, Foy, & Eisler, 1976).

Looking—The duration (in seconds) that the patient looked at his partner while talking and the total time the patient talked were timed separately. Looking percentage was computed by dividing the duration of looking while talking by the total duration of talking (range = 74.0-99.7; mean = 92.2%).

Appropriate requests—A request for the respondent to change his behavior which did not imply harm (e.g., "Please move, I have to sit down.") (range = 88.9-99.0, mean = 93.4%).

Inappropriate requests—A request for the respondent to change his behavior which directly or indirectly threatened that psychological or physical harm might follow the respondent's noncompliance (e.g., "Move, or I'll throw you off the bus!") (range = 85.2-97.5, mean = 90.7%).

Irrelevant comments—Any verbal statement unrelated to the theme of the situation (e.g., commenting about the weather when requesting repayment of an overdue debt (range = 90.0-96.3, mean = 93.2%).

Hostile comments—A threat or comment likely to provoke a nonproductive counterattack (e.g., "Go to hell!") (range = 84.0-96.3, mean = 90.8%).

Compliance—Compliance of verbal content was rated on a dichotomous occurrence or non-occurrence basis for each scene. Compliance was scored if the patient did not resist the respondent's position, e.g., if he agreed to have an unwanted frozen dinner or agreed to buy a chair he couldn't afford (range = 90.0-92.3, mean = 91.5%).

Social-skill rating—A global rating of the social skill exhibited by the patient in response to each scene was made on a five-point scale (5 = very skillful, 1 = very unskillful) (range 80.0-100, mean = 85.1%).

Refusal to do scene—Patient's refusal to role-play scene either by walking out of the room, commenting that he would not do the scene, or turning his back to respondent and not saying anything (mean = 100%).

In addition to the laboratory-based social-skills assessment, ward staff were instructed to record any incidents that occurred on the ward. Thus, each patient's chart became a source of data regarding his on-ward social skills. Also, situations were arranged to occur on the ward when the therapists were not present and were observed by nurses, aides, and medical students who would routinely be on the ward. The people observing the situation would report the presence or absence of certain target behaviors, e.g., appropriate requests, as well as provide an overall rating of the individual's social skill in the interaction. These unobtrusive measurement procedures allow for at least a preliminary assessment of social-skill behaviors outside of the laboratory (cf. Frederiksen & Kelly, 1977).

Cognitive Assessment

Patients completed a questionnaire specifically developed for use with clients who have demonstrated difficulty handling social interactions (Eisler et al., 1978). This questionnaire is composed of five items to which the patient responds by circling the percentage of time he expects people to deal with him in a given way, resulting in a description of his general expectations of others. The items presented are:

> In your day-to-day dealings with other people, what percent of the time do you think that they are fearful of you?

> In your day-to-day dealings with other people, what percent of the time do you expect people might try and take advantage of you in some way?

> In your day-to-day dealings with other people, what percent of the time do you expect them to come on in an angry, verbally aggressive or negative way toward you?

> In your day-to-day dealings with other people, what percent of the time do they admire or show respect for you?

> In your day-to-day dealings with other people, what percent of the time do you expect them to be pleasant and understanding of your position?

A second measure of cognitive functioning was obtained by having patients monitor their arousal levels every two hours on a scale from 1 (no tension at all) to 5 (a great deal of tension). Patients also noted the situation in which the rating was made. Patients who participated in physiological assessments were asked to rate their arousal on the same scale immediately before and after each role-played scene.

Physiological Assessment

Information obtained from the behavioral interviews indicated that immediately prior to explosive outbursts the patients would feel "angry," "tense," or "about to explode," and that often during the episodes they were "not aware" of their surroundings and would focus only on the target. In addition, some of the patients' outbursts occurred when they were intoxicated. Based on this knowledge, it was recently decided to assess and compare patients' physiological arousal during angry and neutral role-played situations, both before and after treatment. When relevant, these assessments were conducted under "dry" (the patient had not consumed any alcohol) and "wet" (the patient's BAL was .03) conditions.

Physiological assessment was conducted in a laboratory furnished with a recliner and other comfortable chairs. The patient was seated and hooked up to leads to a Grass Model 7C solid state polygraph to monitor blood pressure, heart rate, and respiration, and a Coulbourn Instruments Autoclinic 2001 to monitor EMG. Leads passed through a wall to the polygraph equipment in an adjoining control room. After the hook-up, the patient was instructed to relax, and baseline measures were taken. Baseline criteria were met when the measures had been stable for at least five consecutive minutes. A total of four alternating neutral and arousal scenes were role-played with a respondent who had not been involved in treatment. Scenes were described over an intercom from the control room and were timed to last for two minutes each. A return to baseline response or a five-minute time lapse, whichever came first, was required before proceeding to the next scene. One minute prior to and immediately following each scene, the patient was asked to rate his stress level on a five-point scale (1 = no stress at all, 5 = a great deal of stress).

"Wet" assessments were conducted after the patient had been pre-loaded with alcohol. He was given enough vodka mixed with orange juice 15 minutes prior to the session to raise his BAL to .03. Blood alcohol level was determined by using a CMI Intoxilyzer Model 4011.

TREATMENT

Treatment was typically conducted on an individual basis during a voluntary inpatient stay on the VA psychiatric ward. Two explosives were treated jointly, combining coaction with social-skills training (McKinlay, Pachman, & Frederiksen, 1977). Each individual worked with his therapist on a daily basis (five days per week) during a total hospital stay of one to three months duration. The entire treatment package consisted of three stages of intervention.

Stage I—Preparation

The first stage of treatment began during assessment of the patient's problem. During this phase the patient and therapist met several times to discuss the program and to conduct the in-depth behavioral interviews. By discussing the history of the behavior and the treatment approach to be used, a rapport was developed which formed the basis for a positive therapeutic relationship (i.e., the therapist became established as a reinforcer). The few in-hospital physical assaults which occurred with these patients happened in this initial phase of treatment. When one of these episodes occurred, the patient was removed to an isolation room on the ward for approximately one hour; in the one severe case, medication and restraints were used. It should be noted that the systematic consequation of explosive behavior played only a minor role in the overall treatment approach.

Stage II—Skill Development

The second stage of treatment consisted of several structured interventions. These interventions were designed to accelerate appropriate behaviors that were incompatible with the individual's previous pattern of explosive behavior.

Social-skills training. Social-skills deficits were treated within a multiple baseline design across either component behaviors or patients. During baseline the patient was instructed to respond to the situation as he normally would, with the exception that if he would physically harm the respondent, he should signal the respondent to leave the room. (The respondent was instructed to leave the room if he ever felt physically threatened by the patient.) Treatment consisted of modeling, instructions, practice, and feedback (cf. Frederiksen et al., 1976).

Before each scene was role-played, a videotape was shown in which another person modeled appropriate responses to the situation. In developing these modeling tapes, care was taken to insure that the model displayed all of the targeted appropriate behaviors (e.g., appropriate requests, eye contact) and none of the inappropriate behaviors (e.g., hostile comments, inappropriate requests). Instructions were given to notice a particular component of the respondent's behavior and a rationale for using the component behavior was explained. The patient would then role-play the scene himself, with instructions to focus on the target behavior. Following role-playing, the therapist and patient reviewed the videotape of the scene, and the therapist verbally reinforced the patient for positive changes while still noting deficiences and suggesting alternatives.

Relaxation training. In order to teach patients to control their physiological arousal, patients were given individual instruction in progressive deep muscle relaxation (Bernstein & Borkovec, 1973). After insuring that the patient could correctly follow the procedures, the therapist provided him with a relaxation tape and the instructions to practice relaxation twice a day. Since the patient had to check the tape player out from the nurses' station at each use, an assessment of compliance could be made.

Cognitive restructuring. Within our model of explosive behavior, the individual's cognitive functioning (e.g., expectations, labeling) plays an important role. This treatment component is designed to provide the individual with more appropriate (i.e., closer to the norm) alternatives. During treatment sessions the patient would describe situations in which his expectations/labeling appeared to be markedly different from the norm. The therapist would then provide feedback on how others might view the situation and explain that the same situation could be labeled in a variety of ways. Each way of viewing the situation would likely lead to a different overt response. Examples of this principle were provided and discussed. In one example used, a situation was described in which an employee's boss walked past him in the morning without saying "hello." If the person labeled his boss as being angry and not speaking to him, he would probably feel fearful or angry himself, resulting in his making a sarcastic remark or avoiding the boss completely. On the other hand, if the employee labeled his boss as being sleepy or preoccupied, he wouldn't feel personally affronted and could continue his work without interference. Whenever personal situations were described by the patient, he and his therapist could then consider alternative (closer to the norm) perceptions of the situation.

Self-management to control abusive drinking. The patients who generally had explosive outbursts while they were intoxicated also received training to control their abusive drinking. Training consisted of eight one-hour classes which taught the patients how to analyze and control the chain of events leading up to their abusive drinking and to control the consequences of that behavior (Keane, 1978). These classes were part of the established Jackson VA alcohol-treatment program.

Stage III—Programmed Generalization

To assist patients in applying their new skills to novel situations and settings outside of treatment, a systematic program for generalization was instituted which included the following components.

Novel and generalization scenes and respondents. During each social-skills training session, novel scenes were introduced to give the patient the experience of practicing his new skills in different role-played situations. These scenes were often composed of incidents that ward staff reported the patient had not handled well. These scenes were videotaped, and the patient received feedback on his behavior. In addition, after training, patients were asked to respond, applying their new skills to untrained scenes, for which they received feedback. To assess generalization across people, occasional role-played sessions and all physiological assessments used a respondent other than the therapist.

Therapist modeling. The patients and their therapists interacted in a variety of situations other than specific training sessions (e.g., daily rounds), allowing the therapists the opportunity to model appropriate responses in their daily lives. According to their behavioral interviews, many of these patients had grown up in families where the parents modeled inappropriate, sometimes explosive, social behavior. Over the course of one to three months, the patient could begin to learn a more appropriate approach as modeled by the therapist.

Fading. As treatment progressed, patients were allowed longer and more frequent passes so that they would have the opportunity to practice their new skills in the outside environment. Upon returning, the patient and therapist reviewed how the patient had handled situations, and analyzed and practiced alternatives to situations which the patient had handled poorly, with the therapist providing social praise for situations the patient reported handling appropriately.

RESULTS

Approximately 50% of the patients who began treatment dropped out. Those who left usually quit during the first week, after the need for their intense involvement in the program became apparent. Consequently, the results presented here are based only on those individuals who completed treatment. While we have no systematic data to predict who stays in treatment and who drops out, it is our impression that individuals are more likely to stay if: 1) There is some contingency on staying in (e.g., the wife will leave him if he doesn't complete treatment); and 2) a positive relationship with the therapist is established early.

Each of the patients who completed treatment and whose data are being reviewed in this section has been presented in previous manuscripts (published or unpublished). The references of prior case studies for each patient are shown in Table 1.

Social Skills

One of the main goals of treatment is to provide the explosive indi-

TABLE 1

References for Previous Data Presentation of Each Subject Reviewed in
the Current Paper

Subject Number	Reference
1	Foy, Eisler, & Pinkston, 1975
2	S1 in Frederiksen, Jenkins, Foy, & Eisler, 1976
3	S2 in Frederiksen et al., 1976
4	Frederiksen & Eisler, 1977
5	Simon & Frederiksen, 1977
6	S1 in McKinlay, Pachman, & Frederiksen, 1977
7	S2 in McKinlay et al., 1977
8	S1 in Rainwater & Frederiksen, 1978
9	S2 in Rainwater & Frederiksen, 1978

viduals with a more adaptive set of social skills. This is accomplished through accelerating the use of appropriate behaviors in previously problematical situations. Probably the most important single behavior in this respect is appropriate requests. By definition, such requests constitute the verbal content of an assertive response. The proportion of role-played interactions during which the individual subjects displayed appropriate requests is shown in Figure 3. All subjects showed very low levels of appropriate requests (eight of nine near 0%) prior to treatment and very high levels (eight of nine at 100%) following social-skills training. Of the six individuals for whom there is follow-up (one to eight months), five maintained very high levels of appropriate requests. The sixth subject dropped to 50% at his six-month follow-up.

While the above data speak to the acquisition and maintenance of a specific target behavior, they do not address the issue of social skill in general, i.e., the combination of all verbal and nonverbal components. To evaluate the patient's overall performance, we have focused on the overall social-skills rating (1-5 scale). This rating takes into account the combination of all the components of social skills. In those instances in which no overall social-skills rating was available, we evaluated the percent of maximum performance on all target behaviors.

The overall social-skills performance for each patient is shown in Table 2. Results are available for performance on training and generalization scenes, both at the end of treatment (post) and at follow-up. In addition, the individual's in-hospital performance, e.g., during rounds, making requests to staff, etc., was unobtrusively assessed (on-ward). Double plusses (+ +)indicate that the overall social-skills rating improved to the

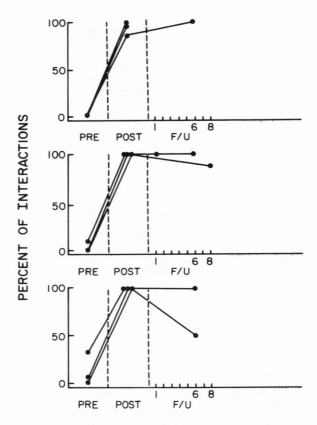

FIGURE 3. Mean proportion of role-played interactions during which each subject emitted appropriate requests during baseline (Pre), at the end of treatment (Post), and during follow-up (1-8 months).

level of 4.0 or better (on the 1-5 scale). The reader may recall that high-assertive but nonexplosive psychiatric patients received a mean rating of 4.15 on this scale, while low-assertives obtained a mean of 1.64 (Eisler et al., 1978). When an overall rating was not available, double plusses indicate that *each* of the target behaviors improved to 80% of the maximum or better. Single plusses (+) indicate that overall social-skills rating improved to a rating between 3.0 and 3.9. When an overall rating was not available, single plusses indicate that each of the target behaviors improved to between 60 and 79%. A negative sign (-) indicates that the overall skill rating was less than 3.0 or that the minimum performance on any of the target behaviors was less than 60%. When no data are available, the block is left blank.

TABLE 2

Overall Social Skills Performance During Training, Generalization Assessment, and Follow-up[a]

Subject	Laboratory Training		Generalization Across Scenes		Generalization Across Respondent		On-ward
	Post	Follow-up	Post	Follow-up	Post	Follow-up	
1	+ +	+ +					
2	+ +		−		+ +		+ +
3	+ +		−		+ +		+ +
4	+ +	+	+ +	+			+ +
5	+ +	+ +	+ +	+ +			+ +
6	+ +	+ +	+ +	+ +	+ +	+	+ +
7	+ +	−	+ +	+	+ +	+ +	+ +
8	+ +	+ +	+ +	+	+ +		
9	+ +		+ +				

[a]Subject's performance is categorized on either mean overall social skill ratings (1-5 scale) or the percent of appropriate behavior emitted.

+ + = rating ≥ 4 or ≥ 80% of maximum on all target behaviors.

 + = rating ≥ 3 or ≥ 60% of maximum on all target behaviors.

 − = rating < 3 or < 60% of maximum on all target behaviors.

Does training improve social skills in the lab and are improvements maintained? As Table 2 demonstrates, social-skills training resulted in improvement for all patients during laboratory training. This improvement was maintained at maximal levels for four patients (one- to eight-month follow-up). Of the two remaining patients, one had an overall social-skills rating of 3.6 (S4) and the other made appropriate requests 50% of the time (S7).

Do these new skills generalize to untrained scenes, a different respondent, and hospital situations outside of the lab? Are these changes maintained? Results of training generalized to on-ward situations in each of the six cases where the behavior was assessed. The improvements also generalized to untrained scenes for six patients. The two patients who did not demonstrate as much generalization to untrained scenes scored 57% on appropriate requests. Maximal generalization to untrained scenes was maintained in follow-up for two patients. The additional three patients demonstrated some generalization in follow-up, with overall social skills of 3.4 (S4) and 3.3 (S8), and 75% of maximum on appropriate requests and eye contact (S7). Each subject demonstrated maximal generalization of improved social skills to a different respondent. This maximal performance was maintained in follow-up by one subject (S7), while a second subject (S6) emitted appropriate requests during 60% of the interactions.

In summary, the results tend to support the notion that explosive individuals can be taught the components of effective social functioning (i.e., "assertiveness") in previously problematical situations. Following training, their overall performance is rated very positively, both during the role-played scenes on which they were trained and during untrained scenes with unfamiliar people. More importantly, it seems that these improved skills generalize to unobtrusively assessed extra-laboratory situations and tend to be maintained across time.

Cognitive

A second important area of outcome is cognitive functioning. Do individuals perceive situations differently after treatment? Results for the three subjects who completed the Generalized Expectations of Others Questionnaire on a pretraining and posttraining basis are displayed in Figure 4. Each of the patients demonstrated changes in the clinically desired direction or maintenance of responses which are already clini-

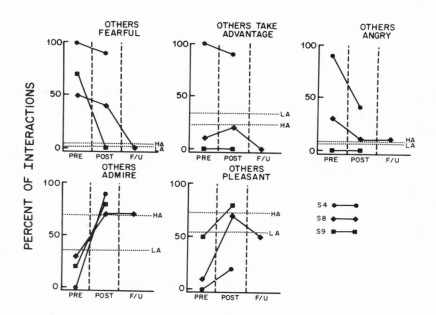

FIGURE 4. Results of the Generalized Expectations of Others Questionnaire for the three subjects who completed it on a pre-post basis. Subject 8 also completed it at a six-month follow-up. Mean scores for high (HA) and low assertive (LA) comparison groups (Eisler et al., 1978) are also indicated by broken lines.

cally desirable. Six-month follow-up data which are available for S8 show further improvement on one item (Others Fearful), maintenance of improvement on two items (Others Angry and Others Admire), and some decrease in improvement on one item (Others Pleasant). Results of the responses to Others Take Advantage are difficult to assess. Two patients reported feeling less taken advantage of than other high-assertives during all phases of assessment. This may indicate, indeed, that other people feared and did not try to take advantage of them; however, any interpretation is speculative.

Physiological

Physiological assessments were conducted on four patients prior to training. Two of these patients completed training and were assessed for physiological arousal immediately after training (S8 and S9). An additional six-month follow-up physiological assessment was conducted with S8.

Is physiological arousal different during role-played neutral and explosive scenes? Results of these assessments vary with each individual patient. Table 3 compares arousal to neutral and explosive scenes prior to training for each of the four patients. If a patient demonstrated 20% greater change score to one type of scene than to the other, the criterion was met for a distinction between the two types of scenes. If more arousal occurred in response to explosive scenes, the block is labeled EXP. If 20% greater change score occurred during neutral scenes, then the block is labeled NEU. When differences between the change scores were less than 20%, no distinction was made and the block was left blank. Subject 8 showed significant arousal to angry scenes on all five physiological

TABLE 3

Comparison of Physiological Arousal to Neutral and Explosive Scenes[a]

Subject[b]	Blood Pressure		Heart Rate	EMG	Respiration
	Sys	Dia			
Drop-out 1	NEU	NEU	EXP	EXP	
Drop-out 2	NEU	NEU			EXP
Subject 8	EXP	EXP	EXP	EXP	EXP
Subject 9		EXP		EXP	EXP

[a]If greater arousal (≥ 20%) is shown during explosive scenes, the block is labeled EXP. If greater arousal occurred during neutral scenes, the block is labeled NEU. If no distinction was made, the blocks are left blank.

[b]The two subjects labeled Drop-out failed to complete treatment.

measures. On the other hand, one subject (Drop-out 2) demonstrated relatively higher arousal to explosive scenes than to neutral scenes on only one measure—respiration. The other two explosives indicated more arousal to explosive scenes on at least two of the five measures (heart rate and EMG for Drop-out 1; EMG respiration and diastolic blood pressure for S9). Two subjects (Drop-outs 1, 2) had higher blood pressure ratings during neutral scenes.

Is physiological arousal to explosive scenes after training different than arousal before training? A comparison of arousal to explosive scenes prior to and following training is displayed in Table 4. A plus (+) indicates that the patient demonstrated at least a 50% improvement in the change score. Zero (0) indicates that the patient had less than a 50% improvement in change score or, for heart rate for S9, no distinction between post-arousal to neutral and explosive scenes. A negative sign (-) represents a 50% undesirable shift in the change score. Results demonstrate that S8 showed a significant change in the clinically desirable direction for all five measures. S9 has improved on EMG, changed in a clinically undesirable direction on diastolic blood pressure and showed no change on the other three measures.

Clinical Outcome

Are behavioral changes maintained once the patient has left the hospital? Follow-up data in the natural environment (Table 5) were obtained by reports from the patient and were validated by at least one of his family members. These data were gathered from six to 48 months post-training on five subjects. The remaining four could not be contacted despite repeated efforts. Results indicate that the severity and frequency of explosive outbursts decreased and family relationships improved for

TABLE 4

Comparison of Physiological Arousal to Explosive Scenes Pretraining and Posttraining[a]

| Subject | Blood Pressure | | Heart Rate | EMG | Respiration |
	Sys	Dia			
8	+	+	+	+	+
9	0	−	0	+	0

[a]+ = over 50% desirable change.
0 = no change.
− = over 50% undesirable change.

TABLE 5
Clinical Outcome Data

| Subject | Follow-up | Episodes | Outcome Variable[a] | | Rehospitalized |
			Family	Job	
1	48 mo	+	+	+	+
2	6 mo	+	+	−	+
4	10 mo	+	+	−	+
5	36 mo	+	+	−	+
8	9 mo	+	+	+	+

[a] + = clinically desirable outcome.
   − = clinically undesirable outcome.

Mother**

Aggression Index

all individuals. None of the subjects was rehospitalized for explosive behavior. However, S4 was readmitted for treatment of continuing depression and S8 was readmitted for alcohol withdrawal. Employment results are less positive. Two patients held steady jobs after discharge, two patients never found employment (S2 and S5), and S4 quit several jobs. In sum, it seems that the available clinical outcome data are very positive with regard to explosive episodes and family adjustment but equivocal with respect to employment.

DISCUSSION

The data summarized in this paper are clearly encouraging. An approach has been outlined that is applicable to individuals with severe histories of violent outbursts. While training was conducted during in-patient hospitalization, the preliminary outcome data are suggestive of broad-based behavioral change both within and outside of the treatment setting. This is especially encouraging since no single therapist treated more than two patients on which outcome data are presented. Yet there are a number of limitations of these data that must be taken into account.

1) The data represent a small number of individuals from a relatively homogenous population (young male veterans, southern residence, severe problems).
2) There was a high drop-out rate. About 50% of the people did not complete the program. This attrition occurred almost exclusively

during Stage I or early in Stage II of treatment. These results are based on those individuals who stayed in treatment.

3) Treatment was extensive (one to three months) and was conducted on an inpatient basis. It is unknown whether the treatment would be as effective if conducted on an outpatient basis. Our impression is that the opportunities for nonlaboratory observation and informal modeling offered by a residential setting are important, especially during the early stages of treatment.

4) While single-case experimental control was used exclusively with the social-skills training data, the cognitive and physiological treatment data were gathered within a pre-post design. Larger samples, better experimental controls and more sophisticated measurement approaches are needed to expand our data base.

5) Independently conducted research is needed, both on the treatment approach and model. While the data reported here were collected by a number of experimenters, the treatment program was completed at the same institution with the same population.

There are at least three major directions in which future research could be directed. The first of these is the development and validation of the model. At almost each point more can be done. A particularly fruitful area might be the cognitive area. These explosive individuals are quite remarkable in their labeling of situations and expectations regarding what is appropriate behavior and what the likely outcome of different actions might be. Perhaps even more exciting are the relationships between the various components of the model. How do the cognitive, physiological, and behavioral response modes interact? To what extent do changes in one system affect the others? Do the consequences of the explosive episodes shape the topography of the episodes, the "amnesia," "blackouts," "remorse," etc.? While much of this work may be difficult to do, it is important. A basic understanding of the processes involved in this behavior pattern is likely to have far-reaching implications for prevention and remediation.

A second and somewhat related direction is the application of the approach to other problems. For example, does this model apply to individuals with less extreme "temper problems"? Can it be used on a preventive basis? Might it also be useful in the understanding of individuals who do not meet the population criteria we specified, e.g., the retarded, the psychotic, the professional criminal? The heuristic potential of the model has yet to be fully explored.

A third line of research is the analysis and improvement of therapeutic effectiveness and efficiency. At this point we have said that our approach *seems* to work with this very difficult group of patients. However, we do not know how it might compare to other potential approaches or even the long-term effects. While the intensive, idiographic research approach taken to date clearly has advantages, it also has inherent limitations. Other types of research, e.g., comparative outcome studies, need to be done. It might also be possible to markedly improve the efficiency of treatment. Our approach has been almost exclusively individual in its orientation. However, the one study that involved using another explosive as a role-playing partner obtained encouraging results (McKinlay et al., 1977). It was found that serving as a role-playing partner, i.e., being almost an "assistant trainer," improved the patient's performance. This also opens the way to working in groups, etc. In sum, it is almost a given that any treatment approach can be made more effective and efficient.

REFERENCES

BANDURA, A. *Aggression: A social learning analysis.* Englewood Cliffs, New Jersey: Prentice-Hall, 1973.

BANDURA, A. Self-efficacy: Toward a unifying theory of behavioral change. *Psychological Review*, 1977, *84*, 191-215.

BERNSTEIN, D. A., & BORKOVEC, T. D. *Progressive relaxation training: A manual for the helping profession.* Champaign, IL: Research Press, 1973.

EISLER, R. M., FREDERIKSEN, L. W., & PETERSON, G. L.: The relationship of cognitive variables to the expression of assertiveness. *Behavior Therapy*, 1978, *9*, 419-427.

FIEDLER, D., & BEACH, L. R. On the decision to be assertive. *Journal of Consulting and Clinical Psychology*, 1978, *46*, 537-546.

FOY, D. W., EISLER, R. M., & PINKSTON, S. Modeled assertion in a case of explosive rages. *Journal of Behaviour Therapy and Experimental Psychiatry*, 1975, *6*, 135-137.

FREDERIKSEN, L. W., & EISLER, R. M. The control of explosive behavior: A skill development approach. In D. Upper (Ed.), *Perspectives in behavior therapy.* Kalamazoo, Michigan: Behaviordelia, 1977.

FREDERIKSEN, L. W., JENKINS, J. O., FOY, D. W., & EISLER, R. M. Social skills training in the modification of abusive verbal outbursts in adults. *Journal of Applied Behavior Analysis*, 1976, *9*, 117-125.

FREDERIKSEN, L. W., & KELLY, J. Social skills and explosive outbursts: An assessment package. In D.M. Doleys (Chair.), *Assessment and treatment of social and assertive skills across populations: Recent Developments.* Symposium presented at the meeting of the Southeastern Psychological Association, Hollywood, Florida, May, 1977.

KEANE, T. M. *Directions in the behavioral treatment of alcohol abuse: Self-management.* Paper presented to the joint meetings of the Mississippi-Louisiana Psychological Associations, New Orleans, October, 1978.

KNUTSON, J. R. (Ed.) *The control of aggression.* Chicago: Aldine Publishing Company, 1973.

LINEHAN, M. M. Issues in behavioral interviewing. In J. D. Cone & R. P. Hawkins (Eds.), *Behavioral assessment: New directions in clinical psychology.* New York: Brunner/Mazel, 1977.

McKINLAY, T., PACHMAN, J., & FREDERIKSEN, L. W. *Coaction: An innovative approach in the behavioral treatment of explosive behavior.* Paper presented at the meeting of the Association for the Advancement of Behavior Therapy, Atlanta, December, 1977.

MATSON, J. L., & STEPHENS, R. M. Increasing appropriate behavior of explosive chronic psychiatric patients with a social skills training package. *Behavior Modification,* 1978, *2,* 61-76.

MEICHENBAUM, D. *Cognitive-behavior modification: An integrative approach.* New York: Plenum Press, 1977.

MISCHEL, W. Toward a cognitive social learning reconceptualization of personality. *Psychological Review,* 1973, *80,* 252-283.

NOVACO, R. W. Treatment of chronic anger through cognitive and relaxation controls. *Journal of Consulting and Clinical Psychology,* 1976, *44,* 681.

RAINWATER, N., & FREDERIKSEN, L. W. *Violent behavior: Assessment and treatment using multiple response systems.* Paper presented at the annual meeting of the Association for Advancement of Behavior Therapy, Chicago, November, 1978.

RIMM, D. C., HILL, G. A., BROWN, N. N., & STUART, J. E. Group-assertiveness training in treatment of expression of inappropriate anger. *Psychological Reports,* 1974, *34,* 791-798.

RIMM, D. C., & MASTERS, J. C. *Behavior therapy: Techniques and empirical findings.* New York: Academic Press, Inc., 1974.

SIMON, S. J., & FREDERIKSEN, L. W. *Social skills training in the treatment of a physically abusive "explosive personality".* Paper presented at the meeting of the Southeastern Psychological Association, Hollywood, Florida, May, 1977.

WALLACE, C. J., TEIGEN, J. R., LIBERMAN, R. P., & BAKER, V. Destructive behavior treated by contingency contracts and assertive training: A case study. *Journal of Behavior Therapy and Experimental Psychiatry,* 1973, *4,* 273-274.

Name Index

289

Subject Index

Italic page numbers indicate material in tables and figures.

Eskalith (lithium), *234,* 236
Ethnicity:
    and employment, 62
    and sex crimes, 147, *148*
Ethnography, 4, 70
Ethology, 4, 38
Exceptional children, vii. *See also* Children
Exhibitionism, 19, 117, *117,* 124, 133, 147
Expectations, 268-69, *268*
    on aggression, 45-46
    rising, theory of, 44
Explosive behavior, 265-87
    assessment of, 271-75
    discussion of, 286-87
    model of, 267-71, *269, 270*
    results of, 278-85, *279-85*
    treatment of, 275-78
Extinction, 36, 43, 45, 252
    and punishment, 84
Extortion, 75

Fading, 278
Families:
    abusive, 83-100
        comments on, 98-100
        nondistressed/distressed, distressed-
            abusive, 88-98, *88, 90, 93, 95, 97, 98*
        observation data on, 87-88
        treatment description, 86-87
    aggression in, 16, 17, 36, 57-58
    and behavior modification, xiii, ix
    crisis intervention in, 175-201, *199*
    dependency in, 188
    pathology in and violence, 17-18, 36
    sizes of and aggression, 36, 57-58
    violence in, 9-11, 17-18, 20, 36
Father Flanagan's Boys' Home, 203n.
FBI, 3, 47, 116, 139, 185
Feedback, 271, 276, 277
    in residential treatment, 215-17
Feminist perspective, 102-14. *See also*
        Sexism
    on rape, 165
    on theories of causation, 104-10
        political, 105-106
        psychological, 109-12
        socio-cultural, 107-109
Fertility rates, 56, 56n. *See also* Birth rates
Fluphenazine (Prolixin), *239*
FPZ, *239*
French Revolution, 12
Frontal lobe abnormalities, 6, 23
Frottage, 19, 117 *117,* 128, *129*
Frustration-aggression hypothesis, 15, 35-
    37

Gangs, street, 68-81
    behavioral analysis of, 71-72, 76-80
    in community, 72-74, 80-81
    incidence of, 68, *70*
    learning in, 75-76
    in media, 68
    and nongang youths, 76-80
    and race, 69
    violence of, 16, 68
Generalization, programmed, 277-78, *281*
Generalized Expectations of Others
        Questionnaire, 268
Genetics:
    and crime, 4-5, 6
    and neural substrates, 230
    and warfare, 4
Geraghty Loma street gang, 72-74
Government, legitimacy of, *43n.*
Grandiosity, 234
Great Depression, 55
Group theory and stages of violence, 11

Haldol (haloperidol), 238, 239, *239*
Hallucinations, 216, *262*
Haloperidol (Haldol), 238, 239, *239*
Height and crime, 5
Hematoma, epidural, 248
Hemorrhage, subarachnoid, 254
Hitchhiking, 149
Homicides, 49, 58, 181, 185, 228
    and cues, 41-42
    of nonstrangers, 102
    rates of:
        long-term changes in, 32, 34
        and population, 51-54, *53*
    year differences in, 54-56, 56n., 59
Homosexuality, *132,* 133. *See also*
        Pedophilia
Hong Kong, gangs in, 69
Hormone changes, 48
Hospital Research Committee, 145
Human-relations/community-relations
        model of police officers, 180
Human Rights Committee, 246
Hyperactivity in children, 235

Ideal mental health services, vii
Illiteracy, 12
Imipramine (Tofranil), *234*
Imitation in gangs, 75, 76
Immigration, 11, 52
Infants, helplessness of, 38. *See also*
        Children
Incest, 102. *See also* Children
    girl-child, 105

Violent Behavior: Social Learning Approaches

Stanford University, 31n.
Statistics Canada, 185
Stereotypes, sex-role, 106, 107, 110
Stimulants, 237
Street gangs. *See* Gangs, street
Stress:
 and aggression, 15-16
 inoculation therapy, 14
Sulfa drugs, 34n.
Superego, 8

Tanzania, 34n.
Teaching-Family Model, 209, 214-19
Temperament, 99
Temper tantrums, 218
Temporal lobe abnormalities, 23, 230, 266
Temporal lobe epilepsy, 230
Testosterone, 235
Theft, 47, 49
 car, 73
Thorazine (chlorpromazine), *234*
Tight, defined, 204
Tofranil (imipramine), *234*
Token economy system, 216
Tokyo, gangs in, 69
Total Aversive Behavior (TAB), 87-94,
 89, 90, 98
Tranquilizers, *234*, 236
Truancy, 73
Twins in genetic studies, 6-7
 identical/fraternal, 7

UCLA Mental Health Clinical Research
 Center for the Study of
 Schizophrenia, 258
Uganda, 34n.
Unconscious and rape, 142
Unemployment. *See* Employment
Uniform Crime Reports (FBI), 3, 47, 49, 53,
 139, 185
United Way, 21
University of California, 227n.
University of Tennessee, 18
 Center for the Health Sciences Special
 Problems Unit, 120-21
University of Texas, 40
University of Utah, 31n.
University of Washington Department of
 Psychology, 138n.
U.S. Census Bureau, 34, 48, 49, 50, 52,
 52, 53, 54, 55, 57, 72
U.S. Department of Justice, 140, 204n.
 Law Enforcement Assistance
 Administration, 80

U.S. Department of Labor, 55
U.S.S.R., mass violence in, 33

Vaccination, 34n.
Validity, 163
 external, 164
 of prediction, 8-9
 testing of, 17
Valium, 236, 237
Values:
 and aggression, 18
 in social groups, 11
Vancouver, British Columbia, domestic
 violence in, 174, 175
Vancouver Police Department, 179, 199,
 199
Vandalism, 47, 49
Variance, 91, *156, 159*
 and covariance, 152
Venereal disease, 146
Verbal resistance to rape, 139, 140, 141
Verbal skills, 108
 of police, 187, 192
Veteranos in gangs, 74, 78
Veterans' Administration, 266, 275
Victim-blame model of rape, 168
Victim precipitation, 109
Videotapes, 21, 77, 86, 119, 149, 192, 196
Vietnam, 34n.
Violence. *See also* Aggression
 of adolescents, 209-13
 definitions of, 3, 32-33
 and demographic analysis, 59-63
 domestic, 102-14
  causes of, 104-12, 113
  research center on, 112-14
 and drugs, 21, 22, 23, 228, 230, 232
 and economic conditions, 16
 etiology of, 24
 in family, 9-11, 17-18, 20, 36
 fictional accounts, of, 33
 in gangs, 16, 68
 and income, 59-63, *63*
 institutional, 21, 22
 in media, 39-40, 103
 and personality, 8
 and police, 181
 and residential treatment, 209-13, *213,*
  219-25
 and self-esteem, *110,* 111
 social psychological analysis of, 59-63
 sources of, 4-15
  disciplinary perspectives, 4-9
  and family, 9-11